ERASMUS
and Jews
the

ERASMUS

and *Jews*
the

Shimon Markish

Translated by Anthony Olcott

With an
Afterword by Arthur A. Cohen

The University of Chicago Press
Chicago and London

B
785
.E64M36
1986
cop.4

SHIMON MARKISH is lecturer at the University of Geneva, Faculty of Humanities. He is the author of several books published in Russian and French and has translated works of Erasmus into Russian.

The University of Chicago Press gratefully acknowledges the generous contributions of Mr. Arthur A. Cohen; Mr. Jack Nash, The Nash Foundation; Mr. Daniel Rose, Rose Associates; and The National Foundation for Jewish Culture toward the translation costs of this book.

Publisher's Note: Translated from unpublished Russian-language manuscript.

The University of Chicago Press, Chicago 60637
The University of Chicago Press, Ltd., London

© 1986 by The University of Chicago
All rights reserved. Published 1986
Printed in the United States of America
95 94 93 92 91 90 89 88 87 86   5 4 3 2 1

Library of Congress Cataloging-in-Publication Data

Markish, Simon Peretsovich.
  Erasmus and the Jews.

  Translated from the unpublished manuscript.
  Bibliography: p.
  Includes index.
  1. Erasmus, Desiderius, d. 1536—Views on Judaism.
2. Christianity and other religions—Judaism.
3. Judaism—Relations—Christianity. I. Title.
B785.E64M32813 1986   261.2'6'0924   85-16454
ISBN 0-226-50590-1

Contents

Foreword to the American Edition

The research for this study was begun in Budapest in 1971 and largely completed there, while the resulting book was written in Geneva in 1974 and 1975. The chronology and place of the work leave a significant stamp on the character of the study, about which I must permit myself a few words of explanation.

I emigrated from the Soviet Union to Hungary with forty years of life and more than ten years of work on Erasmus already behind me. Mine were the first complete Russian translation of the *Colloquia* and the first book about Erasmus written in Russian. Once in Hungary, in an atmosphere of intellectual freedom incomparably wider than that in the Soviet Union, I found it possible to unite the two major interests of my life at that time, Jewry and Erasmus. This was the genesis of the present study, while its actual impetus was Guido Kisch's book *Erasmus' Stellung zu Juden und Judentum* (Tübingen, 1969) (a book I will mention many more times), which I discovered in the library of Budapest University. I should make clear that of the two interests I mention, the greater was Judaism, which could not fully or openly reveal itself in my Soviet preexistence.

While writing in Geneva I tried to fill in the bibliographical gaps caused by the relative poverty of Hungarian libraries in the

most recent works. Nevertheless I realize that certain lacunae—
and fairly substantial ones—remain unfilled.

This book appeared in the French translation thanks to the
approval and support of professors Georges Nivat and Jean
Halperin as well as the publisher Vladimir Dimitrievic; I should
like here to express my deepest and most sincere gratitude to all
three.

The French publication (*L'Age d'Homme* [Lausanne, 1979])
brought me both satisfaction and disappointment. I had imagined
that this chapter from the history of Christian-Jewish relations,
important even if only because of its subject, could not remain
unremarked by Jewish scholars. As far as I know, however, not a
single mention of the book appeared in Jewish publications; all
the reviews and reactions have come from the non-Jewish side.

Thus this American edition is the greater joy for me, undertaken on the initiative and with the assistance of Arthur A. Cohen, the Jewish philosopher and novelist whose name is equally
well-known in America, Europe, and Israel. I am grateful to him
not only for his beneficent attention to my work as a colleague,
an authoritative scholar of Christian-Jewish connections of past
and present, but also, and more important, for his recognition
and evaluation of the Jewish character of this work, a recognition
which in my own view gives this work its *raison d'être;* as I have
already said, of the two components, Erasmus and Judaism, the
latter is of greater importance to me.

The basic text is offered to the reader essentially unchanged
from the French edition; all additions and corrections have been
made in the notes.

Shimon Markish

Geneva, March 1984

I

The Problem Posed

Not once in the entire five hundred years following his birth did Erasmus' judgments on Jews and Jewry attract any special attention; the first work on the subject appeared exactly in that jubilee year, 1969, when the law historian Guido Kisch, author of a well-known monograph on Erasmus and the jurisprudence of his time, as well as of many books and articles on the history of the Jews in the Middle Ages and the Renaissance, published a brochure in which he argued that Erasmus was a convinced and fundamental anti-Semite, able and ready to share the views and program of the later Luther,[1] the same program which, a good many years afterward, the Nazis so warmly approved and to which Julius Streicher referred from the defendant's bench at Nuremburg.[2]

This long scholarly silence is wholly understandable; Erasmus left no works dedicated to the Jews, while his remarks about the past and present of the Jewish people—their religion, culture, language, customs, and so on—are incidental and unsystematic. In fact, the same thing might be said of Erasmus as is said of Calvin in the collection *Christen und Juden*: "If someone should wish to study the Jewish question of the sixteenth century, he ought to turn to anyone but Calvin; whatever Calvin may have said on the subject has no real substantive meaning."[3]

However, Guido Kisch's accusations are equally understandable, since Erasmus (like Calvin) belongs to the ranks of those great leaders of whom answers are sought to all questions, even to those which they have not posed. Acolytes painstakingly collect the passing words of the moment and chance remarks, relating them one to another, so they find themselves a place in a system, becoming included in a tradition and so influencing the future, the pace and direction of the battle of ideas, far more than the specialized treatises of experts and specialists.[4] This means that if Erasmus truly was an overt judeophobe, the fact is very important both for the present and for the future (since even today people speak of the alternatives "Lutheran Europe" or "Erasmian Europe"), even if nothing came from his pen which even remotely resembles Luther's deranged pamphlets *Von den Juden und ihren Lügen* or *Von Schem Hamphoras* (not for nothing did another collection, *Kirch und Synagogue,* characterize Calvin as a virulent Jew-hater who entirely shared Luther's opinion,[5] even though Calvin never showed any curiosity about Jews at all and most likely never met a Jew in his life).[6]

The increased interest in Jewry, particularly in Judeo-Christian relations, which followed World War II can not be considered wholly academic; it was born, first of all, in a feeling of guilt and responsibility among members of the Christian world—"The Jewish question in reality is a Christian question."[7] However, if the evils of the day define the interests of non-Jewish scholars, no less, and perhaps even more, they define the sphere and direction of the interests of Jewish scholars.[8] This topicality though, while not intending deliberate misrepresentation of facts, can lead to the tendentious presentation of facts, which means ultimately to concealment or even distortion of the truth.

For us the danger lies first of all in the unfaded complexes of the ghetto. Too often we, as before, divide the world into those who speak well of us and those who abuse, the first of whom we praise in our turn, while either abusing the second or skirting around them in icy silence. As a rule the neutral figures who have no special interest in us also do not interest us.

With all due care and modesty the author of this study would like to state his deepest conviction, that the evils of the day (or more simply put, the memory of the dead, the existence of Israel, and its struggles) not only define our interests but also deprive us of any right to the servile complexes of the ghetto, even if in the past they were justified by the two thousand years of the Diaspora. In the present it is not persecutors and protectors which we must find but rather the meaning and laws of our own history, which we cannot achieve other than within the history of the majority, in accord with the laws of this "macrohistory."

From here it follows that Erasmus and Erasmism, which have played so great a role in the history of toleration in modern times,[9] belong to the history of European Jewry regardless of the scope of Erasmus' thoughts about the Jews *per se*. It follows then that an exhaustively complete survey of those thoughts, in their historical, psychological, and philological context, is absolutely necessary, on the model, for example, of Reinhold Lewin's *Luthers Stellung zu den Juden*[10] (Kisch not only does not accomplish that task, he fails even to pose it. Kisch works only with material from Erasmus' correspondence, meaning his conclusions and accusations are definitionally without foundation).[11] It is equally necessary to relate and connect this to the Erasmian model of the world, to find its place within the system of Erasmus' world view (or else to demonstrate the inappropriate nature of such thoughts to the system, to show how such thoughts contradict that world view; Kisch attempts this, although without the necessary foundation).

Unlike Lewin[12] though, the author of this study will not restrict the topic of Erasmus' thoughts on the Jews to what Erasmus had to say of his Jewish contemporaries, not because of the poverty of such material when compared to the same for Luther but because of the difference in point of view, in starting position; Luther was a reformer, a politician, a practical man, while Erasmus was a theologian and moralist who effaced all chronological boundaries, mixing all temporal planes in allegorical exegesis. This study will show how Old Testament, Gospel-era, and contemporary Jews obscured one another, coinciding in Erasmus' thoughts and interpretations. It is not possible, therefore, to overlook any aspect, from biblical quotations and allusions to the suspicion that the Imperial troops which sacked Rome in 1527 were full of Jewish mercenaries.

In trying to collect and evaluate as much as possible, it is necessary to keep in mind a certain hierarchy of the Erasmian heritage, so that, for example, a letter not intended for publication may not be placed in the same rank as an epistle Erasmus published himself, and more than once. Apologiae are not equal in meaning or influence to the New Testament paraphrases, the Adagiae, or the New Testament commentary. The anti-Semitic attacks of some letters, on the level of street abuse, "common anti-Semitism" (to use today's term), though foul in themselves and no credit to Erasmus (emphasizing that this is from today's point of view), cannot outweigh the sole and single argument, *ad silentium,* that in the entire commentary on the New Testament there is not a single inflammatory word against Erasmus' Jewish contemporaries, even in those cases where the text under comment provides more than sufficient grounds.

The point of comparison is important in posing the problem, the standard of this or that attitude to Judaism. Kisch compares Erasmus with the model anti-Semite Zasius, contrasting him with the equally model philo-Semite Reuchlin.[13] Unlike Zasius, though, Erasmus never considered the Jews to be slaves, found the idea of forcible baptism of Jewish infants deeply alien, and never approached even close to Zasius' unrestrained cruelty and scabrous style, as this study will demonstrate. Two extremely basic circumstances should be emphasized now, without going into detail—the universal blind hatred of Jews in fifteenth- and sixteenth-century Germany, in no way softened by the humanism of the Renaissance,[14] and the doubtful qualities of Reuchlin's judeophilia. While not wishing to place in doubt Kisch's inarguable thesis that Reuchlin was better, more noble, and more humane than Zasius, that Jews owe him unending gratitude for his consistent and courageous defense of their books and rights, the author also would note that, according to Ludwig Geiger (whom Kisch himself acknowledges as the author of the best monograph on Reuchlin to date),[15] Reuchlin's enemies unjustly accused Reuchlin of shielding Jews and befriending them: "Reuchlin might have defended himself with the words of Jerome, which he accepted and approved: I loathe the circumcised people. He hated this people, seeing in them the enemies of Christians and Christianity, but respected them as bearers of sacred tradition."[16] Whether Reuchlin refuted the persecutors of the Jews from juridical conviction (as Kisch supposes)[17] or from the general tenderness of his nature (as Geiger says),[18] the bounds of his behavior do not exceed the general attitude of the epoch, rather confirming it, as the exception which proves the rule. In the final analysis Reuchlin sought not the peaceful coexistence of Christianity and Judaism but rather, as behooved a good Christian, the conversion of the Jews.[19] Geiger has already seen clearly that Reuchlin and his supporters defended not the Jewish books, and even less the Jewish people, but rather the principles of humanist philology and the right of free enquiry in any sphere[20] (which has become an axiom of modern science). It thus seems premature to speak not only of friendliness but even of the rudiments of toleration.

The point of departure therefore must be universal hatred (sometimes white-hot, sometimes calmer and less passionate), intolerance, and (the inescapable consequence of intolerance) missionary zeal.

The question of the sources and roots of this hatred must be put to the author of a universal history of anti-Semitism, but even our present question cannot be properly posed, in principle, unless we discover the backbone of enmity for Jews which existed at least among that small "community" to which Erasmus belonged, the makers of the Northern Renaissance.

It is widely acknowledged that north of the Alps humanism differed from the Italian version in the sharp expression of its religious coloration. For the English, French, and German humanists Christian faith and Christian piety were not just the rules of the game but rather the game's essence and meaning. For exactly this reason Erasmus was first and foremost a Christian theologian, and only then a philologist, writer, and pedagogue. Christianity was born in the struggle against Judaism, and refutation of the Jewish religion, a polemic with the Old Law, permeated all Christian literature, from the Gospels, through the writings of the Church Fathers and Doctors, through the classics of early and late scholasticism, right up to the works of Erasmus'

contemporaries, his friends and his enemies. It makes more sense
in considering this keystone of Christian dogma, of the struggle
of ideas which never ceased for an instant in the entire history of
the Church, to speak of anti-Judaism, leaving "anti-Semitism" to
mean the xenophobia of the crowd and its practical conse-
quences.[21] Even more appropriate though (at least in Erasmus'
case) is the term "anti-Mosaism," which E. Telle introduced in his
monograph *Erasme de Rotterdam et le septième sacrament,*[22] to
name the cause of Erasmus' hatred for monasticism. In fact, uncompromising hatred for the "letter," the "unspiritual flesh," the
"ceremonies," for empty rituals, in a word for what Erasmus
countless times calls "the Law" or "the Law of Moses," is the
heart of his attitude toward Jewry.

It is relatively simple to trace this feeling, singling it out from
(in Leon Poliakov's felicitous phrase) "the polyphonic passions"
which are judeophobia, and the task is made even easier by Erasmus' unchanging motto "Back to sources!" which permits a de-
tour around medieval tradition and directly addresses the New
Testament and the writings of the Holy Fathers; coincidences between Erasmus and the medieval authorities may be assumed to
be either chance or traceable to the same authority of the past.

At the same time, the indirect, second-hand nature of this feeling should be noted, born as it is in the traditions of the Church
and never leaving that framework. Of bookish origin, its subject is
the Jews of books, not the Jews of life.

Such then are the preliminary remarks; formed in the process
of this study, they never played the role of working hypothesis.

II

Mosaic Law, Judaism, and "Judaism"

The first thing to note about Erasmus' many judgments of the Old Testament is their almost unchanging correlation to various aspects of the Christian religion; in and of themselves Jewish dogma, worship, and ritual do not concern Erasmus.

Of course this is not simply correlation but, primarily, the contrasting of Christianity and Judaism, of which the implacable sharpness is also worth noting. Still, one must begin with the very little Erasmus said about the similarities of the two religions.

Three stages lead to salvation: profession and fear of God; profession of the unity of God; and baptism, profession of the Christian symbols of faith, and the punctilious performance of duty as a Christian soldier. Of these, the first two are common to Jews and Christians.[1] Referring to Apostle Paul's speech in the Areopagus (Acts 17:26), Erasmus divides all world history into three epochs: the Law of Nature (Natural Law), Mosaic Law, and the Law of the Gospels. None of these are fortuitous; each is the fruit of divine planning.[2] The borders between the epochs, wisdoms, or Laws are not impassable; the preceding prepares the way for the succeeding epoch, which then absorbs it, as Moses understood and absorbed all the wisdom of the pagan Egyptians.[3]

The role of Mosaic Law among all the other Laws is delineated most carefully in *Hyperaspistes II* (1527) and *Ecclesiastes* (1535), where, in agreement with Jerome's view that divine providence was alien to no age, tribe, or clan, Erasmus admits that even Natural Law had its saints, to say nothing of Mosaic Law. However, just as Natural Law did not justify, so did Mosaic Law only prepare the way for full justification, preparing the Jews for their encounter with Christ. Mosaic Law more fully taught people the meaning of sin, even though pagan laws had punished many of the same things that Mosaic Law did.[4] All three Laws are the creation of God, but Gospel Law is the last, with no new laws following.[5]

This is the first of the major oppositions, the transitory nature of Mosaic Law versus the eternity of Christ's Law. The time of Mosaic Law has passed irrevocably[6]; the words from the parable of the vineyard owner's tenants—"He will come and destroy those tenants and give the vineyard to others" (Luke 20:16)— denote the complete disappearance of Judaism.[7] In another place Erasmus makes the point even more sharply: "If the Jewish tongue, proponent of carnal rituals and instructions, does not fall silent . . . then the tongue of the Gospels, which proclaims grace, may not speak."[8]

Judaism and Christianity are absolutely incompatible and irreconcilable. "Be either straight Jews, renouncing Christ, or straight Christians, who reject Judaism."[9] The purity of Christianity is measured by its distance from "the Judaic manner," which was so repellent to the faithful Christians of antiquity that they preferred to assume the holy rituals of the pagans rather than be suspected of Judaizing.[10] If Moses forbids plowing with ox and ass yoked together (Deut. 22:10), certainly this means that Christianity and Judaism are not to be mixed![11]

This mutual incompatibility is shown in the oppositions Erasmus repeats tirelessly, without end. In *Hyperaspistes II,* for example, the list of such oppositions takes up an entire page *in folio,*[12] while the foreword to the Epistle to the Galatians requires only two lines: "In that [the Law] was flesh, in the Gospels, spirit; in that, shadows, in the Gospels, light; in that, similitudes, in the Gospels, truth; in that, slavery, in the Gospels, freedom."[13] This short list, however, omits at least three other pairs of great importance: works versus grace, misery versus joy, and limitation[14] versus universality; as well as several other pairs of less importance, though wholly characteristic: rigor versus indulgence,[15] the rudiments of grace versus the fullness of grace,[16] multiplicity (of, for example, virtues, commandments, paths to justification, and so forth) versus absolute unity (Christ combining within Himself all virtues, with "Love one another" as the only commandment),[17] righteousness before men, according to earthly understanding, versus acknowledgment of one's unconditional sinfulness, which means as well the unconditional righteousness of God,[18] and Judaism (as a whole) versus love.[19] This last opposition however even Erasmus doubted, since it contradicts the Gospel texts of Matthew 22:37–40 and Mark 12:30–31, in which Christ refers to Deuteronomy 6:5 ("and you shall love the Lord your God with all your heart, and with all your soul, and with all your mind, and with all your strength") and to Leviticus 19:18 ("You shall love your neighbor as yourself").[20] Still, the authority of the *Enchiridion Militis Christiani* in the hierarchy of Erasmus' heritage unquestionably not only outweighs one of the countless apologiae but also Erasmus' paraphrase of Timothy.[21]

Some of the most important oppositions deserve more detailed examination.

The spirit versus the letter: as early as *Enchiridion* there appears the broad formula, "To revere Christ through visible things, and because of them . . . is to betray the law of the Gospels, which is the law of the spirit, and to fall into a kind of new Judaism."[22] For Erasmus, the difference between Judaism and Christianity forms part of the basic and perhaps most important opposition in his world view, that of the spiritual versus the carnal (or material). Whatever its origin (though unquestionably it is theological) in Erasmus' established system, this opposition acquires not only religious significance but also universal, even cosmic, meaning.[23] Variations on this theme are nearly endless,[24] not surprisingly, given its wide scope; ultimately most particular problems can be reduced to this opposition.

The famous alternatives of justification (or salvation) through "works" (or good deeds) as opposed to through the faith which grace confers may be described by this opposition. The Jews place their hopes for salvation on the obedient fulfillment of corporeal rituals,[25] the "works of Moses" (*opera Mosaica*).[26] The law which sternly demands "works" appeals not to the heart or soul but only to the corporeal ears.[27] With their faith placed in corporeal, material acts, the Jews then expect material proofs from God of His wrath or benevolence, meaning signs and miracles, while the Gospels must be understood through faith and obedience.[28] (The Lutheran doctrine of predestination and salvation through faith alone forced Erasmus to reject radicalism and in part accept works, though with strict distinction, of course, between "Mosaic works," "alien to faith and love," like the "works" people demand of other people, and the Christian "works of love.")[29]

The "works" of the Law are rituals, ceremonies, prohibitions, instructions, and so forth, that flesh of the Law which Erasmus loathed, reviling and abusing it tirelessly, since by usurping piety, "works" force out true reverence, real religion, and spirit.[30] However, because these works were commanded of Moses by God Himself, a contradiction arises, which Erasmus resolved in this way: in the first place, "Mosaic ceremonies" do not wholly coincide with "human ceremonies,"[31] nor wholly with "pharisitical ceremony"[32] (meaning Pharisaism is not wholly identical with Judaism)[33]; and in the second place, "the ancient worship and rituals of the Jews are indeed the will of God, but not the kind will, the benevolent will, or the whole will. God's will made concessions to the stupidity of the Jews, just as it did to the people who demanded a king. Only the New Testament announced that perfect will of God . . ."[34] This theme is connected directly to that of the Law as a stern pedagogue, necessary for a stubborn and nasty child: "The Old Testament makes quite clear that the Jews are an unruly and stubborn people, which is why they are given a heavy and inflexible law. Since they could not learn to submit to God's commandments like native sons, let the sternness of the Law restrain them, like a sort of leg iron and yoke, from evil acts, like bad slaves . . . Centuries too have their age; that was childhood, and the child's tutor was the Law of Moses."[35] Christ was the goal of that education, and the servants of the teacher were the prophets.[36]

The theme of the pedagogy of Mosaic Law (part of the important Erasmian theological category of divine pedagogy)[37] occurs frequently, with perhaps its best expression in passages from the dialogue *Ichthyophagia:* "The bars of the Law, the barriers of rituals, the curb-bit of threats and commandments" were invented to "at least in small part bring reason" to the willful race of man. "Stern slavery in the flesh" was destroyed by the Gospels; the slaves of God became the sons of God. "The power of the commandments withers where the abundance of grace begins." The New Testament did not replace the Old, it fulfilled it; even the prophets "promised a New Testament and a new heart," and condemned the worship and rituals in the name of God himself. "The Jews were not so much released as torn free from the prejudices of the Law, as though snatched away from the breast, native and familiar, but no longer necessary."[38]

The Law was not abolished, but a part of it was made useless and cast-off. This is not to be regretted, anymore than one regrets the flowers when the fruit ripens, just as "no one seeks lanterns or torches once the sun has risen," as the teacher does not regret "when the pupil has become an adult, freeing himself from the teacher's authority and in turning forcing the old teacher to submit to him." The Jews simply did not wish to understand this. "Almost by force they had to be torn from these fantasies or shadows of temporary comforts, in order that they might turn fully to the one whom the Law promised, and vaguely described."[39]

Parenthetically, well before Christ, in deep antiquity, the Jews had violated many prescriptions of the Law, which had not angered God at all. It must be then that "the law which nature itself established and which thus is eternal and unbreakable, must take precedence before a law which did not always exist and which with the passage of time must disappear."[40]

Thus, however contradictory the "Judaic ceremonies" may be of the Law of the Spirit and the philosophy of Christ, in their own time they were both useful and vital, while their abolition is neither easy nor quick.[41]

What part of the Old Law was to be abolished and what part to remain forever inviolate? Those prescriptions of the Law which "more signify sanctity outwardly than express it in substance" are mutable, while those which are "good in and of themselves, and not because their observance has been ordered," must be honored always. The Jews are punctilious about fulfilling the first sort, boasting of it, but forget about the second, "the most important of God's demands on man." Referring to the famous line "For I desire steadfast love and not sacrifice" (Hosea 6:6), Erasmus counts as sacrifice "all which relates to corporeal rituals and which in some way touches on Judaism," but he interprets Hosea's words to be "I desire steadfast love *more than* sacrifice."[42] In other words, even Judaic legalism, even the typical ceremonies and "works" ("the choice of food, special clothes, fasting, sacrificing, prayers said as a duty, Sabbath quiet") are not rejected unconditionally; "These are not wholly to be scorned, in all circumstances, but they do become repugnant to God if a man, relying on the punctiliousness of his sacrifices, is deficient in mercy."[43]

In *Ecclesiastes* Erasmus writes: "The Old Law consists of history, commandments, allegories, rituals, and promises" (the rituals all have allegorical significance as well). Those commandments which encourage good morals and piety are eternal, while those which regulate ritual have lost their literal meaning but retain their spiritual meaning. A Christian is not required to abstain from pork but rather from swinish passions. "Some of them [the commandments of the Old Law] Christians observe even now, some are abolished unconditionally, some are softened, some modified, some abbreviated, while some, on the other hand, are broadened." One must be particularly careful with those Old Testament prescriptions and rules that are dictated by humanity and justice, such as the rules about the sabbatical year, the injunctions not to take clothing as security from a widow, or not to send into battle bridegrooms who have not yet had time to know their wives, the permission to glean a harvested field.[44] The promises of the Law must also be interpreted like the "ritual commandments," in the spiritual sense.[45]

Thus it is not the external side of a ritual, not its "flesh" or "letter" that distinguishes the Christian from the Jew; it is the spirit.[46] It must be said too that the Christian spirit is more ancient than the spirit of Judaism. Not only is the philosophy of Christ which Erasmus and his fellow-thinkers preach not "modernism," on the contrary, it is "traditionalism," a return to sources, to early Christianity, a primary Christianity which is also a return to the beginning of holy history, to the faith of the Patriarchs.[47]

The opposition of works versus grace touches directly upon

another important opposition, the slavery of Mosaic Law versus the freedom of the Gospels.[48] He who fulfills a commandment out of fear of punishment is a slave, while he who fulfills the will of the Lord out of love for him is free.[49] This freedom through grace is limited however by a significant amendment: "On hearing that Christ has repudiated the entire Law [the attack on the reformers—S.M.] the unwashed mass understands this to mean that each may do as he sees best, although there is now less freedom for transgressions."[50] In essence, in spirit, though not by the letter or the flesh, the freedom of the Gospels is actually more severe than the Law,[51] which is not surprising; since Christians are incomparably higher and more complete than Jews, more is asked of them.[52]

The dolor and gloom of the Law is continually contrasted to the ardor of grace, which also relates to the "spirit-letter" pair. "Sorrow is native to the Jews; to the Christians, rejoicing. But what for the Jews, subjects of the flesh, is a source of sorrow, is for Christians, who live by the spirit, a source of joy."[53] It must be recalled that from the very beginning of his literary career until its very end, Erasmus spoke of the joyous character of Christ's philosophy and of Christianity as "true epicurianism," in contrast to the gloom and fanatical asceticism of the monastic life.[54]

Perhaps no opposition is repeated more often than the "shadow of the Law versus the light of the Gospels," with many variations, showing the wide semantic field of this pair. Variants like darkness, shades, prototypes, symbols, riddles, and so on separate at first glance into two large groups, the first where the Law is the murk of dawn, replacing the black of paganism and foretelling the rising sun of the Gospels, beneath the rays of which the Christian should be ashamed to slumber like a Jew[55]; and the second, what in the Law is darkly hinted, heralded by suggestion, or promised, is in the Gospels said aloud, fulfilled, and brought before one's eyes.[56] The significance in Erasmian theology for this opposition is particularly great, because with the opposition "spirit-letter" it forms the basis of allegorical exegesis, which the next chapter treats in more detail.

Taken to its logical conclusion, that same opposition says that the flesh also equals death, so in literal interpretation the Law is death. "The Jews interpreted Mosaic Law literally, although death lies within it, while the spiritual interpretation holds life."[57] To believe in "Mosaic ghosts" is to perish, though only once the Gospel truth has shone forth,[58] which addendum is absent from the preceding quotation. It is also absent from the following one, a most curious passage in the paraphrase to the Epistle to the Galatians (3:10) where, on the authority of the Apostle Paul, Erasmus says, "All who depend upon fulfillment of Mosaic Law but do not fulfill it are under a curse. The Jews themselves can not refute this, since it is written in Deuteronomy, chapter 27, that 'Cursed be he who does not confirm the words of this law by doing them.' It is not that justification is heralded for him who observes the Law, but that a curse is laid on him who does not observe. But is anyone able to observe the entire Law, whose injunctions stimulate a passion for sin, while giving no strength to overcome temptation?"[59] (This last phrase belongs wholly to Erasmus, as commentary, not paraphrase, but it is strictly orthodox, traceable to Romans 3:20, 4:15, 5:13, and 7:8, as well as to 1 Corinthians 15:56. Erasmus enjoys repeating and extending the idea, and not only in his New Testament paraphrases).[60]

The polemic with Luther, who predicted unconditional perdition for all who had not recognized Christ, forced Erasmus to clarify his own view. "I never held that before the flood of Gospel light the Jews could not save themselves by observing the strictures of the Law, if lacking only the hypocrisy but possessing the faith and mercy required in those times."[61] Other citations[62] confirm that "never." It is worth noting Erasmus' amusing vacillation in the numeric evaluation of those saved by the Law; in 1516 he held the number of such was insignificant (*pauculi*), while in 1527 and 1536 he spoke of a great many (*multi*). The Old Testament Jews after all remained the chosen people; no matter how cruelly God punished them, they remained ever his children, even if unrepentant.[63]

On the whole though it is clear that Erasmus views the Old Law with irritation and malice, most obvious in the tone of those throwaway, apparently insignificant but venomous phrases of which Erasmus is such a master. He calls Judaism a superstition (*superstitio*), a coarse, insignificant religion (*vappa Legis Mosaicae*), an inside-out religion (*praepostera religio*), a perverted (*perversa*), empty (*inanis*) religion, a primitive and muddle prejudice (*rudis quaedam et confusa de rebus divinis credulitas*), while the Law of Moses is bitter and useless (*amara et inutilis*), bloody and unforgiving (*sanguinaria et inclemens*).[64] However, when the theologians of Paris deemed one of these attacks heretical, blaspheming the perhaps superannuated but nevertheless divine Law, Erasmus replied that he had meant only the worship, and not even the whole worship, but only ritual sacrifice, which among the Jews was coarse to the point of superstition, almost indistinguishable from paganism.[65]

Erasmus condemned not only the unbearable weight of the Law, heavier than any of the world's yokes,[66] not only the "biased judgments" it contained,[67] not only Jewish "zeal," meaning undue passion in religious matters,[68] not only the tyranny of the priestly class,[69] and more, but he even spoke without particular respect for the fundament of fundaments, the Decalogue. In his view, the commandments of the Decalogue were overly carnal,[70] appropriate to a coarse and bumptious people. Only three of the laws command something estimable; the remainder prohibit crimes.[71] Erasmus even cast doubt on Jewish monotheism, since if Jews acknowledge neither the Son nor the Holy Ghost, then they revere not one God but some form of mutilated God.[72]

Before seeking an explanation for this exaggerated anti-Mosaic sensitivity, a connection should first be made to Erasmus' moralism and individualism. The moralist systematically destroys and shatters, as may be seen with a glance at Erasmus' invectives against rulers (surprisingly sharp in tone) as well as his explanations on the point.[73] The principle of "without respect of persons" is inverted (there being no persons, criticism may be pitiless, since it is impersonal), constantly concluding with disclaimers of the type "I mean the crowd, the great unwashed, the majority, and not the small number of those better." Thus in discussing the Jews' false hopes for a "fleshy" Messiah Erasmus notes that it was the crowd who awaited such an Annointed One.[74] Castigating the Jews during his polemic with Noël Bédier, Erasmus several times stressed that "I speak of the majority of this people," "I mean the Jewish mob, not the Prophets or those elevated in spirit, of whom there were astonishingly few,"[75] and so forth. Note again the curious move to quantitative evaluation; in a similar context, in 1532, Erasmus speaks not only of the small number of better people who opposed the crowd but of the "many" who had.[76] In this connection it is useful to recall how Erasmus judged his own, Christian mob: "From ancient days the most important culprit of bad living and bad opinions is the crowd . . . As for the Christian crowd, remember that never, anywhere, even among the pagans, was there ever anything more corrupt in judgment or morals . . . After all there is not the slightest doubt that faith without morals worthy of that faith is not only useless but even worsens the condemnation."[77]

It is not the task here to summarize systematically Erasmus' concept of the Law, first because that would be a theological concern, and second because it has already been done, in Kohls' well-known monograph *Die Theologie des Erasmus*.[78] Since Kohls analyzes only Erasmus' early works, through *Enchiridion*, with conclusions which in no way differ from my own observations, it may be taken as proven that Erasmus' idea was already fully formed in his early years, remaining unchanged to the end, which for present purposes is essential. Far more important is that Erasmus' understanding of the Law and, in part, the sharply stressed contrast of Law of the spirit and Law of the flesh both spring strictly from Erasmus' Christology and Christocentrism[79]; in other words, it has no significance in and of itself, rather being the necessary consequence of an idea central to Erasmus' theology (and hence his entire world view).[80]

Of course the question of roots, origin, and formation of this central idea lies far beyond the bounds of the present study, but, as the preceding chapter has already noted, the foundation laid by the New Testament and the Church Fathers for Erasmus' anti-Mosaism unquestionably does demand our attention. Many of the blocks of that foundation appear in the notes; the number of citations could be enlarged, but there are enough for certain conclusions that touch upon the present theme.

First, despite all of Erasmus' erudition in the literature of the Church Fathers, it is rather Scripture itself (source of sources) that, in large part, defines his views of Mosaic Law. Erasmus' anti-Mosaism corresponds almost entirely to the anti-Mosaism of Paul, not the original Paul, the Paul whom church historians are now reconstructing, but rather to the "Apostle of Gentiles" and savior of the young bride of Christ from the threat of "new Judaism," the Paul who springs from the pages of the epistles ascribed to him, and from The Acts of the Apostles. The whole of Erasmus' position may be found in the short summary that precedes Epistle to the Romans in Erasmus' edition of the New Testament: "He [Paul] humbles the arrogance of the Jews, who in relying on the Law destroyed the whole essence of the Law, faith in Jesus Christ. He holds that the ceremonies of the Law are antiquated . . . that there is no longer a place for Sabbath rest, circumcision . . . dietary laws . . . slaughter of innocent animals [in the Temple] . . . These shadows of things dispersed when the light of truth first shone. The true sons of Abraham are those who summon the faith of Abraham; truly the Jews are those who proclaim Christ, truly circumcised are those who have cleansed the spirit of base passions . . . No one may achieve true justification through the Law of Moses, but only through faith . . . Rejoicing at the rescue of the pagans, he [Paul] mourns like a father at the blindness of his own people, even though he is everywhere met with the most stubborn callousness. He tries to smooth this stubbornness . . . averring that not all are blinded and that the Hebrew nation will eventually come to its senses, attracted by the faith of the Gentiles . . . He exhorts the Jews not to harbor hate for the Gentiles who are accepted into the brotherhood of the Gospels."[81] At the very beginning of his commentary to this most important of epistles, Erasmus says that Mosaic Law had dug incredibly deeply into the Jewish soul, giving rise to a serious danger that the Gentiles might also be led into slavery to the Law. Only Paul saved Christianity from that danger.[82]

Here, in short, are not only the subject of this chapter but also the broader subjects to be considered, up to and including the main one, that for which this book was written, the problem which pulls together all the threads—the problem of Erasmus' relationship to Jews of his day, the problem not of theological and abstract anti-Semitism but of concrete and political anti-Semitism.

Further, if Erasmus' position is not fully logical, even contradictory, the cause is not the internal contradictions of the Erasmian model of the world, nor a reaction to the Reformation; the cause is rather, first and foremost, the contradictory nature of the New Testament itself (or, more precisely, of Paulinism) and of early Christian ideology. Like Paul, Erasmus in effect springs from the irreconcilable antithesis Law versus Christ, which leads logically to rejection of the Old Law *in toto,* the Decalogue not excepted. Paul could not and did not wish to follow this path to its end; instead he combined a rigid theoretical anti-Law position with a neo-Law practice,[83] replacing the "Law-Christ" antithesis with that of "Moses' Law versus Christ's Law."[84] Erasmus obediently follows the wanderings of Scripture and Tradition, but aversion to ritualism—*any* ritualism—remains at the core of his emotional "I," always making itself felt.

Only one of the several echoes of this basic contradiction need be noted; the logic of Pauline theory leads to the idea of the absolute, unprecedented novelty of Christianity (a truly *New* Testament, breaking with all that is old, which it no longer needs), while those same demands of practice (as it were, the "antilogic" of life) force a search for sources in the past, in the history of Israel, the chosen nation of God, and in earlier episodes of biblical history.[85] The result of such searching is, on the one hand, symbolic interpretation of the events, figures, and rituals of Jewish Old Testament antiquity (which become prototypes of the Christian future) and, on the other, the idea of a renaissance in Christianity, a return of the ancient faith of the Patriarchs and even of Adam. Erasmus saw both conclusions, using them in the widest possible ways, although they fail to remove the contradiction. The Christian humanist bows before the past, yet the desire to "snatch from one's self the ancient Adam," to repudiate the *entire* past at once, is no less sincere than the bowing.

Third, in the first centuries of its existence Christianity defined itself solely in relation and opposition to Judaism, not as a theologians' whimsy and not as a conditional device but in a real battle with a real and very active opponent.[86] Erasmus continues this tradition of the early Church, but the sixteenth century is not the third or fourth, so the idea of the struggle against Judaism had either to lose all meaning entirely, becoming simply a rhetorical figure, or be infused with a wholly new content.

And a new content it acquired. What most facilitated this was Erasmus' peculiar concept of historical time (or even apprehension rather than concept). Erasmus saw no sharp temporal boundaries dividing one historical period from another; various temporal planes jostle, efface, and mingle with one another, creating a certain extratemporal or unitemporal continuum, in which the past intrudes actively and dynamically into the present, conditioning it.[87] Erasmian "antiquity" is also in this continuum, combining traits of antiquity and early Christianity from several periods and of various sorts, to make an antiquity which never existed in reality anywhere, at any time.[88]

This mixture of temporal planes is the basis for endless moralizing. The past becomes a bottomless well of examples, not simply instructive but of burning significance; it becomes a sort of norm. But if this norm exists (what above is called the ideal "antiquity," infused with the philosophy of Christ), then there must also be an antinorm, equally ideal, and which equally never existed anywhere, at any time, and also is composed of anachronistic and variegate elements. Following the tradition of the early Christians, as discussed above, the name of this norm then becomes "Judaism."

In allegorical and moralistic exegesis, which by nature require the complete rejection of time and its sequence, the Jews of the Old Testament, the Gospel era, and the present day all merge and fuse. One and the same line of the Psalms may be interpreted first as a reference to Christ, then to King David, and finally to contemporary Jews.[89] The blood of Christ is not only upon those who crucified him and upon their descendants but also upon their ancestors, whom the Crucified in his unutterable mercy had redeemed by harrowing Hell.[90] Even now the synagogue may "burst with envy" at the luxurious revelry of the Church, in which the synagogue refuses to take part, while alongside, as before, the pagans "die of starvation."[91]

This composite, syncretic Judaism is not only contrasted to an equally composite Christianity for didactic purposes, as a kind of warning, but also is interwoven with it; infected by the Jewish vices, Christians are no better than the Jews, and the drama of Christ's passion repeats ever and anew each day. Apostle Paul's struggle with the Judaizers, a competition between those who "clutch the flesh of the Law in a death grip" and those who profess the spiritual freedom of the Gospels, is a battle which "will never end among Christians."[92] In fact, Erasmus repeats constantly that all the ill we speak of Christ's enemies and tormentors may be applied to all times, and first among them, to our own, for every age has its Pharisees and scribes, its Herods and Judases; in every age the crowd is ready to cry "Crucify Him!"[93] Those who are now crucifying Christ in the souls of men (heretics who seduce away true believers, despoilers of virgins, slanderers, and so forth) are scarcely less dangerous than Christ's murderers in the flesh.[94] The Christianity of today is full of Pharisees, alongside whom the New Testament Pharisees appear exemplars of rectitude and sincerity; were Christ to return to earth today, these new Pharisees would deal with him even more severely than the old ones ever did.[95] "The Jews who lived in hopes of life in heaven and who kept spiritual vigil abided in the New Testament, while those today who measure piety by external rituals and have no fill of earthly blessings, who are cold to mercy and not to revenge, these stay still beneath the Old Testament, for they have not yet snatched from themselves the ancient man."[96]

Just as diffuse as the attacks against Jews in these contrasts (since any sort of fault can easily be ascribed to an antinorm) is the amorphous and infrequent praise, in contrasts of the type "even the Jews are better than we are." Thus while excoriating bad servants of God Erasmus reminds readers that even the Old Testament priesthood was forbidden to have wealth or keep mistresses.[97] Immediately after that point he also speaks of how pitilessly the tithe is gathered, under threat of excommunication, without regard for poverty or hungry children, indiscriminately from victims of fire and shipwreck alike; he concludes, "Even among the Jews you won't find such examples."[98] The Jews loathed tax collectors, while among the Christians they are in great regard, and not surprisingly; merchants and money changers, whom neither Aristotle nor Cicero wished to have numbered among the respectable citizens, now are almost the highest of all in the state.[99] The Old Law categorically forbids loaning money at interest to members of one's own tribe, a foul crime among the Jews, while the Christians condemn usury in words but suck the blood from all about them like spiders.[100]

Paradoxical though it may sound, the idea of Judaism grows firmer according to its distance from its direct meaning, just as "Jew" becomes a derogatory label for bad Christianity. In such an instance we are correct to speak of "Judaism" (or "new Judaism," as Erasmus says often enough). This "Judaism" is the dominance of ritual at the expense of the essence of Christianity. As early as the fall of 1501 Erasmus wrote that, if someone who is saving himself from the sins of this world should fall into the clutches of the monks, "they bind him to some petty observances of human, not divine origin, and plunge the poor fellow into a kind of Judaism, teaching him how to tremble, not how to love."[101] This letter is a sort of introduction to the first edition of the *Enchiridion;* three years later, in the year when *Enchiridion* saw the light, Erasmus defined the task he had set himself in the book: "The *Enchiridion* I composed . . . solely in order to counteract the error of those for whom religion consists of rituals and observation of corporeal things, more than Jewish, I would say . . ."[102] In fact, this polemic (true, more hidden than open) with "Judaism" is an important part of *Enchiridion.* Erasmus does not condemn "material ceremonies" altogether; they can be symbolic and an aid to piety. They can be indispensable for "the young in Christ," up until they mature and grow strong; nor is it bad if those who have "achieved maturity" continue to observe them, so as not to lead the weak into temptation. These ceremonies however may not become a goal in and of themselves; they are but the first step toward salvation. "To worship Christ through visible things and because of them, and to place in that the zenith of religion, is to take pride in it and to condemn others, to quail reverentially and even to forget about everything on earth, while also (to speak directly) leaving Christ . . . means to betray the Law of the Gospels and to fall into a type of new Judaism no less dangerous than the great and scandalous sins of the soul. It is true that the second ailment leads more quickly to death, but for that reason the first yields to cure with greater difficulty"[103] (a portion of this key statement has already been quoted above).

With variation, this motif extends the length of Erasmus' creative life. It would be difficult to name a work (save possibly the pedagogical and philological ones, most narrowly defined) which does not attack "new Judaism," at least in passing; more often the attack is fundamental and significant. A few details merit closer attention.

First, it must be stressed again that Erasmus considered such attacks a direct continuation of the Apostle Paul's battles with the

Judaizers of early Christian society. No matter how Paul strove to teach Jews not to trust "works" and to direct them toward "spiritual things," "the Christian mass, as I see, once again slid in that direction." And not just the masses, but also the priests, a large part of the theologians, and a countless flock of monks.[104] Paul saved Christianity, which had once again been ready to succumb to the slavish and base Law of Moses, but "even today we are distinguished from the Jews more by the sense of the rituals than by their number, so far has Christ moved away with the passage of time."[105] Significantly, in his commentary to the New Testament and particularly in his New Testament paraphrases, Erasmus speaks of the Apostles' opponents in the same tone and with the same words as he uses to characterize his contemporaries.[106] This may explain what could be called the "Judaization" of the paraphrases, their wealth of reminders, references, and details (sometimes neutral but generally negative) about Jews. Christ's threats to the Jews are far more fearsome in the paraphrases, and the accusations are sharper. For example, in the Gospels Matthew 12:39 reads, "An evil and adulterous generation seeks for a sign; but no sign shall be given to it except the sign of the prophet Jonah"; in the paraphrase this becomes, "A base and perverted people, boasting that their father is God, . . . although they more resemble those who forsook God to worship the Golden Calf, who rose up against Moses . . . Their father is Beelzebub, and full of his spirit, they rebel against the Spirit of God! This people shall have no heavenly sign; they are not worthy of it, for they devote themselves utterly to the earth, but there shall come a sign to them from the earth . . . but if even then they choose not to convert, then they shall perish."[107]

The "Judaization" of the Epistles is even more characteristic. Peter's first epistle contains no "Jewish" places at all, save for a hint in 1:18 ("the futile ways inherited from your father"); in the paraphrase Jews and Mosaic Law are mentioned thirty times, of which only five are neutral. The rest are hostile.[108] Similarly, in the original 2 Peter has no references, there are eight in the paraphrase[109]; 1 John has none in the original, nine in the paraphrase[110]; Colossians has three in the original, twelve in the paraphrase[111]; Hebrews has seven, its paraphrase has forty-two.[112]

This forcing of "Jewish material" is a product not of enmity for the Jews, even if they were directly responsible for the crucifixion of Christ, but rather from the evil of the day. This is an open polemic with the "New Judaism" which was corroding the Church. It was not by chance that the paraphrases enjoyed such success among Erasmus' contemporaries and those following, a success extraordinary even within the context of Erasmus' very great popularity.[113]

Those who are hopelessly mired in ceremony have no right to the name of Christian, so Erasmus openly calls them Jews.[114] Further he announces, "Judaism I call not Jewish impiety, but prescriptions about external things, such as food, fasting, clothes, which to a certain degree resemble the rituals of the Jews."[115] Is it possible to be any clearer about the target of Erasmus' anti-Mosaic barbs?

"Judaism" also resembles Judaism genetically; as has been shown, the bars and chains of the Law are God's concession, an answer to the base morals of the Jewish people. In the same way, human frailty forced the Church to retain some traces of Judaism; our spiritual weakness does not permit us to maintain the heights of Gospel freedom and thus we need the same fetters as were placed upon the Jews.[116] Ideas of the necessity and even utility of the hobbles of "new Judaism" were born in the polemic against Luther, in which they were employed. In one of his anti-Luther addresses of 1526 Erasmus said that the crowd either holds fast to the old ways, not permitting the bishops to improve anything, or are so given to all sorts of scandal that, "if you relax even slightly the reins of Judaism [*si quid relaxes Judaismi*], the crowd, just like a horse that has thrown rider and tack, will plunge into the most horrible impiety and rather than return from Judaism to Christianity, they depart into paganism."[117] However, even this danger could not force Erasmus to refuse battle with "Judaism." In 1529 he writes, "In this desperate storm there is nothing better than to preserve equilibrium, so as not to fall again into that Judaism which some are proselytizing, and not to tumble into anarchy and paganism."[118]

Most Jewish of the "new Judaism" Erasmus saw in the codification of the fast. Christian fasting is an even more onerous superstition than the Jewish "choice of foods."[119] "Of all that which has crept its way into the life of Christians, there is nothing more remote from true piety, nothing closer to Judaism, than the choice of foods."[120]

The most dangerous and zealous carriers of the "new Judaism" are the monks. Erasmus' frequent and pitilessly cruel antimonastic invectives generally also include accusations of "Judaism."[121]

"Judaism" is one of the greatest threats to Christianity. In the famous "Ut fici oculis incumbunt" (*Adagia,* n. 1765, first in the 1517 edition, expanded in later editions) Erasmus sketches an apocalyptic picture of general degradation; after showing the unbearable tyranny of mendicant monks, he concludes, "What have we then? A crowd of impious and idle monks burden the land, rulers hold sway over their people, the bishops over their flocks, the people over their shepherds, while the purity and freedom of the Christian religion slips little by little into Jewish ceremonies."[122] If the "Jews" are not restrained, if no limit is set to their "ceremonies," the freedom of the Gospels has perished irredeemably.[123] It is wholly natural then that Erasmus saw the battle with "Judaism" as among his most constant, important tasks, as well as a major contribution. "With my labors," he wrote in 1521, "I followed no other goals than to resurrect the humanities, which among us are almost consigned to the grave; further, to rouse the world, sunk in Jewish ceremonies, to take trouble about true evangelical piety; and finally, to return theological tasks . . . to the sources of the Holy Scripture."[124] Erasmus formulates almost this same program, in somewhat wider form, seven years later, but in an entirely different political, clerical, and psychological situation, just before his flight from post-Reform Basel. "Here . . . is the essence of what I always did, with the aid of my books. I bravely took arms against war . . . I tried to urge a theology withered in sophistic distinctions back to its sources, to the simplicity of ancient times. I tried to restore their former sheen to the Doctors of the Church. I taught the humanities, once all but pagan, to serve Christ. As far as I was able I assisted the new flowering of languages. I held up to shame the false judgments of mortals about many, many things. I roused a world sunk in a slumber of almost Jewish ceremonies and directed it toward pure Christianity, at the same time never condemning the ceremonies of the Church."[125] Again, about six years after that, Levinus Ammonius, Erasmus' old, devoted friend and a learned Carthusian, confirms that self-evaluation: "You strove as you were able to resurrect the humanities and authentic Christianity, which the thoughtlessness of some had disfigured (how criminal!) with Jewish prejudices."[126]

So, for all the chronological unaccountability of Erasmus' concept of Judaism,[127] the last link in this chain, "new Judaism," is sufficiently distinct from "Jewish impiety" in a strict sense; this latter becomes an object of emotion only as and to what degree it is warmed by hatred for the former. Looking to the sources, to "antiquity," the Christian humanist and disciple of the Brethren of the Common Life there finds unending struggle with Jews and Judaizers; while "resurrecting antiquity," meaning transporting it to his own era, Erasmus brands the sins of the Church of his own day with the shameful mark of Judaism. Despite the "renaissance," this is as much a mark of medieval thought[128] as those Jews whom the Renaissance painters put, in modern dress, into their biblical and Gospel paintings. Neither the costume of the day nor the stain of Judaism were simple conventions or props, but knee breeches and a fashionable tunic did not prevent an audience from recognizing Joseph or the Prodigal Son; so too could Erasmus' readers understand the distinction between Judaism and "Judaism," even without its quotation marks.[129]

There is no doubt that anti-Judaism belongs to the defining particularities of Erasmus' world view, and Telle is absolutely correct to speak of the "anti-Judaic evangelism" in Erasmus.[130] However, to see this anti-Judaism as the result of hatred for Jews and their religion, as Telle does,[131] means to simplify unforgivably a complex and contradictory subject, as well as, in part, to confuse cause and effect (as this chapter has tried to show). Telle is also inaccurate in saying that for Erasmus Judaism became a "universal word or sign, signifying all that he did not like . . . all that seemed to him senseless, outdated, burdensome, or the blind obedience to human rules."[132] This would be some sort of Judaism without bound, an amorphous world evil. Only a madman could suspect Erasmus of such Nazi-like Manichaeanism.[133] For Erasmus "new paganism" is a danger no less real and, apparently, no less dangerous than "new Judaism," as is demonstrated by the *Ciceronianus* and the whole line of struggle against the "Ciceronian apes," as well as by the many remarks, in several other contexts, including some having to do with Judaism. Some of these last have appeared in this chapter; two others should be added:

"Impiety has come to such a state that it appears boldly in people, here open Judaism, there undisguised paganism."[134]

"I grieve that in these years [the last four hundred years] human piety has cooled, as souls yield either to the blandishments of the world or to Judaism."[135]

If "the world" in this alternative means anything other than the "undisguised paganism" of the first quotation, then the number of Christianity's enemies (meaning only original and permanent ones) simply multiplies. To paganism and "the world" would have to be added, at the very least, heretics.

Thus for Erasmus Judaism is not a universal label but rather the mark of the "letter," the "flesh," the power of law, the dominance of ritual, first and foremost a moral category, not a historical or religious one; it is applicable primarily to the lives of contemporary Christians, not to the ancient Hebrews, to the Church, not the Synagogue, and in that is its *raison d'être*.

This is the ideological foundation beneath Erasmus' attitude toward Jews. The first story of that structure (as well as an important part of its foundation) is Erasmus' attitude to the Jewish part of the Bible, to the common heritage of Jew and Christian.

III

The Old Testament

T he assertion that Erasmus did not like and did not know the Old Testament has become a tradition studies only rarely fail to mention.[1] This thesis, based largely on two remarks, from November 1517 and March 1518,[2] would seem a misapprehension. It is in no way surprising that a Christian humanist professing the *philosophiam Christi* and very close in his worship to the ideas of Thomas à Kempis would place the New Testament higher than the Old, but to emphasize this circumstance, as Aldridge does, for example, is to force an open door. On the other hand, to assert, as Renaudet does, that Erasmus read neither Genesis, the historical nor juridical books of the Bible, the prophets, nor even the Song of Solomon, is to ignore Erasmus' entire theological practice, for he refers endlessly to Genesis, to the Prophets, and to the historical epos of the ancient Hebrews, to the monuments of legal thought, and even to the Song of Solomon. As for the excerpts from Erasmus' letters, both are from the time of one of the crises over the Reuchlin affair; indeed deeply hostile to the Old Testament, both passages may easily be explained by the circumstances of the moment and by Erasmus' psychological makeup, just as they must be seen against the background and in the context of Erasmus' other opinions of the Old Testament.

Many times Erasmus states definitively that the Old Testament is important and necessary in its entirety, to the last jot and tittle. Everything in Scripture is fruitful.[3] The divine writings are rich

with hidden wisdom which reveals itself to an experienced eye in
every line.[4] "All that is written and described in the Old Testament is written and described for our edification."[5] Even the long
lists of incomprehensible and alien-sounding Jewish names
should not tire the pious ear: "Just as we revere a repository of
sacred objects without knowing precisely what the objects
are . . . so must we piously hear out or repeat these names, the
secret of which we are not able fully to explain."[6] The Old Testament is not only for instruction; it is also for imitation. "In truth,
there is nothing in the holy books which does not have some
relevancy to our doctrine."[7] Erasmus finds justification even for
the cruelty of the Old Testament, that eternal stumbling block for
Christian meekness. God does not forget charity, Erasmus asserts,
even as he destroys the impious. Pharaoh, swallowed by the Red
Sea, was incapable of correction; left among the living, he would
only have piled sin upon sin, making his eventual punishment that
much worse. "So too must be judged the other examples of severity which the books of the Old Testament contain, those whom
fire devoured, earth swallowed, the sword destroyed, and vipers
killed."[8] In *Ecclesiastes,* after recounting St. Augustine's *"De utilitate credendi,"* Erasmus concludes, "Augustine suggests this cor-
rectly; it is necessary first to love the Holy Scripture, and only
then to study it. One must also learn that there is nothing false in
Scripture, nothing frivolous or born of human minds; it is entirely heavenly philosophy and worthy of the Holy Ghost, in
whatever form it may appear."[9]

Like the Old Law, the Old Testament also has its flesh and
spirit; the true meaning of the ancient Scripture is revealed only
in the depths of the spirit, freed from the covering of flesh. As
early as the *Enchiridion militis christiani* Erasmus states that to read
biblical history without searching for its hidden meaning is no
more useful than to read the pagan authors. In such a case the
books of Kings or Judges are no more instructive than Titus Livy.
Pagan works lack no examples of good morality, just as the Old
Testament has no lack of "apparently senseless things and even
things harmful to mortals, if judged superficially . . . Thus one
must ceaselessly examine the hidden spirit, discounting the flesh
of the Scripture, particularly in the Old Testament."[10] The same
appears at the end of Erasmus' creative life, in *Ecclesiastes,* which

gives a list of apparently senseless Old Testament stories, concluding that it is the habit of Scripture to conceal holy secrets beneath
a pitiable exterior.[11] To take comfort in the dead letter and, even
more, to make it an example for imitation, means direct perdition
for the soul.[12]

Erasmus brought his beloved image of the "*sileni Alcibiadi*" to
the Old Testament, symbol of the dialectic duality integral to everything in the world.[13] "There are also *sileni* in the secret Writings. If one remains on the surface, much seems laughable, but if
you penetrate deeply, to allegory, you bow before divine wisdom.
Take the Old Testament. If you see nothing save stories about
events [*praeter historiam*] [there follow examples, Adam made
from clay, Eve from Adam's rib, the tempting snake, the angel at
the gates of paradise—S.M.], don't you have to see this as a fable
from the workshop of Homer?" When you read of Samson, of
David's fornications and his old man's weakness, about the
prophet Hosea marrying a whore, aren't all these unsuitable
things hard for tender ears? "But God Immortal! What brilliant
wisdom lies beneath this base covering!"[14]

Though paying due regard to the pagan heritage and objecting
to discounting the ancient writers in comparison to the books of
Moses,[15] the Christian humanist still asserts decisively the su-
premacy of the Bible, placing it higher than the best works of
Greece and Rome. This idea sounds particularly clear in the polemic with the "new paganism" of the humanists. "History, if you
remove its authenticity, is not worthy even of the name of history.
Now, if you please, compare Herodotus' fables with Moses, compare the creation of the world or the flight from Egypt with the
fables of Diodorus, compare Judges or Kings with Titus Livy,
who often contradicts himself . . . to say nothing of departures
from the truth . . . Compare the psalms, where everything is
holy, to Pindar's flattery; compare the Song of Solomon with
Theocritus' songs . . . Divine wisdom has its own fluency, and it
is not surprising if that differs from the fluency of Demosthenes
or Cicero, since one homage befits the spouse of the greatest of
kings, while the other befits the girlfriend of a boastful soldier. I
am ready to assert that even if someone should wish to compare
word for word, figure for figure, meter for meter."[16] This same
idea appears both before and after *Ciceronianus*. For example, in

Chapter III

Parabolae (1514) Erasmus writes that just as the opal combines the virtues of many precious stones, so "in Holy Scripture you will find at once all that might attract in any of the pagan writers,"[17] while in a letter from 1 March, 1533, Erasmus writes, "Those who read the histories of the Old Testament almost as they would those of Livy or Sallust are seriously in error. After all, the holy tales are incomparably richer and more full of philosophy!"[18]

It is absolutely clear, *a priori,* that the Old Testament is important for Erasmus not in and of itself but as a gigantic allegory about Christ, a collection of prophecies about the eventual victory of Church over Synagogue (surely the deep orthodoxy of this position, as well as its agreement with the Church Fathers and medieval tradition needs no explanation). In the actions of Christ there is almost nothing not raised earlier by the Old Testament prophets.[19] The Pentateuch and the prophets foretold and described Christ precisely.[20] "The entire Old Testament is a prophecy about Christ . . . the whole Scripture is full of mystery."[21] The Savior Himself, the evangelists, and Apostle Paul all revealed and interpreted these ancient prophecies in abundance, both the oblique (the "mute," in Erasmus' terms), meaning symbols and allegories, and the direct (the "spoken"), meaning those directly from the name of Christ, even when spoken long before his coming (such as Isaiah 61:1–2, for example).[22]

For present purposes though another orthodox thesis is more important, that of the commensurability, even (with certain reservations) the equal significance of both Testaments, or at least the complete inadmissibility of contrasting them. As early as the *Enchiridion* Erasmus insists upon a single method of study for the entire Scripture, moving from the dead letter to the living spirit: "This is not only for the Old Testament, but also for the New."[23] In *Querela Pacis* (1517), which finds considerable fault with the bellicosity of the ancient Hebrews, Erasmus says, nevertheless, "All the books of the Christian, whether Old Testament or New, speak of nothing save peace and unanimity."[24] If he wishes to be truly useful to his listeners, the gospel tutor (*doctor Euangelicus*) must refer both to the books of the Old Testament and to "Evangelical philosophy."[25] "We are obligated in significant measure for our faith in the Gospels to the Old Testament."[26] God's mercy infers not only the New Testament but also the Old.[27] *Explanatio*

Symboli Apostolorum (1533) insistently stresses the "miraculous harmony" between both parts of the Christian Bible, while Christian faith itself is defined as "a divine gift . . . thanks to which man reveres as unshakable truth all that God commanded and promised in both Testaments."[28] If the Old Testament is sterner than the New, then this very sternness, fulfilled with New Testament meekness, in some circumstances is necessary and salutary for the Christian.[29]

Among the impressive multitude of these and similar pronouncements, remarks of a programmatic or sharply polemical character naturally call particular attention to themselves. The most important programmatic statement comes in *Epistola de Philosophia Euangelica,* one of the forewords to Erasmus' edition of the New Testament. "Hardly any of the evangelical writings impart anything beyond what was imparted many ages before in the books of the Old Testament, and in some case, by the works of the philosophers . . . The worthy law of love, which alone encompasses all the laws, is it not revealed directly and clearly in the Old Testament? [Erasmus cites Deuteronomy 6:5] . . . And the worthy admonitions to evangelical love, urging us to charity . . . for the poor, are so clear in the books of the Prophets and the Old Testament that they could not be more clear and evident [Erasmus refers to Isaiah 1:17 and 58:6] . . . Christ teaches, 'Give to him who asks,' while Deuteronomy speaks of the very same, with even greater urgency (*efficacius*): 'Let there be among you no poor man, so the Lord your God may bless you.' [There follows a whole series of examples, to prove that all the principles of the philosophy of Christ had already been formulated in the Law and the Prophets, not excluding even the principle of not resisting evil with force] . . . There is no lack in the books of the Old Testament even of examples of evangelical perfection. After all, even Moses demands to be stricken from the divine book if God will not forgive the rebellious people their sin, and Aaron defends those who conspired against him. There are even examples of brave men who surrender life itself for righteousness, like the martyrs of the gospel."[30]

The *Epistola* ends by contrasting the Testaments, showing that the Old Testament was a shadow, a preparatory course for the philosophy of the Gospels. "Christ brought nothing which was not preceded by a shade or spark in the books of the Old Testament." Erasmus states too that Jewish righteousness was confined to the narrow limits of one small people, while "Christ desired to make his philosophy the common property of all people of the earth."[31]

The polemical attacks are also very interesting. *De magnitudine Misericordiarum Domini Concio,* first published in September 1524, and immediately acquiring great popularity and wide circulation, asks, "Where are these madmen—yes, madmen, and not heretics—who make of one God two? The God of the Old Testament, who is only just, but not good, and the God of the New Testament, who is good, but not just? . . . Where is that mad Manichaean who teaches that He who speaks so lovingly with us through the prophets, who gave us the Law of Moses, is somehow not the real God, but one of the evil demons? There is one and the same God in both Laws, one Truth."[32] Even more clearly (for present purposes), Erasmus writes eight years later, "Those too who accept the books of the New Testament but reject the Old Testament are singing falsely, who distinguish between the God of the Old Testament and of the New."[33]

It is only against this background that one may or should examine Erasmus' attacks against that part of the Bible which is common to Christians and Jews.

Such attacks are few and, more important, are not of a type. Sometimes the note of condemnation sounds so indistinctly that one may doubt whether even to call it an attack, as in *Institutio Principis Christiani* (1516), where Erasmus notes, "The prince should be warned not to consider as obligatory for imitation all that he reads in the holy books. Let him learn that the wars of the Hebrews, the bloodshed and cruelty to enemies, must be interpreted allegorically, or such reading is destructive (*pestiferam*)."[34] This warning should not be disregarded simply because the number of biblical examples in *Institutio* is small compared to those taken from classical antiquity.

There are more definitive examples to address, five in all. Two are the hostile references in the letters, mentioned at the beginning of this chapter; the other three, taken from the works, are significantly less hostile.

Ecclesiastes (1535) cites the differences between "Jews" and "pagans" in the ancient Church, telling how the apostle reconciled the factions by convincing the first not to demand observation of the Old Law and the second to respect the Law as "holy and good" but to interpret it allegorically.[35] In doing so, Erasmus expanded the viewpoint of the extremist "pagans" who "out of hatred for a superstitious and vain people" (that is, for the Jews) had gone so far as to reject the entire Old Testament. "It is absolutely obvious that they were confused, first, by the visage of certain tales which seem either insufficiently true or insufficiently responsive to the greatness of Holy Scripture." (Then Erasmus introduces examples of such stories, "almost the entire history of the creation of the world," the family life of the patriarch Jacob, the amorous adventures and revenge of Samson, the curses in Deuteronomy 27, and so on.) "In the second place, [they were confused] by the multitude of commandments about leprosy, sacrifice, food choice, clothing, and so on . . . Third, by the savage revenge accorded those who had violated the strictures, and by the severity of other injunctions, which seemed remote from humanity." (As examples he used the Flood, the punishment of those who worshipped the Golden Calf and rebels against Aaron and Moses, the massacre of Achan and his family in the seventh chapter of Joshua, "the order to destroy utterly so many peoples and to hate so many others forever," the death of Uzzah for touching the Ark of the Covenant with his hand, in 2 Kings 6.) "There is no end to such examples, while in the New Testament the truth is simple and obvious, without a hint of superstition or savagery, but all is filled with sincerity and meekness."[36]

It is not difficult to demonstrate that both this passage from *Ecclesiastes* and the quotation above, from *Institutio,* might simply be included in the context of general considerations of the flesh and spirit of Scripture. At the same time, while it is not hard to notice Erasmus' sympathy for the extremists' doubts about the full divinity and divine inspiration of the Old Testament, it is no more than that vague sympathy which came so naturally to Erasmus, as the opening of this chapter points out.

The words of the *Ratio verae Theologiae* (1518) are much more resolute; the books of the New Testament are "so much more important for our confession of faith that today they might almost suffice alone [without the Old Testament] . . . Once, in order to

bring the Jews to faith, it was necessary to rely on the authority of
the Old Testament; now we are connected to the Jews only to a
negligible degree, and among the other peoples the Jewish books
do not enjoy the same respect. However, I do not deny that an
extraordinary amount of useful material may be extracted from
them, if they are interpreted allegorically, referring either to Christ
or the morals of men, but even this is measured, infrequent."[37] It is
significant that these resolute words first appear precisely in 1518, or
just after the two anti–Old Testament passages in the previously
mentioned letters; it is curious to contrast them with a similar place
in the commentaries to the New Testament (1519 edition): "And in
general I would more readily approve appropriate (*pro rei commodi-
tate*) meditations on the Old Testament books than that their authority equals the magnitude of the Gospels, or even almost
exceeds it. In fact, what else [besides Old Testament texts] are read
in the temples today?"[38] For all its obvious coolness to the Old
Testament, this quote does not contradict Erasmus' general views
on Scripture, as the one before it obviously does, by presenting the
Old Testament as something with which the Christian may
dispense.

Thus too is Erasmus' revolt against the Old Testament tight-
ened into one chronological knot, the end of 1517 and the beginning of 1518.

The sacramental phrase, "In my opinion the entire Old Testament could go to the devil (as long as the New remains untouched) rather than disturb the peace of Christendom over the
Jewish books,"[39] appears in a letter to the Cologne humanist
Johann Cesarius, dated 3 November 1517, one of the series "dedicated" to Johann Pfefferkorn, the obscurantist protagonist of the
Reuchlin affair.[40] It is well-known that Erasmus studiously kept
out of this noisy matter, stressing his own neutrality, and that he
was very displeased by the coarseness of *Epistolae obscurorum viro-
rum,* particularly since they mentioned his name.[41] He spoke out,
for Reuchlin and against the obscurantist from Cologne, only
once the matter was ended and Reuchlin himself was no longer
alive.[42] Even in August 1519, in a venomous, murderously sarcastic letter to the inquisitor Jacob Hoogstraten in answer to
Hoogstraten's book *The Cabala Refuted, or the Cabalistic Blasphemy of Johann Reuchlin Capnion,* Erasmus maintained outward

decorum and a respectful tone, once again refusing to judge who was truly in the right.[43]

The anti-Pfefferkorn series (to be examined in detail in Chapter 5) is full of hatred for all things Jewish, in the coarsest invective, while the letter to Hoogstraten is courteous and superficially dispassionate, but in both instances Erasmus violates his own neutrality, for reasons which in both cases are identical; each had touched Erasmus personally. In the *Cabala Refuted* (which appeared in April 1519) the inquisitor of Cologne accused Erasmus of heretical views on divorce, as expressed in his commentaries on the New Testament.[44] In the beginning of 1517 the productive convert Pfefferkorn published a polemic under the title *Streydt puechlyn vor dy* [sic] *warheit* (since his Latin was poor, the convert wrote only in German), in which he called Erasmus a runaway monk.[45] Word of this reached Erasmus in the very beginning of November (or perhaps just before); on 2 November 1517, he wrote his most faithful admirer Gerard Lister, who at the time was running a school in Zvolle: "My learned friends tell me that one Pfefferkorn, once a damned Jew and now a most damnable Christian, has published a book in German in which like a mad dog he tears the whole learned world to pieces, and me with it."[46] Erasmus' extreme sensitivity, his irascibility, his inability to keep his counsel, his need immediately to whitewash himself while blackening his opponent have all been remarked on by a number of scholars.[47] He answered both men who had insulted him at once, but the highly placed and influential Dominican he answered directly and with restrained (if fully sensible) ardor, while replying indirectly to the fanatical neophyte whose only strength was his personal commitment and the tireless energy which so often characterizes the newly converted (the foul "Jew" was so base that it was beneath educated people to argue with him)[48]; moreover, Erasmus replied to Pfefferkorn as though hiccuping with hatred, cursing without restraint anything which might in any way be connected with the man who had insulted him. As a result, not only did the unlucky tribe from which the scoundrel had sprung get blasted, but so too did the Old Testament. In these paroxysms of judeophobia Erasmus descends to the level of the great unwashed, the dense and somnolent crowd which he himself disdained and could not endure, to the level of that everyday anti-

Semitism which remains unchanged in shape even today, of which more will be said later.

However, implicit in such rashness of temper is also short duration and superficial emotion. In fact, after a two-week eruption, Pfefferkorn disappeared from Erasmus' sphere of interest; in August 1518, in a letter to Willibald Pirckheimer devoted almost entirely to the Reuchlin business, Erasmus gives but a single sentence to Pfefferkorn: "Even to mention him I regard as an evil omen."[49]

A second attack on the Old Testament, dated 13 March 1518, may also be explained by an eruption of this common anti-Semitism. Erasmus wrote to Wolfgang Fabricius Capito (Köpfel), Hebraicist and reformer-to-be, a companion of Bucer; Erasmus condemned Capito's interest in Hebrew and advised him instead to apply himself to Greek, after which Erasmus denounced the Jews and all their literature, worrying whether "that pestilence that was long ago suppressed" (that is, Judaism) had been given "a chance to rear its ugly head." He ends his philippic by saying, "If only the Church of Christians did not attach so much importance to the Old Testament! It is a thing of shadows, given us for a time; and now it is almost preferred to the literature of Christianity. Somehow or other we are all the time turning away from Christ, who was enough for us, all by himself."[50] In this instance, the cause of the "eruption" can be determined with less precision but still reliably enough.

At this time Erasmus was working on the second edition of his commentary to the New Testament. Among the many attacks the first edition had suffered were reproaches about not knowing Hebrew; mistakes in the "Hebrew part" of the commentaries had been found. Erasmus' main Hebrew consultant had been Johann Oecolampadius, soon to become a famous reformer in Basel; in preparing the second edition, Erasmus again requested help from "my Theseus" (as he always flattered Oecolampadius, until breaking with him after many years). The same day that he wrote to Capito he also wrote to Oecolampadius: "Since you accept the name 'Theseus,' prove yourself fully a Theseus. Many people attack the Hebrew commentaries which I added, relying on you . . ."[51] It is possible to imagine how often Erasmus cursed both Oecolampadius and the Hebrew wisdom that had brought him under the heat of criticism, to which he could not even reply independently.[52] Although he wrote to his former "Theseus" Erasmus did not count on the help of Oecolampadius, who then had no time for him; in fact, Erasmus had already supplied himself with a new helper, Matthias Adrian,[53] a christened Jew and professor of Hebrew at the Collegium Trilingue in Louvain, the man who a few years earlier had taught Capito Hebrew. Relations between Adrian and Erasmus were sunny until just before 13 March 1518, when there was the first unpleasant incident. The letter to Capito, up to the beginning of the anti-Semitic passage quoted above, is wholly devoted to a description of this event, an ugly scene caused by Adrian asking Erasmus to be a witness and arbitrator in Adrian's argument *in absentia* with Capito; the letter then concludes with that judeophobic passage. The primitive logic of the letter is plain; two unpleasant sensations more or less connected with Judaism (the scandalous visit by the convert and the memory of his own weakness in Hebrew) were enough to call lightning down upon all things Jewish at once. Parenthetically, the storm passed as quickly as it had gathered. Already by 26 March Erasmus was enthusiastically praising both Adrian and the studies in which he was engaged.[54]

All this would seem to lead to three conclusions. First, the only serious attack on the Old Testament is that from *Ratio verae Theologiae*, since the letters to Cesarius and Capito in no way belong in the ranks of the works written for publication, and indeed they were not printed in Erasmus' lifetime. The *Ratio* though was distributed extraordinarily widely, both in Erasmus' lifetime and after his death. Second, this single serious attack is in some way connected to the two judeophobic "eruptions," occasioned and conditioned by them; the chronological proximity of the three cannot be fortuitous. Third, to speak on such a basis of Erasmus' dislike or even hatred of the Old Testament is as incautious as, for example, to speak of Erasmus' hatred for Germans, based on the fact that in the middle of 1523 he cursed German coarseness, drunkenness, and poor personal habits,[55] or that in April of 1524 he wrote, "If I had known the sly character of the Germans, I would sooner have settled among the Turks than here" (meaning Basel).[56] After all, Erasmus also calls himself a German countless times, repeating "our Germany," praising the successes of the

German humanities. Also, there is not the slightest doubt that
both these "jabs" at Germany were caused by two conflicts with
Germans that were extraordinarily unpleasant and difficult for
Erasmus, those with Ulrich von Hutten and Heinrich von
Eppendorff.

For the same reasons there seems little need to ascribe too
much significance to Erasmus' attempts to falsify the Old Testament (though no reason to minimize it either). In the New Testament commentaries Erasmus insisted that the Old Testament
teaches "love your neighbor and hate your enemy,"[57] for which
he was accused of lying by the Paris theologians; he clumsily justified himself by agreeing that there is no such literal text in Scripture, but insisted that many places in Scripture lead to such an
idea and that this is not a commandment but a permission, a concession to the human frailty of the Jews.[58] In fact, this is not even
deliberate falsification or an attempt to discredit the Hebrew part
of the Scriptures, but that same vehement irritability about the
Law of Moses which the previous chapter discussed, which those
same Paris theologians considered excessive.

"Erasmus and the Old Testament" is the subject for an enormous study, probably of several volumes[59]; the present study will
touch, and that only fleetingly, upon just certain aspects.

Canon

As a philologist Erasmus could not fail to doubt the authenticity
of those parts of the Christian canon the Jews rejected, doubting
them equal in value to the other Old Testament books. This philological conviction was particularly firm while Erasmus was
working on the New Testament and the writings of St. Jerome.
In his foreword to the second volume of Jerome Erasmus writes
of the hierarchy of authority within the Hebrew canon (Jews revering highest the "Law and the Prophets," the "hagiographies"
second, and the "Apocryphae" third), noting sympathetically that
Jerome also followed the Hebrew tradition, not hesitating to
cross out doubtful episodes in Daniel and radically reviewing the
order of the Book of Esdras.[60] Somewhat farther down the same
foreword Erasmus declares categorically that the "approval of the

Church is of course very important, but if it gives equal significance to the Hebrew books and the four Gospels, it of course
does not wish to give Judith, Tobias, or the Wisdom the same
weight as the Pentateuch of Moses."[61]

Erasmus says approximately the same thing (but more generally) in *Ratio:* "If you wish, it would be entirely wise to establish
the famous succession of authorities among the holy books as
well . . . First place among them would be given to those of them
which the ancients never doubted. For me at least, Isaiah deserves
greater respect than Judith or Esther."[62] The quotation further
up, from the commentaries on the New Testament, condemning
misuse of Old Testament texts in Church services, concludes with
a direct, and for the times very daring, condemnation of the
Christian canon: "After all, we include in our canon even those
books of the Hebrews which they did not wish to include in their
own! The Christians are better disposed to the books of the Jews
than the Jews themselves!"[63]

Erasmus' position in *Free Will* (1524) is somewhat sharper. He
wonders how the Jews could exclude the Wisdom of Jesus ben
Sira after accepting Proverbs and the Song of Solomon, but he
accepts all the other exclusions as wholly explicable.[64] Toward the
end of his life, however, Erasmus seems to retreat even further,
into an unreasoning orthodoxy; "They sing falsely . . . those who
approve of some books in the canonical scriptures and condemn
others, when there is among them the most complete harmony."[65] This retreat though (as often is the case with Erasmus) is
fortuitous, temporary. Already in the following year, 1533, writing
of the late additions to the Christian canon (that is, of the books
rejected by the Jews), Erasmus says that "whether the Church
took these books as equal to the others, the spirit of the Church
only knows."[66] At the very end, in *Ecclesiastes,* Erasmus writes
with his former lack of ambiguity: "If you will, I would advise
that proofs from Scripture come primarily from such books as
never evoked the slightest doubt from the Jews, Greeks, or Romans," and Erasmus follows this comment with a curtailed Jewish
canon, leaving out the Song of Solomon, Ecclesiastes, and
Proverbs.[67]

On the whole then it may be considered proven that for Erasmus the Old Testament canon was the Jewish one, not the

Church variant (though of course it would be wrong to see anything in this other than faithfulness to the traditions of the Church Fathers and philology). Nevertheless, in practice Erasmus often refers to a number of "insufficiently canonical" books of the Old Testament, citing copiously from both Wisdoms as well as from Proverbs. In fact, the "list of literature" recommended for the future ruler in *Institutio* begins with precisely these three books[68]; not only the classics (Plutarch, Seneca, and so on) but also the Gospels themselves must cede first place to the Old Testament Apocrypha and the "somewhat doubtful" Proverbs.

PSALTER

This book of the Bible deserves particular attention both from general considerations (no Old Testament book was as well-known to Christians nor had as much influence on Christianity) and because Erasmus interpreted the Psalms (i.e., they were the point of his direct contact with the Old Testament), as well as because Erasmus loved the Psalter almost as fervently as he loved the Gospels themselves. A letter to Pope Hadrian VI, on 1 August 1522, states that all of Scripture is music which can heal souls that are suffering discord (a hint at Luther's schism), "but by my reckoning there is nothing more effective than the Psalms, in which the divine Spirit deigned to reveal to us the most secret joys of its mysteries."[69] Another example of Erasmus' esteem comes as the conclusion of a list of the possible ways in which a single psalm might be interpreted: "Such is the fertility of Blessed Scripture that at the same time it feeds the young with milk and supports the strength of adults with more fleshy food, and nourishes [the souls of] the completed with higher knowledge. Yes, for hidden in it is an inexhaustible lode, in which the deeper you penetrate, the more astonishing seem the riches."[70] Erasmus could not have spoken more respectfully or reverently even of the New Testament; these panegyric lines recall the intonation of *Paraclesis*. Still, a discordant note can intrude upon praise of the Psalter: "[Psalm 38] has something Judaic to it, that is, lamenting and mournful, when under the grace of the Gospels everything has become livelier, gayer."[71] Then, further on, "But there is something Judaic yet in this psalm, not an example of evangelical perfection for us, but an example of man, who struggles still with his own flesh."[72] This discordant note though must be seen not so much as an attack on the authority of the Psalms so much as a passing remark (the quotes above are the only ones of their sort), in the spirit of the major contrasts discussed in the previous chapter (dolor of the Law versus the rejoicing of Grace, completeness of spirit versus incompleteness of flesh).

Erasmus interpreted only eleven Psalms, not the entire Psalter, not because the Old Testament as a whole interested him less than the New (which is Guido Kisch's explanation),[73] but because of objective difficulties. "Many times various people, among them the King of England, have asked me to publish a commentary on all the Psalms, but I was frightened off, among other reasons, because in my view it is impossible to accomplish such a task worthily if you do not know fully Hebrew literature and history, and also a heap of commentaries can dim the prophetic word."[74]

ORIGINAL AND TRANSLATIONS

This is the subject of the last, primarily philological chapter of this book. Here it is enough to caution that Erasmus the philologist *a priori* could not doubt the value and importance of the original, while Erasmus the theologian could not deny the authority of the Septuagint and the Vulgate, which had entered solidly into Church tradition. The result is a wholly curious collision.

OLD TESTAMENT EXEGESIS

Essentially this same collision may also be noted in Erasmus' exegesis. Chapter 2 has mentioned allegorical-moralistic exegesis, which mixes all temporal planes and cancels all historical concreteness. This method of understanding and interpreting the ancient texts, however, directly contradicts the scientific, philological method the humanists of the Renaissance had succesfully applied to the classical writers, which Erasmus, first among the Christian humanists, had applied to the Greek sources of Christianity and to the works of the Church Fathers. Naturally Erasmian exegetics is a subject in its own right, far beyond the scope of the present study.[75] It should be noted however that Erasmus' attraction to allegory was not a childhood disease or an old man's failing, so that attempts to resolve this contradiction by relying on the evolution (or regression) of Erasmus' world view[76] will lack foundation. In fact, Erasmus many times (and not simply in his prime years) protested against excessive allegorization, insisting on the necessity of a thorough understanding of the "historical" (literal) meaning of the text, and he polemicized against overly daring allegories even among the Church Fathers.[77] Still, Erasmus always considered allegory a method of vital importance for true theology. Ardent tirades in defense of allegory and attacks on those who refuse to move from the literal meaning to a hidden one are just as much a feature of *Ratio verae Theologiae* (1518) as of *Ecclesiastes* (1535), of the commentary on Psalm 1 (1515) as of Psalm 33 (1530),[78] and if Ecclesiastes abounds in cautions against unrestrained allegorism,[79] there are no fewer warnings of the opposite sort.[80] And how could it be otherwise? As the previous chapter has shown, the ascent from the letter to the spirit is one of the pillars of Erasmus' world view as a whole and of his theology in particular.

This is extremely important for Old Testament exegesis, because the holy history of the Jewish people is interpreted as a prototype of the incarnation and earth life of God-as-Man, as well as of the history of the Church. Christ himself, as well as his Apostles, gave the first examples of such interpretations.[81] The figures and events of the Old Testament become precisely the same "shades," "hints," and "phantoms" as the "shadow of the Law" compared to the "Light of the Gospels." So to exclude the spiritual[82] meaning from Scripture becomes "impiety" and "Judaism." The "historical" meaning is the body of Scripture, while its hidden meaning (*sensus reconditior*) is its soul.[83] For this reason the Jews are decidedly incapable of understanding Scripture, remembering their Prophets to no purpose; in order to understand the ancient prophets other, newer prophets are necessary. If the Jews who read daily in their books of Christ not only fail to recognize him but pursue him with implacable hatred, it is solely because they have no prophecies of a new and higher order to reveal the hidden meaning of Scripture.[84] It is but one small step from here to complete textual violence, the very sin of which Erasmus accuses others. Nor does he refuse the step: "Of necessity we depart from the literal meaning every time the words of Scripture . . . reveal an obvious falsehood (*falsitatem*) or absurdity (*absurditatem*), or when the sense contradicts the teaching of Christ and pious habit."[85] Philological and theological impediments are swept into a single heap; medieval exegesis prevails over the "new theology," herald of which had been Erasmus himself. This though should not be surprising, given the starting point of Erasmus (and Christianity as a whole) that the Old Testament is the source of attestations of Christ in some continuum not bound by the laws of historical time. It is not at all unexpected to read something of the following sort: "Often the future appears to prophetic eyes in the form of the past or the present. This is why the divine Scriptures about the future often tell of something as though it were taking place right then, or indeed had already occurred. We see Christ, returning with glory from Hell, through the eyes of faith. He [the author of Psalm 85] saw this with his prophetic eyes as though it had already happened, and this was no less truthful than if it had already occurred."[86] The often fantastic practice of allegorization found, largely, in the interpretations of the psalms is thus not surprising.

Erasmus' attitude to Jewish exegesis, both medieval and late classical, is taken up in the last chapter of this book, while the problem of sources as a whole will remain untouched.

THE OLD TESTAMENT FIGURES

Accordingly, these are allegorized following early Christian tradition as well as that of the Church Fathers (see preceding chapter). Without going into detailed analysis of particular figures (Erasmus treats not only the major heroes of holy history but also many secondary ones, such as Judith[87] or the mother of the Maccabees), a characteristic duality of attitude even to the most "Christianized" figures should be noted, such as to Abraham, "father of all who believe without being circumcised," and for Paul, beyond need of circumcision (Romans 4:11–12). Even the authority of Paul himself does not keep Erasmus from a critical correction to Romans 4:16 ("and . . . [the promise] be guaranteed to all his descendants—not only to the adherents of the law but also to those who share the faith of Abraham, for he is the father of us all"). Erasmus wrote, "You must imagine two Abrahams in one. As God created two Adams, an earthly one and a heavenly one, so did He, as it were, create two Abrahams, justified in noncircumcision by faith, and so the spiritual father of pagans, and justified in circumcision by faith, who . . . is the father of believing Jews."[88] The principal or substantial (if one may so speak) division here is of the spiritual and fleshy, the incompatibility and irreconciliability of New and Old coming into contradiction with the compromise of Paulinism. Erasmus himself recognizes the contradiction, however, for the 1516 edition of this commentary ends with the thought, "Incidentally I see that the majority hold another opinion."

Aversion for the law of Moses extends to Moses himself, where Erasmus' ambivalence becomes lopsided, tilted toward the negative. Naturally Erasmus does not lose sight of the fact that Moses is a favorite, beloved of God, that Moses was a prototype of Christ before Christ's birth in the flesh (*Christi typum gerebat*), that to curse Moses is a great impiety,[89] and so forth, but first there is always the contrast of Moses versus Christ. The contrast repeats itself countless times, sometimes extending to the most detailed contrasting of the "true Moses" (*verus ille Moses*), meaning Christ, with his prototype[90]; Erasmus reminds his readers particularly insistently that Christ was the son of God while Moses was a slave, a servant (a formula borrowed from Hebrews 3:3–6). It even happens that when carried away Erasmus joins the chorus of impious scoffers, for example, openly placing Moses in the same ranks as Christ's enemies: "He who thirsts has nothing to ask of Moses or the Pharisees or the scribes or high priests. Let him come to Me."[91] (This is a paraphrase of John 7:37, with Erasmus putting his at least ill-considered words into Christ's mouth.)

Unlike Moses, David is praised without restraint, as the greatest credit to the Hebrew race since Abraham[92] (although Erasmus' praise for Abraham is incomparably less frequent than for David); he is not simply a prototype for Christ, he is also identified with him terminologically.[93] Still, even the "royal prophet" earns words of criticism. "We prefer Solomon, a lucky and peaceful man, to David, victorious and red with blood."[94] Like Moses, David also sometimes grieves God with his deeds.[95] Here only the conjunction of beloved David with hated Moses is remarkable; much more remarkable is Erasmus' statement, "Although King David in much resembled Christ, he also preserved within himself something as well of the Jewish tribe, and was not always a man pleasing to God." This is followed by a list of David's sins, concluding with a contrast to Christ, in whom all is complete, for all time.[96] It is not the contrast of the mortal "slave" with the Immortal Son that is important but rather the explanation for incompleteness, which is a product not of human weakness but of membership in the Jewish tribe. It seems though that *Judaicae gentis portio* must be understood and interpreted in a larger context, against the background of Erasmus' understanding of "Judaism" as an antonym for "Christ's philosophy" and not as a national category.

PHILOLOGICAL EXEGESIS

This—textual criticism in the modern sense of the word, observations of a historico-literary nature, largely stylistic, and real commentary—is no small part of the "Old Testament material" in Erasmus. For example, Erasmus took a lively interest in the question of the authorship of the Psalter, the boundaries between the Psalms, and the numeration of the Psalms.[97] He said that if the works of Greek literature, particularly the tragedies and Homer, could move a reader to tears, then the Old Testament books enjoyed no less emotional power, as an example mentioning Genesis 42 (the story of Joseph's brothers in Egypt).[98] He demonstrates the connection between Old Testament oratory and classical rhetoric,[99] showing the great artistry of the Hebrew style, which grows from the quantity and variety of ways in which the very same thought may be expressed.[100] He also shows the polyphony of the Old Testament (how the voices of the different personages sound different).[101] Erasmus refutes those theologians who consider it blasphemy to speak of hyperbole in Scripture, since the holy books contain all the tropes which grammarians had been able to discover among the poets.[102] Interpreting the Psalms, commenting on the New Testament or paraphrasing it, and commenting on Jerome's letters, Erasmus very often explains Jewish antiquity, the music, daily life, religious practices, and so forth, as a rule doing so in a straightforward manner without passing from explanation to evaluation.

As a conclusion, I shall attempt to trace the contours of the most complex and laborious problem in the material under consideration, that of Old Testament citation, parallels, and allusions. It has already been shown that the very abundance of such would seem to refute the assertion that Erasmus was not interested in the Old Testament. Two such dissimilar works as *Enchiridion* (1504) and *Lingua* (1525) are equally impossible without Old Testament quotation. *De Magnitudine Misericordiarum Domini Concio* (1524) has 103 Old Testament references against sixty New Testament ones. Abundant Old Testament citations are given very close analysis in both *Hyperaspistes* (1526 and 1527), especially in the second.

There is no book in the Old Testament to which Erasmus did not refer in some context or other. It is interesting though to note which books he preferred, apart from those which were his lifelong favorites (Isaiah, Proverbs, the Psalter, and others). In *Ecclesiastes,* for example, of the twelve minor prophets, only half are used—Hosea, Joel, Micah, Habakkuk, Zechariah, and Malachi. The selection of examples in *Lingua* is instructive: referring to the danger of garrulousness and counseling that the tongue be kept still, Erasmus refers thirty-four times to the Old Testament, fourteen of them to Jesus ben Sira, eight to Proverbs, three to Job, two to Ecclesiastes, and once each to Genesis, Psalms, Isaiah, Jeremiah, Hosea, Amos, and Zecharaiah.[103] When speaking of how to combat an evil tongue, he refers five times to Isaiah, four times to Jesus ben Sira, twice each to Psalms, Proverbs, Jeremiah, Job, and Malachi, with a single reference to Ecclesiastes, Daniel, and Nehemiah.[104] The degree to which this selection reflects Erasmus' world view and the degree to which it reflects tradition (the influence of the *Liber sententiarum* and so forth) should be determined; the paucity of Old Testament material in the letters is very striking. And these are examples only of questions that present a scholar with a purely quantitative processing of quoted material.

It is no less interesting to determine the function of such references (moral injunctions, practical advice to preachers, factual commentary, grammatical or stylistic parallels, and so on). Such a classification would help to refine Erasmus' attitude to the Old Testament texts.

Also interesting are Erasmus' system of references and the accuracy of his quotations. Inaccurate references and fractured quotations occur fairly often,[105] and Erasmus even excuses his own negligence (or, as he calls it, "slips of memory") by saying that they in no way affect the essence of what he is saying.[106]

Again it must be emphasized: if much of this chapter is sketched fleetingly and casually, the cause is not inattention but rather the fact that Erasmus and the Old Testament is a subject for another book, unlike the present volume in breadth, in nature, and in its goals. It is a primarily theological subject, one which touches the very heart of Erasmism.

IV

The Jews of the Gospel Era

Although the concepts "Jew" and "Judaism" have an atemporal, ahistorical character for Erasmus, they nevertheless show a certain concrete foundation, which as Chapter 2 notes is the Christian's Holy Scripture, the New Testament and, first and foremost, the epistles of Paul. The syncretic images of eternal Judaism and the Synagogue, unchangingly and uniformly opposed to Christianity and the Church, from its very birth right through to the present day, are drawn primarily from the Jews of the Gospels, the contemporaries of Christ and the Apostles. Their portrait there, as it appeared to Erasmus, bears careful examination.

By the time of Christ, Jewry had traveled far from its great ancestors, and for the worst, leaving the faith and piety of the patriarchs and prophets; one of Erasmus' most frequent criticisms of Gospel Jewry is degeneration.[1]

Relying solely on works of piety, Jews were aspiritual and without grace. Paul strove constantly to "tear them away" from blind faith in "works" to bring them to spirituality,[2] and each time he used the words "graced" or "in a state of grace" he opposed them to the "self-assurance of the Jews, who in hoping for their works considered grace unnecessary"[3] (Jewish faith in works is contrasted with the ideas of grace, selection, predestination, and so on, as well as with the other apostles).[4] Aspirituality leads to coarse materialism; Jews were unable to understand Christ's words about "the bread of God" and "the bread of life" (John

6:30 ff.) because they interpreted them in their "alimentary sense" and "loving satiety more than salvation, they more quickly sought a good provider than a savior."[5] Faith in works is one of the most important reasons for Jewish opposition to the teachings of Christ.[6] Not for nothing did Christ "find in the Jews only the appearance of religion, while that faith's fruits, for which only he thirsted, he found not."[7]

Not understanding that all men are sinful, that all need the glory of God,[8] Jews were full of obdurate[9] self-satisfaction, self-glorification, and impertinent arrogance.[10] Most of all they preened on their origins; true, "this ailment is common to all men, but Jews, who boast endlessly of their father Abraham, suffer more seriously than the rest."[11] They consider themselves holy by right of birth,[12] but "only themselves; the Canaanites, the Samaritans, and other . . . peoples they considered unclean, dogs."[13] Even Christ was not spared this Jewish failing. In discussing Matthew 15:26 ("It is not fair to take the children's bread and throw it to the dogs") Erasmus remarked, "This Christ said in obedience to the feeling, common to all Jews, that only Jews are holy and beloved of God, while they consider all others dogs."[14] The theme of Jewish xenophobia arises very often[15] in Erasmus, but almost always in opposition to the New Testament lack of distinction between Jews and Hellenes.

This theme is connected to another, no less frequent theme, of jealous ill-well for pagans "permitted access to salvation" alongside the chosen people. This at first glance would seem to mean the Hebrew Christians, who are called "Jews" in the apostolic epistles, and thus to mean one concrete and limited period in the history of early Christianity. In fact there are references to that effect,[16] but the question is more widely posed, touching on the interminable problem of the "Jewish character." The Jewish people always suffered from envy, the sister of slander, as Erasmus declares in *Lingua*.[17] The Jews always swore that the Messiah was promised to them alone and would not agree to share him with anyone,[18] for which reason they preferred (and still prefer) to forgo salvation entirely *(carere salute)* rather than share it with the uncircumcised.[19] In this way "Jewish jealousy" becomes a reason (almost the entire reason) for Jewish unbelief[20] and (what perhaps is even more curious) so brings into action the very important opposition "limitation versus universality."[21] As the commentaries to Psalm 85 (1528) put it: "The Jews strove to keep the pagans away from the grace of the gospels . . . but the Lord keeps no one from His grace, not the Jew, not the Greek, not the Asiatic . . . No sex, no age is kept from God's charity, which once was narrow, anointing only the Jews, but later flooded over all peoples of the earth. It was precisely this about which the Lord prayed to His Father, as He went to his martyr's death, that God's name be called not just in a tiny corner of the earth, in Judea, but among all peoples of the earth, so that all might know His mercy, love of man, and charity."[22]

Self-satisfaction leads to unbounded devotion to all that is one's own,[23] first of all to one's religion. "There is a certain particular stubbornness in this people, and not one other people has clutched its religion so tightly, as . . . Joseph Flavius shows in . . . 'Jewish Antiquities.'"[24] That same stubbornness, without parallel among all other peoples, was shown by the Jews in their struggle with the Gospels of Christ.[25] It makes sense that Jewish stubbornness, for which God often reprimands His people in the various books of the Old Testament, attracts Erasmus' attention in general.[26]

Unlike the classical tradition, for which "Jew" was a synonym for naive credulity,[27] the New Testament and early Christian tradition portrayed Jews as stubborn skeptics and unbelievers. Erasmus makes no mention of the contradiction, in this instance allowing no concessions to antiquity. Skepticism[28] is a consequence of aspirituality; Jews did not believe God's promises and vows, always demanding "signs," material and palpable, always demanding miracles.[29] It is to expose aspiritual Jewish skepticism that the resurrected Christ orders the Apostles to touch his hands and feet (Luke 24:39–40).[30] This, in part, is the cause of Jewish deafness and blindness to the teachings of Christ,[31] "in part" because they "persisted in their disbelief, blinded by hatred, envy, vainglory, greed, and other base passions."[32] Erasmus terms "persistent maliciousness" the fact that the "light of the Gospels" not only did not illuminate the souls of enormous numbers of Jews but blinded them the worse.[33]

Erasmus remarks too on the mercenary nature of the Gospel Jews,[34] their peevishness, their predisposition to complaints,[35] to

despair,[36] ingratitude,[37] vengefulness,[38] rebelliousness and cruelty.[39] A defender of peace, he readily condemns the bellicosity of
the Jews,[40] although that stems not from the time of the Gospels
but from much earlier. However, bellicosity is an integral part of
the syncretic portrait of the Jew, so it should be noted that, while
condemning the trait and contrasting it with Christian love of
peace, Erasmus also admits that the Jews waged war on the direct
orders of God, but he places such orders in the same rank as the
customs and commandments abolished by "the philosophy of
Christ" and Church practice, such as circumcision, animal sacrifice, polygamy, divorce, and so on.[41] Second, he emphasizes with
particular insistence that the Jews battled impious believers of
other faiths, while Christians were fighting one another.[42] Third,
and especially curious, when necessary Erasmus also can turn to
Jewish bellicosity as a positive example. In the well-known work
of 1530, "Must There be a War against the Turks?" (*Enarratio
Psalmi 28*), Erasmus wrote, "At one time, on God's inspiration the
Jews waged bloody war with other tribes, and Moses himself,
with the aid of the Levites, killed twenty-three thousand of his
own people for worshipping the calf. But, doubt some, has this
right to battle passed to the Christians? . . . However, if someone
removes wholly from the Christians the right to war, then he
must also remove from the authorities the right to punish the
guilty."[43]

The traditional, standard nature of this list of accusations is not
in doubt. To be convinced of that one need only leaf through the
New Testament. Erasmus follows the age-old clichés strictly,
adding nothing from himself. In this regard perhaps the most
obvious are the recountings (in the paraphrases of the New Testament) of those portions of Paul's epistles that enumerate the sins
and failings of the Jews, such as 1 Timothy 1:10 or Titus 3:3.[44]

Words of praise for Jews, for all their small number, are much
less standard. Erasmus approves of Jewish love for children ("This
people was philoprogenitive like no other")[45] and their marriage
laws and customs, not only agreeing that the purpose of marriage
is the production of offspring while barrenness is a shame and
punishment from God,[46] but occasionally even remarking on divorce without condemnation,[47] saying that in some instances the
Church ought to permit couples who were unlucky through no

fault of their own to have what was permitted among Jews for the unjust embitterment of husbands.[48] Erasmus liked how the Jews strove to prepare for battle even when God himself had ordered them to attack the enemy and promised victory; the careless lazy man is unworthy of God's promises.[49] He praised the Jewish rule which dedicates holidays to the study of Scripture, contrasting that with the empty amusements to which Christians devote themselves on holidays, so scolding the Christians with the Jewish example.[50]

Erasmus also appealed to positive Jewish examples in polemics. Among other arguments in favor of translating the Scriptures into new languages was: "Among the unenlightened Jews the Prophets were read to all listeners, without exception, and all understood the language, while Christians are not permitted to read the holy books."[51] Erasmus, however, rejected the demand to open Scripture for all, in its entirety. "I will not repeat here that the Jews permitted certain holy books, Genesis among them, to be read only after age 30."[52] Parenthetically, praise on the formula of "even the Jews are better than us" approaches cliché, but moralistic cliché this time, not the theological cliché of which Chapter 2 has already spoken. To what is said there might be added the daring assertion from the dialogue *Ichthyophagy,* that Christian ritual was so burdened with "the rules of men" (that is, with late additions unknown to the early church) as to make it heavier than the Jewish ritual.[53] The daring nature of the statement, however, is mitigated by the dialogue form, which permits the author to hide behind the backs of his characters and so not express his own thoughts directly.

Despite their clichéd quality, the "panegyrics" are most important, having as their source certain well-known New Testament passages, such as, for example, Romans 9:4–5. Erasmus' paraphrase of the two verses: "This is a people whom God once singled out from all others and loved especially, counting the other peoples, the pagans, as foster children, cherishing only this people as his own children. This people has a particular glory and a particular honor because, despising idols, they worshipped the true God. The Law, made and given by God, belonged to them first. They made testaments and agreements with God. They have a worship and a rank of priests by the prescription of God; they heard the Prophets' words many centuries before the coming of Christ . . . They carry their stock from the gloried luminaries and pillars, most beloved of God, of our tribe, from Abraham, Isaac, Jacob, and the rest, from those roots which Christ Himself did honor by his birth in the flesh, so that they, *volens-nolens,* are kin and close to Christ."[54] Similar passages may be found outside the paraphrases as well.[55]

The New Testament (both the Gospels and the Epistles) often call Christ a Jew. Erasmus does not pass this by in silence, a shameful fact for the many anti-Semites among the Christians; he mentioned it not only in the New Testament paraphrases[56] but also in other connections where it might have been possible easily to do without that clarification.[57] Further, as has been shown, Erasmus did not hesitate to imply that Christ was guilty of the taint of a "general Jewish fault," national self-satisfaction.

This brings up the most important question of this chapter, the murder of Christ and the guilt of the Jews. It is worth re-emphasizing that the importance of the question is doubled by Erasmus' chronological Daltonism; that crowd which cried "Crucify him!" before Pilate's praetorium merges and mingles inseparably with their tribe-fellows Matthias Adrian and Johann Pfefferkorn, who were Erasmus' contemporaries.

The bulk of the material for this question comes from the New Testament paraphrases. In the other works the problem of Jewish guilt and responsibility for the passion and crucifixion of Jesus is treated superficially or not at all, which is particularly surprising in the case of the New Testament commentaries. Not one of the famous anti-Jewish verses or passages (such as Matthew 27:25, John 8:41, or James 5:6) receives real comment, just as those places that touch on the mystery of the future salvation of the Jews are left almost without explanation. This means that in the period of his "acme," the years when he worked on the New Testament, Erasmus in general was not particularly interested in the Jewish aspect of the New Testament and post–New Testament history (that is, in Judaism, as distinct from "Judaism"). Thus it cannot be so much that his interests changed as that this abundance of thoughts about the guilt and fate of the Jews was caused by the nature of the paraphrases, "unbroken commentary" which did not permit willful omissions.

The first question was, Who precisely is guilty? The entire Jewish people, or some one of its parts? And does not at least some part of the guilt fall on the Romans? In the paraphrases the usual list of Christ's enemies is *Pharisaei, Scribae, Sacerdotes, Seniores, Primores populi;* more infrequently it is *Herodiani, Saducaei, Templi primates, Pontifices, Legis periti, principes Sacerdotum, principes Judeaorum.*[58] Rarer still, it is *Judaei.* "The high priests and elders of the people," Erasmus says, "primarily conspired against Jesus because they feared losing their benefits and their influence."[59] After listing all the participants in the drama of Christ's Passion, from Judas to Pilate, Erasmus concludes that "in each of them was Caiaphas, and in Caiaphas was Satan."[60] Erasmus even said (paraphrasing Mark 15:10–11) that the people would have agreed to Pilate's offer to release Jesus "if it were not for the implacable envy [or hatred] of the high priests."[62] What examples there are of another sort are almost always conditioned by the textual source. Thus when Erasmus lists Christ's killers as "the priests, Pharisees, scribes, and elders of the people, as well as the people themselves,"[62] it is because Acts 13:27 speaks of "those who live in Jerusalem and their rulers." In the paraphrase of John 19:11, where Erasmus without the slightest apparent cause places the words, "The Jewish nation, guilty of my death,"[63] into Christ's mouth, the groundlessness is only apparent; the Gospel According to John differs sharply from the synoptic ones in its anti-Jewish spirit,[64] and Erasmus, a great philologist with an unfaulted sense of the text, in good conscience reflects that distinction.

The guilt of the Jews emerges with particular clarity in those instances when Erasmus writes of Pilate and the Romans. Strictly following the Augustinian tradition,[65] adding nothing of his own, Erasmus wholly whitewashes the Romans, placing full responsibility for deicide upon the Jews. He not only excuses Pilate,[66] he even praises him;[67] while the Jews are not just wholly at fault, they even attempted in advance to put their guilt off onto others, which was the very reason why they took Jesus to Pilate, to make it appear the pagans had killed him, not the Jews.[68] They did not wish to enter the praetorium, to avoid sullying themselves before Passover, but "their spirit was in the praetorium, was in the hands of the soldiers who on their own initiative were disposed to crime, but whom the Jews further incited."[69] A simple glance at the paraphrased verse Mark 15:16 shows how greatly Erasmus strengthened the anti-Jewish tone of the original, a tendency which may be felt throughout the episode of the Passion. It turns out that the Jews not only urged the legionnaires on but also allotted Jesus the place on Golgotha between the two robbers, as well as offering him the spongeful of vinegar and gall[70] (compare with Matthew 27:27, 38, 34). Pilate also has Christ flagellated to satisfy Jewish bloodlust[71] (compare with Mark 15:15). Nor did the Jews stop at urging the Romans on; they even bribed the tormenting soldiers[72] (compare John 19:2). John 18:31 reads, "Pilate said to them, 'Take him yourselves and judge him by your law.' The Jews said to him, 'It is not lawful for us to put any man to death.'" Erasmus' paraphrase of the same verse reads, "So spoke the shameless people, murderers of so many prophets, flattering themselves with the hope of remaining pure of the crime, even though by all possible means they drove the innocent man to destruction, as though the killer is only the executioner who nails him to the cross with his own hands. They [the Jews] had the soul of a murderer and the tongue of a murderer; they hired a traitor, they hired the cohort, they hired false witnesses and invented false crimes; they jostle and cow the judge, but imagine themselves unstained by crime."[73]

Still, none of this is Erasmian invention or initiative; Erasmus is obediently following the Augustinian tradition, born in the period of the reconciliation of the Roman Empire with Christianity, which became almost dogma in the Middle Ages, withering only in our lifetime with the resolutions of Vatican II. Beyond the active sphere of the tradition, outside the juxtaposition of Jews and Romans, the tone softens noticeably, becoming calmer and more reserved. Thus the famous line, "His blood be on us and on our children" (Matthew 27:25), Erasmus paraphrases, "But even these words of Pilate, 'I am not guilty in the blood of this Righteous Man,' did not frighten the unhappy Jews . . . They called destruction down upon themselves and their descendants. But Christ, more merciful to them than they to Him, closed the path to forgiveness to no one, if the guilty would but come to their senses. And in fact very many of those in the crowd who cried then, 'Crucify, crucify him!' later bowed before the Cross of Christ."[74]

The traces of another tradition (and a newer one, formed fully only in the eleventh century) in the paraphrases are very interesting, the concept of the "blessed guilt" (*felix culpa*) of the Jews, which had enriched the world.[75] In a way the approach to the idea lies in a reasoning far from fine theological distinctions, dictated only by elementary logic, as in the following (which, it is true, refers to the tormentors of the Apostles, but without stretching it could also be applied to those who crucified Christ): "There were in the crowd people who still did not believe that Jesus was the Son of God, and this error in some way lessened the savagery of their crime . . . There were also those who were simply mistaken, thinking that they were offering God a welcome sacrifice, destroying those who would undermine God's established Law."[76] However, even the truly guilty were serving God's design. No matter what Jewish cleverness concocted for reviling Christ, "He turned everything to his own glory."[77] For our salvation Christ made use even of the vile hatred of Judas.[78] He "died not through the will of the Jews, but through the will of the Father, and by his own will, when he wished and as he wished."[79] The devil attempted to destroy Christ "through his servants, the Pharisees, scribes, and high priests. But here too the Lord with divine art overcame the cleverness of the enemy. He made into our salvation that which [the enemy] had invented for destruction."[80]

This then is the picture painted by the paraphrases, which may be fleshed out further with quotes from other works; these are few, but quite important, since such instances are not dictated by the duties of a commentator and hence appear *motu proprio*.

At the very beginning of his theological career, in 1499, Erasmus took up a discussion with John Colet about Christ's sorrow and worry in the Garden of Gethsemane, and the words, "My Father, if it be possible, let this cup pass from me" (Matthew 26:37–39). Colet, following Jerome, said that Christ was suffering fear for the Jews, not wishing his death to become the cause of their destruction.[81] Erasmus though held that the Savior's sorrow before death was the fruit of his human nature, which could not but fear death; in the end Erasmus agreed to combine and thus reconcile the two positions.[82] He concludes the discussion by saying, "Let us say that of two circumstances which are not essentially related but which by chance would coincide [*ex duobus illis quae se fuerant non rerum cognatione, sed eventu consecutura*], namely his death and destruction at the hands of the Jews, Christ desired one, death, but not the other, that the Jews would kill him at their peril. He could after all have died at the hands of madmen; he could absolve the sin of his murderers. There is no crime so heavy that it cannot find forgiveness."[83] Then Erasmus made an important clarification, which, as is seen above, also appears much later in the paraphrases, that the death of Jesus is the intention of the Father, not of the Jews.[84]

The *Interpretation of Psalm 1* (1515) contains an affirmation that the Jews were guilty in the mocking of Christ by the Roman legionnaires and in the choice of execution methods and that, although the torments and death on the cross were necessary to bring about all that had been prophesied about Christ, this still does not excuse the Jews, since they acted consciously and of their own free will,[85] so the Jewish people deserve the fatal punishment they brought down upon themselves.[86]

However, in addition to his commentary on the New Testament (1535), interpreting Peter's words about "the definite plan and foreknowledge of God" (Acts 2:23), Erasmus says, "With these words Peter shows that nothing in Christ's deeds was by chance, that everything was shaped by the unbreakable plan of God, and at the same time he lessens the guilt of the Jews, who, although they did not know it, were serving the divine plan."[87] In 1525 (*Interpretation of Psalm 4*) Erasmus apostrophizes the Jews: "Do not despair of salvation because you crucified the Son of God; your crime was admixed with error."[88] Two years later, in *Hyperaspistes II,* Erasmus let drop a remark which was of astonishingly good sense for a theological discussion. "Not all Jews reviled Jesus with blasphemy, not all of them sent the innocent man to death, to say nothing even of the Jews who lived far from Palestine and scattered throughout the whole world, who had no idea what was happening in Jerusalem."[89] However, the next year, 1528 (*Interpretation of Psalm 85*), Erasmus repeats the idea of the Jews' general guilt and the universal conspiracy[90] of Jews, source and supply of which was the Old Law, which they understood incorrectly, interpreting it solely in its corporeal sense, without spirituality.[91] All efforts by the Jews to excuse themselves are categorically rejected: "The Jews say, 'We killed a man, we didn't know it was God.' That may be, but you killed a man who was innocent and your benefactor; you did not balk at that at which Pilate balked, seeking reason to release the guiltless man, or at which Pilate's wife balked—both a woman and a pagan. Your hatred held above all, blinding you utterly, for otherwise you might have seen something in Jesus greater than a man . . . We, they say, didn't kill him. No, you killed him with your shouts, killed him the more foully because long ago you coveted his soul with [various] devices, with your insolent cries you forced the just rulers to serve as the instrument of your crime."[92]

Erasmus' last utterance on the subject, however, is more favorable for the Jews: "As Paul says, if they had known [Him] they would never have crucified the Lord of Glory." Had it not been for Satan using the weakness of human nature, the Jews would never have caused the sacrifice through which, incidentally, they might if they but wished it free themselves from their many centuries of slavery to that same Satan.[93]

The picture thus is maculate, if not chaotic. This very maculation would seem to imply a lack of interest in the problem of Jewish responsibility for deicide, a conclusion strengthened by considerations of a general nature. As is known, Erasmus primarily saw theology as a path to piety, to Christian virtue, a guiding principle, directions, a redeeming example, and not speculative musings far removed from the needs and troubles of the world.[94] The Jews who had crucified the Savior in the flesh occupied him incomparably less than the new Pharisees and new Jews (meaning bad Christians) who ever and anew crucified Christ in the souls of men (see Chapter 2). This was the center of his attention, while the former occupied a modest corner in the periphery.

It is also impossible not to note the individualism and sober judgment so typical of Erasmus which may be heard in some of the quotations above.

As a whole it would seem that all this speaks to a certain similarity of Erasmus' position to the views of one of the most attractive figures of the early Middle Ages (from the Jewish point of view), Pope Gregory the Great, who accused not just the Jews of Christ's crucifixion but also the Romans and the Christians, whose sins crucify Christ in each generation of man, and who always pointed out that the Savior was sent to suffer on the cross by the Pharisees, not the entire people.[95]

The tragedy of the Jews though, Jewry's incomparably bitter and awful fate, is defined not only, and even not so much, by deicide as by their stubborn unbelief, their blind and categorical unwillingness to see in the crucified Jesus the very Messiah whom Jews had anticipated for so many centuries. Here Erasmus' thought follows strictly the plentiful and well-known New Testament texts, but occasionally in details and nuances Erasmus shows an extraordinary liveliness and even enthusiasm. This is understandable, since the subject is not a passing confusion or burst of passion, evoked by the inadvertent will of God, but is about a conscious choice of paths, about free will, that is, it is not primarily a theological puzzle but a living problem, standing constantly and with unchanging sharpness before the Christian as much as before the Jew.[96] Of course, it is not necessary to recall as well that it was the discussion of free will which finally and irredeemably tore Erasmus away from Luther and the Reformation.

At first the Jews did not recognize the Messiah in his humble and pitiable form, but this mistake was only the pretext of their future doom.[97] Both in and beyond the paraphrases Erasmus wrote unflaggingly of the stubbornness and ill-will of the Jews, who had not responded to any of the calls to salvation. They were the first summoned to enter the kingdom of God, first through the Prophets, then through John the Baptist, then through the lips of Christ himself, and finally by the apostles, and so they may appeal to no one if having so often despised the mercy of God they suffer deprivations without number. The whole fault lies in their obstinate evil will [*obstinata malitia*].[98] Christ ordered the apostles to take the message only to the Jews, so that later they could not excuse themselves; thus it would be plain to all that they had lost the kingdom of God through their own depravity [*perversitas*].[99] Erasmus' paraphrase of the well-known verse "O Jerusalem, Jerusalem . . . How often would I have gathered your children together, as a hen gathers her brood under her wings, and you would not!" (Matthew 23:27) reads, "I have not overlooked a single means of your salvation, while you did not overlook a means of bringing doom upon yourself and the loss of salvation. He though to whom is given freedom of choice [*arbitrii libertas*] cannot be saved by force. My will must be answered by your will."[100] This highly curious remark anticipates by at least two years the tract *A Diatribe on the Free Will;* that does not touch on the problem of Jewish unbelief, but *Hyperaspistes II* (1527) examines it in detail,[101] giving full development to the thesis advanced five years before.

That discussion is based primarily on an analysis of the second chapter of Romans. Failure to accept the truth of the Gospels, Erasmus states, annuls any claims the Jews have to blessedness or election. He who does not believe and does not wish to believe in the Gospels is not capable of receiving grace.[102] God did not inspire this unwillingness in the Jews but simply foresaw it[103] and so opened the doors of salvation to the pagans, even though they had known neither the Law nor the prophets. "God consecrated the pagans into the Gospels, but he did not force them; and He did not refuse the Jews by force, but since they stubbornly resisted the Gospels after so many beneficences and so many clear miracles, since they had already destruction as vessels of anger ready for destruction, He made of them a warning example for all and each, to show how dangerous it is to scorn God's grace, which is offered us."[104] Thus the fall of the Jews and the elevation of the pagans is the result of the unbelief of the one and the belief of the other. "At work here is free will which, if it wishes to, responds to the knocking of grace standing at the doorway, and so accepts the grace which justifies man, or may turn away if it wishes and make a man unworthy of grace."[105]

It seems indisputable that Erasmus saw the conscious and attributable guilt of the Jews, the source of their sufferings, humiliations, and repudiations to be in their unbelief, not in the murder of Christ. He urges Christians to consider this Jewish unbelief precisely because it conceals a terrible but instructive lesson for the future. However, it is clear too that for all its instructiveness the lesson does not inspire hatred, does not kindle the base and vile passions of the crowd, and does not urge pogrom. Further, the lesson is more suited to evoke pity for obsessed blind men; in fact, one of the epithets Erasmus most often links to the word "Jews" (beside "unbelieving" and "blind") is "unhappy." It is equally clear that Erasmus' position is not at all suited to serve as a foundation, or even part of a foundation, for serious anti-Semitism, theoretical or practical.[106]

The problem of guilt and punishment touches not only the Jews of the Gospels but the Jews of Erasmus' time as well, inasmuch as the guilt remains unexpunged, the unbelief remains undefeated, and the punishment continues to press down upon the condemned. To an even larger degree this relates to the great mystery of the future salvation of Israel, for which reason it will be left for the following chapter ("The Jews of Erasmus' Day"). In conclusion, however, a few terminological questions should be considered in the present chapter.

Works on the history of Jewish-Christian relations pay great attention to Christian authors' use of the words "*Judaei, Hebraei, Israelitae*" to denote various periods in the history of the Jewish people. By the time of the New Testament (John and Revelations) "*Judaei*" is invariably derogatory, as distinct from "*Israel*."[107] In the works of the Church Fathers before Augustine "*Hebraei*" and "*Israel*" are used for Jewry before Christ, while "*Judaei*" applies to contemporary Jews and thus has a pejorative tinge. In Augustine "*Israel*" is positive, "*Judaei*" derogatory, and "*Hebraei*" is neutral.[108] However, indiscriminate use of all three terms is also a fairly ancient tradition (dating from the fourth or fifth century), to which Pope Gregory, among others, adhered.[109] Erasmus shows a mix of the two traditions, which even in the primacy of the first shows the influence of the second. Unquestionably the term "*Judaei*" predominates in the New Testament paraphrases, but occasionally Jesus' contemporaries are called "*Hebraei*."[110] On the other hand, Jews throughout the full course of their history are called "*Judaica natio*,"[111] while in the *Interpretation of Psalm 4* (1525) Jews of Jesus' time are called "*populus Israeliticus*."[112] In *Vidua Christiana* (1529) Erasmus writes that Judith fasted every day save on the Sabbath, the beginning of the month, and on the other holidays, "when the *Judaei* were forbidden to fast."[113]

It would seem even here that the search for sources surely would lead back to the New Testament. In fact only John distinguishes systematically between "*Judaei*" and "*Israel*"; Acts, for

Chapter IV

example, has Peter in the second chapter using both "Men of Judea" (2:14) and "men of Israel" (2:22) in the same sense, and Erasmus preserves both in his commentaries.[114]

Still, there are abundant examples of Augustinian use of the three words. Writing of the practice of the Old Testament Jews to marry beautiful non-Jews (Deuteronomy 21:11–13), Erasmus says "Israelites," while using *"Hebraei"* for the exodus from Egypt (*Enchiridion*, 1504).[115] "He whom the Greeks call *'christum'* and the Latins *'unctum'* [Anointed One], the Hebrews [*Hebraei*] call *'messiah,'* the word which Judeans [*Judaei*] use for the specific designation of the great prophet . . . promised for the salvation of all peoples. Anointment among the Hebrews [*Hebraeos*] was not solely for kings . . ."[116] The first *"Hebraei"* here means the users (or initiates) of the Hebrew language (just as frequently occurs in Augustine),[117] *"Judaei"* means the contemporaries of Christ, and the second *"Hebraei"* means Jews of the Old Testament. "For how many centuries did the Hebrews [*Hebraei*] wait for their . . . Messiah? But what was it the crowd waited for? Some sort of great king who would greatly expand the border of his kingdom, who would free the Judeans [*Judaeos*], showering wealth upon his people, putting to fire and sword the pagans who knew not the Law of Moses."[118] Here *"Hebraei"* means Jews throughout their history, while the crowd thirsting for the liberation of the Judeans are those who failed to recognize Christ in his humble and far from kingly guise. The same usage is followed in this quotation, from the commentary to the New Testament (1516): "The Jewish people [*populis Hebraerum*] . . . were called 'circumcision,' the other people 'foreskins,' but it was only among the Judeans [*Judaeis*] that the former name was considered an honor and the latter shameful."[119] In *Lingua* (1525) the example of hypocrisy among the Judeans [*Judaeos*] is the Pharisees; the Proverbs were written either by Solomon or some other wise Hebrew [*Hebraeus*]; the Golden Calf was made by the people of Israel [*populus Israeliticus*]; Judeans [*Judaei*] accused Christ of many crimes; the wise Hebrew [*Hebraeus*] Ecclesiast writes that . . ."[120] From the letters: the Hebrews [*Hebraei*] once again gained freedom in the desert; the wise Hebrew [*Hebraeu*] Ecclesiast.[121] These are but a few examples, taken at random, without particular method.

62

Erasmus also follows New Testament word use in calling Christianized Jews "Judeans," which often leads to confusion (as occurs as well in the New Testament itself). Paraphrasing Acts 8:38, which recounts how the apostle Phillip baptized the eunuch, Erasmus adds on his own that "the Judean [baptized] the Ethiopian."[122] Somewhat further down, however, paraphrasing Acts 9:21 in which the citizens of Damascus marvel at Saul's sudden conversion, Erasmus writes, "How did this happen, that he so quickly expunged the Judean in himself?"[123] Erasmus shows particular relish in calling "Judeans" those new converts who still keep allegiance to the Old Testament law.[124] Striving to avoid the ambiguity and muddle which in some cases seriously threatened comprehension,[125] Erasmus sometimes offered the necessary clarifications. Romans 15:25 ("I am going to Jerusalem with aid for the saints") Erasmus expands with the explanation "to tell the Christian Jews [*Christianis Judaeis*] living there about the pious acts of the Macedonians."[126] 1 Corinthians 9:20 ("To the Jews I became as a Jew, in order to win Jews") Erasmus renders as "I adapted myself to the Jews . . . as if I were a real Jew [*vere Judaeus*], although I knew that the Law of Moses has been abrogated."[127] In Acts 21:39 Paul says of himself, "I am a Jew" [*Ego homo sum quidem Judaeus*], which Erasmus paraphrases as, "I am of Jewish origin" [*sum homo genere Judaeus*].[128]

Use of "Israel" and "Jews" to mean Christians, a terminology that reflects the early Church's battle with Judaism over the Old Testament heritage,[129] a battle ended in the Middle Ages,[130] was something wholly natural to Erasmus, used as it were automatically, without confusion. Erasmus often repeated that "Jews" in Hebrew means "believing"[131] [*confitens*], a name of which those who deny Christ are unworthy.[132] "We call ourselves Jews, meaning believers."[133] "Let us also be Jews, in order to sing a psalm to the Lord. Jew means believing."[134] Combinations like "the true Israel," "spiritual sons of Abraham," "truly circumcized," and so on, are both extremely numerous and fairly broad but not relevant to present purposes, save to note the curious contrast of "the Jewish people versus the spiritual Israel,"[135] the explanation of "holy Israel, meaning eternal truth, able neither to err nor cause error,"[136] and Erasmus' apostrophe to "sons of Zion," a Christian preacher addressing his Christian audience.[137]

Worth noting too is Erasmus' use of "Israel" to mean the Church.[138]

For present purposes the question of the relationship between Church and Synagogue is also primarily one of terminology, both posed and answered in the spirit of the centuries-long traditions of Western Christianity. Before Christ a gathering of the pious, an assembly of the holy, was called a "synagogue," after Christ it was a "church."[139] The synagogue gave birth to Christ, a Jew in the flesh, and so it may bear the name "mother of Christ," but at the same time it must be called the "servant of Christ," while the church earns the name "bride" and "daughter" of Christ.[140] All the same (and occasionally even in the same work) Erasmus speaks of the synagogue as the wife or bride of Christ which has destroyed its beloved.[141] Erasmus notes that "synagogue" and "church" [ecclesia] mean essentially the same thing, but dissemination of the gospels demanded a change of name, since the gentiles hated both the synagogue and the Mosaic Law it professed.[142] Directly thereafter though Erasmus indicates a difference in meaning; the noun "synagogue" comes from the verb "coerce," "assemble by force" (cogere), while "church" comes from "summons" (evocare). Thus the first term befits the Jews, "a stubborn and rebellious people," kept within the confines of the Law by fear of punishment and hopes of earthly reward. The gentiles responded eagerly to the call of the Gospels, while the Jews refused to exchange their empty ceremonies for true piety, their shadows for the light, their letter for the spirit. To submit under threat is the way of servants, while to obey voluntarily is that of sons.[143] As the "mother of Christ" the synagogue is the prototype of the Madonna.[144] The image of the synagogue also turns up in various allegories of the Gospel; if the young ass on which Christ enters Jerusalem (Mark 11:2ff.) is the future Church of the Gentiles, then the synagogue is an old she-ass[145]; if the poor widow who gave two copper coins to the temple treasury (Mark 12:44) is the church, then the synagogue is the haughty matriarch who boasts of her husband, Moses, and of her children, the Prophets.[146] The synagogue of the Jews is narrow, while the church of the Christians can accommodate all the peoples of the earth.[147] There is another contrast, the kingdom of the synagogue versus the kingdom of God,[148] which was undoubtedly sprung from the New Testament phrase "synagogue of Satan" (Revelations 2:9 and 3:9), which Erasmus often repeated.[149]

As ever, there is also anachronistic moralizing; the tasteless waters of the synagogue are drunk by those who are mired in ceremonies, relying on "works" and human efforts[150]; any whose spoiled palate still savors the soulless letter belongs yet to the synagogue.[151]

Almost no coarse or derogatory epithets are used for the synagogue.

What are the usual epithets for Jews? It is not worth citing Jewish faithlessness (*increduli, incredulitas*), blindness (*caecitas*), or envy (*invidia*) of the gentiles, since the epithets are too common and too frequent; they also have been mentioned above, as were the "unhappy Jews" (*miseri, infelices*).[152]

Jews are stubborn (*obstinati, pervivaces*),[153] intractable (*natio intractabilis*),[154] ungrateful and forgetful (*ingrata gens, populus ingratus et obliviosus*),[155] corrupt (*Judaeorum perversitas, improbitas*),[156] impious (*impii*),[157] hopelessly superstitious (*Judaeorum invicta, invincibilis superstitio*),[158] arrogant (*superciliosi*),[159] malicious (*Judaeorum malitia*),[160] suspicious (*Judaeorum perversa suspicio*),[161] slanderous (*calumniatores*),[162] coarse and stupid (*duri et crassi*),[163] savage (*Judaeorum saevitia*),[164] rabid (*Judaeorum rabies, furor*),[165] jealous (*Judaicus livor*),[166] of hopelessly base nature (*invincibilis Judaeorum importunitas*),[167] despised of all peoples (*contempti ab omnibus nationibus*),[168] as well as pitiful, abject, and sterile (*deplorati, abjecti, steriles*).[169]

Not what could be called an overly flattering list. Still, almost 100 percent of this abuse is the work of St. Augustine,[170] which became the common property of the entire medieval Christian West. Almost every time a medieval Christian writer who was using Latin wished to heap evil abuse on the Jews, he did so with formulas and terms from Augustine.[171] A comparison of this list with that in Blumenkranz' book on Augustine (see n. 170) will show how modestly Erasmus dipped into that common store.

V

The Jews of
Erasmus' Day

*L*et us begin with a detailed summary of all the material, in chronological order.

Erasmus first speaks of Jews contemporary to him in his famous essay on the adage "Dulce bellum inexpertis" (1515): "When has the sword, murder, arson, plundering turned conquered people into good Christians?! Openly to be a Turk or a Jew is a lesser evil than to pretend to be a Christian. I prefer a real Turk to a false Christian."[1] It is characteristic, almost symbolic, that Erasmus' first and almost fleeting mention should be inscribed in the broad context of Erasmian ideas, the rejection of force in matters of faith, true and false Christianity, internal reality and deceitful exterior.

The first edition of the New Testament commentary (1516) leaves the subject of contemporary Jewry untouched, which *argumentam a silentio* would seem weighty evidence of Erasmus' utter indifference to the Jewish question, in today's sense, since all problems that disturbed Erasmus found some reflection in the commentaries. There are, however, two exceptions; the foreword, titled "Paraclesis," asks, "Mohammedans remember their teaching, and Jews study their Moses from the cradle on. Why is it we don't manifest the same with respect to Christ?"[2] and the remarks on Matthew 1:21 include "the madness of the Jews of our day" who claim that Christ had a name other than Joshua ben Nun (Book of Joshua) and Joshua the High Priest (Ezra 3:2, 10:18, *et al.*).³

The first hostile remark comes in February 1516, when Erasmus writes to Wolfgang Fabricius Capito (see Chapter 3) in praise of his theological and philological work: "There is still one misgiving in my mind: that under cover of the reborn literature of antiquity paganism may try to rear its ugly head . . . or that the rebirth of Hebrew studies may give Judaism its cue to plan a revival, the most pernicious plague and bitterest enemy that one can find to the teachings of Christ . . . Lately there have been published several pamphlets which breathe the unadulterated air of Jewry. I watch our great hero Paul [the Apostle] toiling to defend Christ against Judaism, and I feel that some men I could name are slipping back into it secretly. Then I hear of people who have other schemes afoot which can add nothing to our knowledge of Christ but merely throw dust in men's eyes."⁴ The context shows that primarily this is "Judaism," the tyranny of rituals in the Church, not the living Judaism of living Jews; after all, no one can doubt that what Erasmus means here by paganism is not the worship of Athena Pallas or Jupiter on the Capitoline but the "neopaganism" of the Renaissance. Strictly speaking, this citation from the letter to Capito should have no place in this chapter, but it is included solely for polemical reasons, since Guido Kisch uses it as an example of Erasmus' ardent anti-Semitism.⁵

However, that same year, while praising France, Erasmus exclaims in the first lines, "France alone remains not infected with heretics, with Bohemian schismatics, with Jews, with half-Jewish Marranos, and untouched by the contagion of Turkish neighbors."⁶ Almost the same appears the next year, in 1517, in *Querela Pacis:* "Nowhere [save France] do the laws blossom so, nowhere is such purity of religion preserved, uncorrupted by the traffic with the Jews which has occured among the Italians, uninfected by neighboring Turks or Marranos, which have happened in Spain or Hungary."⁷ That same year, 1517, has the first judgment about God's wrath, applicable equally to Jews of the Gospel and Jews of the day. Paraphrasing Romans 9:22 ("What if God, desiring to show his wrath and to make known his power, has endured

with much patience the vessels of wrath made for destruction")
Erasmus wrote, "With great leniency God supports and long endures the unbelieving stubborn Jews, as vessels which deserve
soon to be broken, and He endures in order that all may clearly
see that they deserve destruction, who despite all summons and
blandishments are incapable of correction: equally He endures so
that others will see their punishment and be in awe of almighty
God, who may not be provoked with endless sinning."[8] The moralistic and pedagogical interpretation here (especially in the second half) is interesting, a sort of variant on the Augustinian
concept of "the Diaspora for witness." Augustine saw the meaning of the Jewish Diaspora in the Jews' transportation of Christianity's holy books throughout the entire world, testifying to the
authenticity of Holy Scripture.[9] Erasmus' idea here might be
called "Diaspora for edification," which replies as nothing else can
to the very broad moralism of Erasmism.

The letters of 1516–1517 also contain the first surviving remarks
from Erasmus' personal acquaintance with christened Jews, scholars of Hebrew. In March 1516 (or 1517) Erasmus was seeing Paulus
Ricius in Antwerp, a Hebraicist and physician, personal surveyor
to Emperor Maximillian (they had first met in 1506, in Pavia).
Erasmus was enchanted beyond words: "I was so attracted by
Paulus Ricius in our recent conversation, that I have a kind of
great thirst for more frequent and intimate talk with him. Besides
his knowledge of Hebrew, what a lot of philosophy he knows,
and theology too! And such an upright character, a great desire to
learn, an open readiness to teach, a modest manner in debate.
Personally I liked him long ago at first sight in Pavia, when he
taught philosophy there; and now that I see him at close quarters,
I like him still more. At last I find in him an Israelite indeed [*is
demum vere mihi videtur Israelitam agere*]."[10]

In 19 October 1517 Erasmus wrote of meeting Matthias Adrian
(see Chapter 3), not nearly as rapturously as about Ricius but
wholly positively: "There has lately arrived here one Matthias
Adrian, by race a Jew [*genere Hebraeus*] but in religion a Christian
of long standing, and by profession a physician, so skilled in the
whole of Hebrew literature that in my opinion our age has no one
else to show who could be compared with him . . . Not only has
he a complete knowledge of the language; he has also deeply ex-

plored the recesses of the literature at first hand and has all the books at his finger tips."[11]

Both these remarks on converts are curious not for their friendly tone but for their, as it were, clarification of racial properties; christening does not remove his Judaism from a Jew, and Jewish origin remains an important, perhaps even necessary, characteristic of the new convert.[12] This is important to remember when turning to the first truly judeophobic eruption, over the convert Pfefferkorn, in November 1517. Chapter 3 has already offered a psychological explanation for that eruption, but Erasmus' attitudes to the Reuchlin affair as a whole bear somewhat more detailed examination.

Erasmus did not wish to take part in the affair, not solely for his constant dislike of any "party" or affiliation[13]; he also had understood very early that what the obscurantists and Reuchlin's supporters were fighting over was not the Jewish books but the renaissance of philology, intruding into theology, and he feared for himself and his own works. As early as May 1515 he wrote that Reuchlin's enemies had puffed their bonfire up out of trifles, that *Augenspeigel* would have gone unnoticed had they not raised the cry themselves. All people may err, so it was possible Reuchlin too had made some mistakes, which was not for Erasmus to judge. Better not to call attention to minor sins of that type. This whole conciliatory and ambiguous exclamation, however, ends entirely unambiguously: I fear for my Jerome (that is, the scholia to the first four volumes of the works of St. Jerome, which appeared the following year), for the hostile theologians will find more than enough ground there for attack.[14] In 1519 he wrote that "they confound the cause of the humanities [*bonarum literarum*] with the business of Reuchlin and Luther, though there is no connection between them."[15] It is clear that Erasmus did not consider the Jewish side of the affair important for *bonae literae* nor of interest to himself, so the manner in which he behaved in the matter, in a cowardly way or wise, consistently or deviously, has only tangential importance for present purposes, which are that in the anti-Pfefferkorn letters Erasmus' personal offense with the convert is aggravated by the conviction that if not for that foolish, totally unnecessary fight over burning the Talmud and other Jewish books, frontal and direct confrontation with the conservatives could have been avoided,[16] which would have been to the benefit of the reviving sciences.

The cruelest and most detailed denunciation of Pfefferkorn and Jewish deviousness comes in the letter to Willibald Pirckheimer of 2 November 1517. The foul convert deserves not even the name of half-Jew, since he has shown himself a Jew a hundred times over! "My life upon it, he had no other motive in getting dipped in the font than to be able to deliver more dangerous attacks on Christianity and by mixing with us to infect the entire folk with his Jewish poison. What harm could he have done, had he remained the Jew that he was? Now for the first time he is playing the part of a real Jew, now that he has donned the mask of a Christian; now he lives up to his breeding. The Jews brought false accusations against Christ, but it was Christ alone; this man lets loose his fury against so many upright men of proved integrity and learning. He could render to his fellow Jews no service more welcome than to pretend he was a turncoat and betray the Christian polity to its enemies . . . the horrible fellow reasons somewhat like this: "If however my tricks are detected and my machines made public, and the whole Christian world abhors me, I am absolutely certain of glory among my fellow Jews, who will then understand that when I left them, it was not with hostile intent."[17] In a letter of the same day, to Gerhard Lister, Erasmus exclaims, "A poisonous fellow, unworthy to be pitted against such opponents, fit only for the hangman." He adds, "It was indeed worth his while to be dipped in the font! As a Jew in disguise he could throw peace among Christians into confusion."[18] The next day he wrote: "I wish he were an entire Jew—better still if the removal of his foreskin had been followed by the loss of his tongue and both hands. As it is, this angel of Satan transformed into an angel of light is attacking us under our own colors and rendering his colleagues of the circumcision the same service that Zopyrus did to Darius,[19] the father of Xerxes . . . What more could these curtal wretches hope for, or Satan their leader, than to see the unity of simple Christians rent in twain like this?"[20] Again, on 3 November: "If the world can once understand how crooked he is and can see that under the pretext of defending the Christian faith he is proceeding to overthrow Christianity. This will be very popular among his colleagues of the circumcision, for whom he has done as Zopyrus did for Darius. My life upon it, if he could be opened up, you would find not one Jew in his bosom but a thousand . . . If only the old saying were not so true, that a bad Jew always makes worse Christians! . . . What could suit the Jews better (for it is their battles he fights while pretending to oppose them) than for concord among Christians to be rent asunder like this? . . . If only he were still an entire Jew, and we were showing more caution in admitting the others!"[21] November 4: "Why do men who are genuine Christians keep their claws off that Jewish scab? [*ab ista Iudaica scabie ungues absti-nent*] . . . I am surprised that on this point government and the bishops are asleep . . . they do not see that from this hellish seed, which Satan, the friend of the Jews, has begun to sow with his own hand, a monstrous jungle will grow up unless timely steps are taken."[22] Finally, 15 November Erasmus writes to Reuchlin himself: "This half-Jew Christian by himself has done more harm to Christendom than the whole cesspool of Jewry [*Iudaerum sen-tina*], and clearly, unless I am mistaken, is playing the same game for his nation that Zopyrus played for Darius, though this man is much more treacherous."[23]

Two details in this flood of invective call for attention, the idea of a Jewish conspiracy, and the assertion that Pfefferkorn convert-ed only for appearances in order to serve his people better and more effectively. The *idée fixe* of a Jewish conspiracy already had existed many centuries,[24] part of the complex of folk or everyday anti-Semitism, and continues even to the present day, in the form of the *Protocols of the Elders of Zion* and the "world-wide Zionist conspiracy," which the Arabs, their protectors and clients tirelessly expose. This is the same sort of folk myth as ritual murder or profanation of the Host, all accusations against which both secular and religious authorities were struggling.[25] Howev-er, as has been shown, for Erasmus conversion did not destroy Judaism, so he is fully consistent in speaking of Pfefferkorn's ser-vices to "his people." But this is not the main point, which is that the source of the news about Pfefferkorn's false conversion was the "judeophile" himself, Reuchlin.[26] As early as 1512 Reuchlin had announced that Pfefferkorn had returned to Judaism, which news was seized and trumpeted high and low by all Reuchlin's supporters.[27] It seems then that even in this case Erasmus invented nothing himself, only using a ready stamp, as might be expected in a chance eruption.

In order to finish with Reuchlin it is necessary to break the chronological order of this summary, to mention the letter of 11 August 1519 to Jacob Hoogstraten, already mentioned in Chapter 3. Categorically refusing to say which was correct, Reuchlin or Hoogstratten, Erasmus equally categorically condemns the malevolence and unseemly tone of the attack by the inquisitor of Cologne on his opponent (though recall that Erasmus had no less decisively condemned the coarse unruliness of speech among the Reuchlinists). He praises Origen, who in his polemic with Celsus did not once offend that enemy of Christ. "He who carries hatred in his soul has no faith even in the most righteous matter . . . With your usual keen thought you should have reasoned whether this booklet of Capnion's had anything in it able to cause the Christian religion a heavy loss. However, it speaks only of how Jews should not suffer greater restrictions than those they deserve. Was it worth striving so hard to blow up hatred for the Jews? Is there really someone among us who lacks sufficient aversion for this sort of person? If being a Christian means hating Jews then all of us here are remarkable Christians."[28] The sarcasm of this last phrase is clear enough even in so small a context, but it becomes obvious when just above this there appears a precise, and hence not accidental, parallel to it, save in a serious vein: "If Christian piety permitted the cursing and defaming of anyone at all, then Origen would have cursed Celsus."[29] Since Origen in no way denounced Celsus, cursing is not a sign of piety, so it follows that hatred for Jews is also not a sign of a good Christian.[30] It ought also to be noted that the whole letter to Hoogstraten is a brilliant example of Erasmus' irony, apparently naive and inoffensive, but in fact deadly offensive.[31] For example, "There are various opinions about your morals. Some say that you are a reasonably calm and intelligent man, though quick to take offense. Many people though say that you have no soul other than ambition and greed, that because of your savage, more than tyrannical character you are trying to put yourself above all others, while your insatiable greed and self-interest make you want to get your hands on the Jews' property. It is my habit always to try to give the benefit of the doubt, so that in this case, even though I could not disprove all the accusations, I tried as I could to soften them."[32] While observing outward respectfulness, Erasmus addresses the inquisitor as though he were a total idiot, playing him like a great bullfighter plays a huge and wild bull, who in reality is helpless.

In short, there are no grounds for seeing echoes of the anti-Pfefferkorn explosion in the letter to Hoogstraten. Not only is Christian hatred of Jews not approved, it is condemned, along with all other hatred.

Chapter 3 has treated the 1518 explosion, as reflected in the March 13 letter to Capito, at some length; the text of the second (and judeophobic) half of the letter reads: "I could wish you were more inclined to Greek than to that Hebrew of yours, with no desire to criticize it. I see them as a nation full of most tedious fabrications, who spread a kind of fog over everything, Talmud, Cabala, Tetragrammaton, *Gates of Light*, words, words, words . . . Italy is full of Jews, in Spain there are hardly any Christians. I fear that this [that is, the study of Hebrew and its literature—S.M.] may give that pestilence that was long ago suppressed a chance to rear its ugly head. If only the church of Christians did not attach so much importance to the Old Testament! It is a thing of shadows, given us for a time; and now it is almost preferred to the literature of Christianity. Somehow or other we are all the time turning away from Christ, who was enough for us, all by himself."[33]

To the direct causes of this eruption which have already been discussed might be added another one, more remote, but therefore more general. Less than a year before this letter to Capito, Erasmus' beloved friend and sometime tutor John Colet, dean of St. Paul's in London and head of the group later termed the Oxford reformers, wrote to Erasmus about Reuchlin's book *De Arte Cabilistica:* "My dear Erasmus, of books and knowledge there is no end. Nothing can be better, in view of this brief life of ours, than that we should live a holy and pure life and use our best endeavors every day to become pure and enlightened and perfected. These things are promised us by Reuchlin's Pythagorical and Cabalistic philosophy; but in my opinion we shall achieve them in no way but this, by the fervent love and imitation of Jesus. Let us therefore leave all these complications behind us and take the short road to truth."[34]

It is just these ideas that are easily recognizable in the reproof to Capito over his attraction to Jewish studies. The new worship (*devotio moderna*) of the Brethren of the Common Life, in whose schools Erasmus spent his childhood and youth, became an integral part of his theological and moral convictions.[35] All things superfluous to practical worship that do not aid in the imitation of Christ, that distract from the sole true path charted by the Gospels and the Epistles, are cut free and discarded, not as an evil to be battled but as something alien and unnecessary. Like Colet, Erasmus does not know real Judaism, its religious or cultural heritage, *nor does he wish to*. Despite the verbal sharpness (caused by the confusion of a term that has at least three meanings: the Judaism of Gospel times, "new Judaism" within the Christian church, and the culture and religion of modern Jewry), Erasmus is not manifesting hatred here but rather disaffection on grounds of principle.

Ratio Verae Theologiae of the same year (1518) has a direct confirmation of this fact. Erasmus wrote, "Once, in order to bring the Jews to faith, it was necessary to turn to the authority of the Old Testament; now we are attached to the Jews only to an insignificant degree."[36] Behind this statement of the facts lies complete indifference to it; the Jewish and Christian worlds have nothing in common, and Erasmus is totally unconcerned about how the gulf dividing them might be bridged. The Jewish world isn't even a curiosity for him, and he doesn't think about how to join this world to the Christian one, about how to convert the Jews. Remember that in the anti-Pfefferkorn letter Erasmus had already complained that Christians were sometimes too careless in their zeal to join the Jews to the true faith; on this subject the second edition of New Testament commentary (1519) makes a detailed and highly important pronouncement. Commenting on Matthew 23:15 ("you make him twice as much a child of hell as yourselves") Erasmus writes, "The bad pagan made a worse Jew. If you will, this speaks to our ways; after all, we consider it a great business to bring a Jew to baptism. Of course, we are all obligated to desire that all the Jews should come to their senses, but some men seek their personal glory in this and so lead the new convert along the wrong roads, teaching them something other than real Christianity. In truth, how can we make others Christian, if we aren't first Christians ourselves? So it happens sometimes that in place of a criminal Jew we get an even more criminal Christian, as Spain can attest. There are those too who act on a new plane, making Christians by force of arms, and under the guise of spreading the faith they trouble only to enrich themselves. However, you gain nothing in this way, save sorrow in pure Christian souls. This is like the way some monks behave, who, some from slyness, some from pious but unthinking zeal, convert all whom they can to their rules of life, particularly those who in their surmise will prove useful to them, and so stoop to astonishing devices to lure the young and simple, who know neither themselves nor true religion."[37]

This text not only shows uncompromising condemnation of forced conversion (Erasmus decidedly follows the "soft" line of the Western Church, represented by Pope Gregory the Great, the Venerable Bede, Bernard de Clairvaux, Eugene III's papal bull *Sicut Iudaeis,* and Thomas Aquinas)[38] but also doubts the goal of Christian missionary work among the Jews.[39] (No doubt too the subtext here is also based on Paul's prophecies from Romans 11, concerning the conversion and salvation of Israel at the end of time. There the apostle speaks of a "mystery," but a mystery is a miracle of God, in which we have no right to interfere.) It is also significant here that "fishers" of Jewish souls are compared to greedy or overly zealous monks who use all means, fair and foul, to pull the young and inexperienced into the monastery. Erasmus considered himself a victim of such tricks, so the accusations of monastic trickery and hypocrisy is one of his most beloved hobby horses. This suggests that the subject of forced conversion truly disturbed Erasmus, part of the broader subject of violence against the helpless, which it appears he interpreted not so much a Jewish question as a Christian one. After all Marranos are mentioned critically not because they are former Jews or secret Jews but because they are "criminal Christians."

Thus when Erasmus, defending Luther in a letter to Albrecht von Brandenburg on 19 October of the same year, writes of Luther's enemies that, if they wish in fact to prove themselves great theologians, they should turn the Jews to Christ and correct the morals of the Christians rather than demand the blood of Luther,[40] the words are either empty eloquence or (more likely) a joke.

Also very significant is one phrase from a letter of 1 November 1519 to a Czech correspondent who complains of the religious discord in Bohemia and Moravia, saying that the people had divided into three sects, not counting the Jews, the epicurians who did not accept the immortality of the soul, and heretics.[41] Erasmus replies, "The trouble would not be so heavy if everyone were to share a common error. Now, though, as I hear it, many of you are not only in rebellion against the Catholic church but also are fighting one another . . . As for Jews living amongst you, you are not alone. They also live in Italy and Germany and in other countries and, most of all, in Spain."[42] In other words, whether actual or former (as in Spain), Jews have no influence on your troubles; they are not the problem and present no danger.

1519 is also the year of the passing remark in the paraphrase of 1 Corinthians: "Now there is no other people who are farther from God than the Jews."[43]

Erasmus in his *Interpretation of Psalm 2* (1522) mentions contemporary Jewry twice, each time in a wholly traditional spirit, enumerating the deprivation of the Jews in contrast to the brilliant successes of Christianity. "What say you, unhappy Jew? You see that God has made dust of all your plans? You see that all your trickery has come down on your own head? You see that you have fallen into the pit you dug for others? You see that the Temple was razed to its foundations so that even its traces cannot be found; that your religion has wholly flickered out; that priests, Law, states, cities, people, country, all have disappeared, that nothing remains save a handful of wanderers and exiles, witnesses to the former madness and former misfortunes, and that they remain only on the guarantee of Paul, whom they persecuted with mad cruelty, and because of the charity of Christians, whom they hate rabidly. Here, unhappy Jew, is that innocent blood which you called down upon your heads and the heads of your children! Here is your King Caesar, whom you preferred to Christ! And still you won't come to your senses and don't wish to acknowledge your blindness? Still you breath hatred for the King of the Jews, whom we worship?"[44] Further on Erasmus speaks of the wrath of God, which Augustine understood as the blindness of stubborn men who did not wish to repent of their sins. "We see this wrath (and grieve over it) in the remainders of the Jewish people, for they see that all that their prophets foretold of the Messiah was fulfilled in Christ, for it is clear from Gospel history that there is no other Christ than that which the whole world now reveres. They understand not only that God has mocked them but also that they are a mockery to all the peoples of the world, and still even today they curse Christ in their synagogues and wait for who knows what other sort of Messiah, whom they shall never see, save on the Day of Wrath, and will never hear, save in that hour when with His wrath He will discountenance all the impious. And though they understand, seeing their own deprivations, that the wrath of God obviously hangs over them, still their spiritual blindness is such that even so great a torment cannot bring them to their senses."[45]

Both these comments are so clichéd as to be without interest, save for their remarkable tone, not of passion or hatred but rather of contemptuous pity.

The remaining remarks from 1522 deal with Jewish moneylenders mentioned in passing—just the two words—in a list of the sins of Rome,[46] and words from a polemic against Spanish critics of his commentary on the New Testament, when Erasmus caustically proposed they forget their differences for a joint attack on heretics: "As far as I am able I shall pounce on those who clutch the Gospel scriptures too tightly and who are overly alarmed at Judaism. Let Zuñiga and Carranza fling themselves after heretics of another sort, who have already littered the fields of the Lord more than enough. Certain Jews, half-Jews, and quarter-Jews are getting ever stronger, pushing their way among us, bearing the name of Christian but carrying all Moses in their souls . . . So they are a particularly dangerous threat to the Christian cause and profit more from slander than from usury. No one could defeat them better than Zuñiga and Carranza."[47] The sharply satirical tone is set in the very first phrase (the absurd proposition of attacking loyal defenders of Gospel truth and enemies of "Judaism"). Erasmus also seems to have meant something other than Spanish Marranos when he wrote "heretics of another sort"; Erasmus' polemics against Zuñiga hint several times at Zuñiga's Jewish origins, as will be shown below, in the analysis of this polemical device. The contrast of slander and usury is comprehensible now; in the Germany of the end of the fifteenth century and beginning of the sixteenth, "Jew" and "usurer" were synonyms,[48] which Erasmus ignores, discarding that dependable and well-known anti-Semitic argument (which, parenthetically, he never used). Erasmus is only concerned that the "Jew" Zuñiga and his defender (which act makes him also a Jew!) Carranza were trampling the fields of the Lord, slandering good Christians (meaning Erasmus).

The final reference of 1522 comes in the paraphrase of Matthew, where Erasmus says Jesus scolded the Jews for obstinance and corruption, but their sinful and unhappy blindness grew seven times worse after Jesus, so that their troubles today are much worse than they were in olden times.[49]

Most of the material from 1535 comes from paraphrases of the Gospel, not original and for the most part without interest. Again there is the blindness of the Jews, who see worse than the blind man of Mark 10:46, and who boast of their knowledge of the Law, and so become leaders of the blind.[50] Again there are the deprivations and humiliations of the Jewish people, who have become like the barren fig tree.[51] Again Erasmus is astounded at the unbelief of the Jews, who refuse to heed the prophecies of Moses and Elijah about Christ, revering, in their own words, the Father, but refusing to worship the Son.[52] The Jews wanted to rule independently at the "wedding feast" (Luke 14:8–11), as a result of which they lost their place entirely at the feast of nations, or else they occupy the very last place.[53] They refuse the resurrected Christ because they never really believed (*non vere credidit*) Moses and the prophets.[54] The episode with the blind man who prayed for sight and received it (Luke 18:35–41) "is often put as an example to the Jews, so they might either heal themselves of their unbelief or else in the future show clearly that they are rejected as they deserve, for they do not wish to be healed."[55] The cause of Jewish unbelief is that Jews even now remain on the earth (unlike the short Zacchaeus, who climbed up the fig tree, in Luke 19:4), meaning they are mired in the flesh of the Law.[56] Even today the Jewish people stay clear of the Gospel kingdom, stubbornly hate Christ, and in refusing to serve him "serve all the tyrants of this world, serve Satan, most savage of the tyrants."[57] Today, after the appearance of the Savior, to follow the Law while denying Christ is not only useless but also destructive (*exitiabilis*).[58]

In all these general remarks (one might almost say banalities) only the decided absence of agitational purpose is remarkable, the lack of an "incendiary" start, or attempt to rouse hatred for contemporary Jews. From this point of view another excerpt from the paraphrase of John is particularly meaningful, for it hints at the theory of the eternal enslavement of the Jews. This theory was elaborated in the thirteenth century, reflecting the claims of religion and temporal authorities on the Jews as a sort of income-producing property,[59] but the arguments over the idea had not died down even by the beginning of the sixteenth century, when Erasmus' friend Ulrich Zasius was an ardent adherent and defender of the idea,[60] taking it to such far-reaching conclusions as the right of the ruler to baptize Jewish infants by force. Erasmus, as has been said, limited himself to a hint, a mere mention without further development. "Jews desperately hated the rule of Caesar, but moved by [another] hate they loudly renounce their Messiah and accept Caesar as their ruler. 'We have no other king save Caesar,' they say. Such was their thirst for revenge that they condemned themselves to eternal slavery solely to destroy Christ, the source of freedom."[61]

1523 was also the year of a small exegetical work, *Precatio Dominica*, which rapidly gained wide popularity and was translated into all the languages of western Christianity. It speaks *inter alia* of the Jews, who do not cease reviling the Son of God in their synagogues, their revulsion falling also on the Father. Jews consider the name of Christian more shameful than that of thief or murderer, and mock Christ's cross. However, all these accusations (again 100 percent cliché) conclude not with exhortations to revenge or punishment, or even with a call for missionary activity, but simply with a prayer, that God might have mercy on them (*misereatur et istorum tua clementia*), enlightening them with his Spirit and convey them faith in his Son, so that all people and tongues, every sex and age would be all together, to praise the most holy name of God.[62] One other passage does not name Jews but unquestionably implies them: "Many peoples are even today under the power of the fearful tyrant Satan . . . Many do not know what freedom, what high worth, what happiness it is to bow before Your heavenly kingdom, and thus they prefer to be slaves of the Devil rather than your Sons."[63]

Among the correspondence from 1524, a letter from Conrad Mutianus Rufus, canon of Gotha, to Erasmus is of particular interest. Despite sympathy for Reuchlin's and Erasmus' views on the dissemination of education and reform within the Church,[64] on this occasion Mutianus Rufus expresses sharp dislike for the carriers and disseminators of Hebrew learning as well as for the Jews themselves. "The Jews, bad Christians,[65] endanger us, destroying the simpletons of little faith with rare cleverness, under guise of piety. You could easily punish their acts and evil deeds with your divine fluency, if you were to write something against [empty] prophecies and against Moses, so that those criminal circumcized all wrapped in the holy books won't be able to give us poison in place of curative potions and can't upset the calm of society. By my reckoning the state which accepts Jews so they can lend money is making a mistake. Also mistaken are people who let a baptized Jew lead public education. People of this sort tend to Luther, giving advice and enjoying respect . . . They propound and interpret the Old Testament and no one suspects them of a thing. We though should worship Christ in the way of our ancestors."[66]

This letter juxtaposes well with the letter to Capito of 13 March 1518 (quoted above), showing the same fear of a "renaissance of Judaism," the same distrust of the Old Testament. The accusation that Luther was harboring converts and Jews apparently is connected to Luther's judeophilic views of that period, as reflected in his *Dass Jesus Christus ein geborener Jude sei* (1523), as well as with the number of first-class Hebraicists Luther had about him. For present purposes it is much more important to examine Erasmus' reaction to this summons to attack Jews and Judaizing converts. To judge by his writings of the next few years, the reaction was nonexistent. Even if much later Erasmus does come to suspect Jews of deliberate collusion in the "Luther troubles" (see below, 1529), that almost certainly is not the influence of Mutianus Rufus' five-year-old letter. Two remarks of 1524 suggest that, unlike Rufus, Erasmus continued to see no danger in living Jews or living Judaism. "When we see the Jewish people stubbornly clinging to the ceremonies of the Mosaic Law, so that they are deprived of heaven . . . and everywhere on earth are humiliated and persecuted, is this not Absalom we see, caught [in the tree branches] by his own hair?" "And now the Jews grind their teeth at us, but their teeth are shattered, so they can curse us, but never bite us."[67]

A few passages in the *Interpretation of Psalm 4* (1525) concern contemporary Jewry, but they are all of little interest. Jews even today clutch their rituals with a dead man's grip, even though they became unnecessary and useless after the appearance of Christ.[68] Even today Christ calls to the Jewish people, so that they might come to their senses and stop waiting for another Messiah.[69] "Right up to the present day the unhappy Jews suckle the milk of the letter and are unable to leave childhood."[70] They stubbornly take empty phantoms as the truth.[71] It is no wonder that their souls wither and parch, since they are tormented by spiritual hunger and spiritual thirst, because they have deprived themselves of the gospel bread and drink the tasteless water of the letter.[72] Again, the only striking thing here is the didactic abstraction and dispassionate tone.

A short section of *Lingua* (also 1525) is more interesting, for there Erasmus first mentions the sins of the Old Testament Jews, who "commit adultery and walk in lies" (Jeremiah 23:14); he points out that Christ censures exactly those failings in the Gospels, then concludes, "Apparently Jews of today remain the same. They do not recognize their groom, refuse him with a lie, kill him. And they do not cease to steal his sheep, which he redeemed with his own blood; they do not cease blasphemous slandering in their synagogues of the one before whose name kneels all that is in heaven, on earth, and in the netherworld."[73] Besides the sharp, almost provocative mixture of temporal planes (the Jews are crucifying Christ *today*), the most interesting point here is the accusation of successful Jewish missionary activity among Christians. Since the accusation is both wholly senseless and not repeated anywhere else, it either must be understood as a rhetorical flourish (which seems unlikely) or else it refers to the "Judaism" of the Church mired in ritual formalism. If this supposition is correct, then this passage is an example of the way anti-Mosaism and atemporal moralizing can combine to create an obvious absurdity; it is wholly obvious that even the most evil of enemies would

not accuse contemporary Jews of the "more than Jewish ceremonies and little rituals" (in Erasmus' beloved phrase) that burden down the Church.

The next year, 1526, exhibits one of Erasmus' most remarkable
pronouncements on Christian toleration of Jews. The Parisian
theologian Noël Bédier considered an idea from the foreword
paraphrasing Matthew to be heretical. Here Erasmus says that
children should be asked when they are grown to reaffirm the
vow of faithfulness to Christianity their godparents gave at the
christening. Those who refuse to reaffirm the vow should not be
forced but rather left in peace until they change their minds, without recourse to heavy punishments other than refusing them communion. Bédier declared both the proposal to repeat the baptism
vow at a conscious age and this toleration toward possible "re-
fusers" to be heretical. Deflecting the accusation, Erasmus replied,
"No one should be forced to a profession of Christianity. After
all, we don't do that with the Jews (and in my opinion should
not), and they are greater foes of our religion. No one should be
obligated to faithfulness to Christianity who did not approve of
the choice made for him during his infancy. At the same time, no
means should be overlooked to prevent his falling away [from the
Church]. But if someone falls away all the same, let him live
among us as the Jews do, for whom [even] entrance to Church
sermons is not forbidden but who are punished if they spew abuse
on the name of Christ. All this intends to give us true and real
Christians, not coerced and hypocritical ones."[74]

Not only does Erasmus unconditionally condemn the forced
baptism of Jews, he says that the evil "foes of our religion" have
the right to live "among us," without fear, so long as they do not
offend the religious sensibilities of the Christians. Perhaps even
more important, the problem of toleration of the Jews is not singled out but rather is a particular instance, an example of a broader toleration for all those of other persuasions. In other words,
Erasmus here sees the Jewish question in the context of (or in
agreement with) his entire moral system, as a result of which the
results are wholly Erasmian. It is in this same way that the anti-
Semitic attacks and eruptions (both those already cited here and
those still to be cited) contradict this system, precisely as some
(and not many, incidentally) of Erasmus' remarks about the

Hebrew language contradict the principles and convictions of Erasmus the philologist, or his fairly frequent attempts to use the Hebrew original at his own discretion, either ignoring it entirely or else interpreting it with warp and twist dictated by the requirements of theological exegesis. This "antiphilology" by Erasmus is considered further in Chapter 6.

Other remarks from 1526 are "the coarse part of the Law which the crowd followed apparently permitted all that was not punished. That is how the Jews interpret [the Law] even today, just as the Pharisees once interpreted it";[75] "How much more receptive were the pagans to gospel faith during the time of Luke than were the Jews? . . . During the time of Paul, who opposed the Gospels more bitterly than the Jewish people? What they are today we see with our own eyes. No matter how we sprinkle them [with baptismal water], all the same they scarcely endure the name of Christ."[76] This last sentence most likely refers to the Marranos, so to see any hint here at Pfefferkorn's wiles or at those of any other clever convert who had irritated Erasmus is without foundation; that would have been possible only with a new eruption, which did not come.

Institutio Christiani Matrimonii, also from 1526, rejects mixed marriages, not solely with Jews but equally with pagans (marriages with pagans were a far from scholastic question in a time of initial colonial conquest). Erasmus refers to the injunction of the Church which forbade a Christian woman "to marry a pagan or a Jew," to Apostle Paul, who permitted marriage "solely in the Lord," and he concludes, "So I am astonished how certain writers of our day affirm that one may marry with a Jew or a pagan. If it is sufficient condition to be man and woman, why a brother and sister are man and woman."[77]

In another instance, one of Erasmus' correspondents was worried that the religious discord would cast the world into a new paganism. Erasmus replied, "You fear paganism, but I see that almost the entire world is seized by Judaism."[78] It is clear that he means "Judaism," or the sentence has no meaning; the quotation is included in the present survey only as a warning against incautious interpretation.

In another polemic against Bédier in the following year, 1527, Erasmus again takes up the question of forced baptism and again affirms his view. "Let us say that an infant from a Jewish or pagan family is secretly kidnapped by Christians and, without the parents' knowledge (or if with their knowledge, then against their wishes) is baptized, as Christians once used to do, according to Augustine. If the child never discovers the fact of his baptism and so persists in his parents' impiety, the fact that he was baptized will have no significance whatever. But if he finds out once he is grown, it is extremely doubtful whether it is just to force him, under threat of punishment, to profess our religion, and in the event of persistent refusal, to punish him as an apostate."[79]

Bédier regarded Erasmus' interpretation of Matthew 13:29–30 as heretical (the parable of the sowers of good seed, where the servants propose to pull up the weeds, but the "householder" won't permit them, fearing the servants will "in gathering the weeds . . . root up the wheat along with them"); he wrote that "the servants who want to pull up the weeds early are those who want to destroy the false apostles and heresiarchs by the sword and [other] capital punishments, while the master does not wish their destruction but is willing to endure them in case they should suddenly come to their senses and turn from weeds into wheat. If they don't come to their senses, then they must stand before their Judge and at the necessary time answer for this . . . In the meantime though the bad which is mixed with the good must be endured, for there is less danger in enduring them than in destroying them."[80] Answering him, Erasmus points out that Bédier is relying on Augustine, who was supposed to have demanded the extermination of the Donatists. He continues, "I might take issue with what Augustine says in the 'Epistle to Boniface,' where he runs to several arguments which, if followed, would require both the Turk and the Jew to be forced to faith under fear of death, if we begin to interpret them to mean that he means capital punishment. But that wasn't what Augustine had in mind."[81] This again demonstrates that toleration of the Jews was not considered separately but was included in the broad confines of the general problem of toleration of those of other persuasions.

Simply for the sake of a complete survey, Erasmus' throwaway remarks ought also to be mentioned; the Jewish people, once the beloved, chosen people of God, now remain the most outcast people on earth[82]; and the Jews still have not ceased to rave about their Moses and Temple.[83]

The interpretations of the two psalms, 83 and 85, published in 1528, contain some extraordinarily curious passages, such as what the *Interpretation of Psalm 83* says about the Marranos: "It is inhuman that we curse as Marranos those people who come from the Jews and who from their native impiety have turned to true piety, when in the event they more greatly deserve respect. If the sons are truly to be guilty for the sins of the fathers, from whom is it we count our own genesis? Is it not from people who scorned the true God to bow down to wood and stone [idols]? Who spilled the blood of martyrs?"[84] This defense of the Marranos, unexpected after the attacks of earlier years (see above, for the years 1516, 1517, 1518, 1522, and 1526), is prefaced by the general observation that God did not hold the pious descendants of Korah guilty for the sins of their forefathers, and "the crowd is unjust in reviling the children for the crime . . . of the parents, as though they had committed the crime themselves."[85] This is truly the Erasmian point of view, springing from the principles of individualism and free will (which in a strange way coincides with the opinion of Zasius, a consistent enemy of the Jews; as was mentioned above, Zasius held that baptism did not change the fact of belonging to Jewry. This membership, however, is not a shameful blot; the convert must be given access to all responsibilities without exception, both religious and worldly).[86] Thus it is sooner the attacks on the Marranos which should be considered unexpected and anti-Erasmian rather than this defense.

The *Interpretation of Psalm 85* once again takes up the problem of Christian tolerance, in the exact sense as before. "[Christ] summoned everyone to the grace of the Gospels but the Jews despised God's mercy and the pagans mocked the Gospels. What did they deserve, besides the cruelest possible destruction? However, the meekness of God long tolerated even these [refractory types] in the expectation that they would wake up and reconsider. The Lord knows in advance who will change in his soul and who will not, and tolerates it all, partly to let his justice be more illustrious, partly to teach us meekness and mercy for sinners, of whom we know not when they might turn to the good. The Jews persist so many centuries in their blindness, yet the Lord tolerates them, everyday summoning them, through his Church, to rebirth. The Christian people also tolerate them, although they revile Christ slanderously and wish ill for all of us, when the Christians could, after all, destroy them without a trace, if they wished. The Jews are insignificantly few in number compared to the Christians; they have no state, no laws, no authority, no ruler, no weapons, no soldiers. They could all be exterminated in a single day, but they are tolerated, in the hope given us by the Apostle Paul, when he wrote to the Romans. The Jews have not stumbled so badly, he says, as to have fallen utterly, and, revealing a mystery, he predicts that when all the pagans enter [the Church], then the Jews will change their minds and all Israel will be saved."[87]

Three main points should be stressed, the call to "meekness and mercy" and the rejection of force, the hope for the mystery Paul reveals in Romans (11:25–26), meaning the conversion of the Jews by divine means, *not earthly or human*, and, finally, the small number of the Jews and thus their imaginary danger to Christianity.

This last point Erasmus reaffirms just below[88]: "There are no pagans among us at all, and either no Jews, or the threat from them is minimal (*minimum molesti sunt*), since they rave slumbering in their dens. And still the fields of the Church as so littered with weeds and nettles that a man wishing to live piously and simply may not find the place where he will not suffer ridicule, burdens, restrictions, theft. If the pagans at one time considered the cross of Christ a madness and the Jews considered it a temptation, that had to be endured; but must we regret that he who was saved by the cross . . . mocks that cross?" This means that if one forgets allegories and didactic examples for a moment simply to look about, there are no Jews to be seen, there is nothing to be said about them, and even less reason to dump the troubles of the Church upon them, when the Church is eaten away from within by sin.

It is wholly understandable then why Erasmus in summoning the Jews to open their eyes threatens them not with human punishment but rather with God's judgment. "O, if only they were discountenanced here and now, so as not to be discountenanced for all eternity! . . . After all, they will see that sign [the

Cross—S.M.] again in the heavens, will see it in the glory of the Father . . . and then they shall be ashamed in the eyes of all peoples and the angels, but they shall be ashamed then for eternity, since that sign, given for their good, they turned into an evil of their own."[89]

Finally, Erasmus repeats again in the commentary on the psalm that the Jews and pagans are repelled from Christ by the sins of the Christians themselves, citing the lines from Romans 2:24: "The name of God is blasphemed among the gentiles because of you."[90]

The *Vidua Christiana* was published in the beginning of 1529; it includes the passage: "Boundless and sorrowful impiety exist, such as should not be given a place, as far as it is possible, in a good gathering. Such is the impiety of Jews and all others who do not fear to sully the glorious name of Christ with impious cursing, or he who is visibly stained by murder, the making of poison, brigandry, fornication, and who are not ashamed of their shame. Their company is to be avoided, save when necessity requires or the hope beguiles that bad might be turned into better. For . . . it is not a sin with that hope to share conversation with heretics and with Jews and Turks. There is a general practice according to which we greet those we meet civilly, as we meet them, even those whose life is not to our liking. There are also closer relationships, which are called . . . friendships. And it is to friendship that they should not be admitted, those who suffer from heavy sins and who give no hope for correction."[91]

Can this passage be called anti-Semitic? It would seem not, since there is no hatred here, no active enmity. Jewry is not inimical to Erasmus but alien (as has been said already a number of times), and he distances himself from it, not permitting it into friendship; he wishes not to enter into company with it save in the hopes of setting it on the path to true faith. He entertained no such hopes, however, and was not filled with missionary zeal.

Two letters from 1529 hint at a sharper feeling against the Jews. On 29 March 1529, Erasmus described the destruction of the Church in Basel as the town underwent Reformation: "This is only the beginning. I fear terribly that this pharisaism will be followed by paganism . . . It seems to me that there are many Jews and pagans mixed up in the troubles here, the first of them hating

Christ and the others believing in nothing at all. It seems to me that they are dreaming up some sort of new democracy,[92] and the whole business is the work of the sliest possible designs of some people whom no one yet knows precisely."[93] Once again the specter of Jewish conspiracy rises up, and this time for no discernible reason. It is of course possible that there simply were no concrete and properly Jewish reasons. 1529 was one of the very worst years of Erasmus' life. The Reformation in Basel forced him to leave the city which he loved almost more than any other, where he had long lived; sick, aged, he was forced to seek a new haven, which turned a man who had been an ideological opponent of the Reformation into its personal enemy. However, it is in the time of those crises which touch the nearest and most direct interests and needs that the temptation is particularly strong to submit to the dark impulses of mass psychology, which seeks and easily finds a universal cause for all its troubles. Whether or not this was it, to judge by the literary production of 1529 (including the surviving correspondence, of which there is a good amount), this gloomy mood did not vent in a new eruption. On 9 June 1529, still in Basel, Erasmus wrote of the situation in Europe: "There are bands of soldiers everywhere, sparing neither friend nor foe. They say that among them there are many Lutherans or Jews. In my opinion, however, they do not deserve even these names, since they believe in nothing at all."[94] Apparently Erasmus didn't believe the rumors about Jewish mercenaries (or Jewish robbers).[95] At the end of the year he even praises the ways of the Jews of his day, holding them up as examples to the Christians: "If the Jews don't permit anyone among them to become poor, how much more does it become those who pride themselves on the Gospels to lessen the need of their brothers with mutual aid!"[96]

The *Interpretation of Psalm 22* is dated February 1530 (or the dedication is), but appeared later, in May. The portion dedicated to the Jews of his own day is consistent, in that abstractly moralizing intonation already familiar from the quotation above. "So now let the Jews, tormented by hunger and thirst, doleful, thin and withered, boast of their repast which they consider holy because they abstain from pork and eel; let them worship their showbread, which none are permitted to touch, save the priests! . . . Let them boast of their sacrifices . . . which they also [like the showbread—S.M.] lost with the destruction of the Temple . . . What do they eat, poor fellows? What do they drink? They chew barley bran, bitter and tasteless . . . and disdaining pork in the flesh, in the spirit they feed on the food of pigs."[97] It is possible to hear not just the distance and scorn in this rhetoric but also a certain portion of compassion; what certainly is not there is hatred or gloating.

The *Interpretation of Psalm 28* ("Must There Be War with the Turks?" printed in March 1530) contains a new and important warning against coercion. "The Christian crowd (*vulgus*) vainly supposes that each has license to kill the Turk as though he were a mad dog, only because he is a Turk. If this were true, each would be permitted to kill Jews, but if someone dares to kill a Jew, he does not escape the punishment of the civil laws. The Christian authorities punish the Jews if they commit a crime against the civil laws to which they submitted themselves, but no one kills for the difference in faith, since the Christian religion is inculcated, not imposed by force . . . The right by which Jews carry punishment equal to that of the Christians was once applied by pagan rulers to the Christians and would now be so applied by the Turks if—which God forbid!—we were to live under their rule in a lawful manner. And they are cruelly mistaken, who believe that they shall fly directly up to heaven if they should fall in battle with the Turks; if your conscience is not clear, then you can't get to heaven even if you were, in the name of Christ, to lay your head on the block before a tyrant who demands that you bow down before idols."[98]

Everything here is clear and unambiguous; the civil laws must be identically impartial to all lawbreakers, independent of their religion (the principle of equality before the law); being of another faith is not grounds for violence; the illegal murder of someone of another faith is not a service but a sin; joining battle against infidels by itself, without personal piety, is not a guarantee of salvation (the principle of individualism). All of this springs organically from the deepest principles of Erasmus' understanding of the world.[99]

Erasmus was more inconsistent about the Inquisition. He referred to the "gentleness of the pillars of the ancient Church" who did not punish by death even converts who returned to Judaism, and to the decision of the fourth Council of Toledo (which Erasmus called the tenth), which in such cases provided for various means of persuasion and coercion but not for capital punishment. "It is well-known that clergy have no right to kill anybody. But now today blasphemy against Christ and the Madonna, even without lapsing [from Christianity] is punished even worse than by death, and he who has fallen into heresy is consigned to be burned even if he is not guilty of blasphemy . . . They also burn the Christian who has turned to paganism. But it would be more just to burn the Jew who accepted Christ as an adult, of his own free will, taught the principles of faith, than to burn him who was baptized as an infant, not knowing [what was happening]. I say all this not to condemn the severity of today's custom, which perhaps is even necessary, but to show that the stronger true piety were to be in the Church, the more it would shun war and punishment."[100]

Thus, on the one hand it seems perhaps overly cruel and even unjust to burn heretics and blasphemers alive, but on the other hand the virulence of the Inquisition is characterized as "perhaps necessary," although scarcely a doubt remains that Erasmus condemns the cruelty. Even the exception he makes for the lapsed convert is wholly understandable; among all the victims of the Inquisition whom Erasmus names here, only the twice-lapsed bears the vows of baptism by himself and consciously, while the act of free choice incurs particular obligations.

There is another short phrase in the commentary on the same psalm: "The Jews live better among us than the Christians among them [the Turks], for they consider the Christians not to be people but work animals."[101] To be a Jew in Christian society is an absolute measure of misfortune and humiliation.

The *Interpretation of Psalm 33*, which also saw light in the first half of 1530, adds nothing new to that which may be found up to that point. Jews even today are deaf, aspiritual, and wait in vain for their Messiah to rebuild the Temple and bring back sacrifice.[102] "The Jews of our day" are still unable to comprehend how the Law God gave for eternity could be revoked, how Christ could be born of a Virgin, and so forth. "O misfortunate ones!" Erasmus exclaims. "Trampling the grace of the Gospels and being trampled by bitter slavery, not only external, which would be but half a misery, but spiritual as well!" If God would but show them mercy at last, they could then justify the name of "Jews," which they no longer deserve, and so on.[103] It is pointless to boast of their great past if they will not imitate their great ancestors, like the Jews of the day who search holy history only for nourishment for their pride.[104] The "unfortunate Jews" are mentioned again, staring enviously at the happiness and blossoming of the Church, while they are poor, homeless, deprived of Temple, sacrifices, and God himself.[105]

The third and last judeophobic explosion came in the middle of March and beginning of April 1531. March 13 Erasmus wrote about the internecine strife which threatened Germany as a result of the religious schisms, mentioning in passing, "Under the pretext of this war the world will be flooded with Jews and heretics."[106] In a letter of April 1 he writes that, no matter how frightening the Turks and the plague, it would be an even more horrible misery if a civil war were to begin in Germany and the bordering countries. This would be a cruel malady, not curable by ordinary means, but "I hate cures which are worse than the ailment itself." If arms were to come into use, then the main portion of suffering would fall on the innocent, and under pretext of defense of the faith, the world would fill up with banditry. Directly following this model Erasmian passage come the words that "Spain is nourishing a quantity of secret Jews, while in Germany a great number of the people are given by nature to banditry and are accustomed to pillaging in war. All these dregs will flood first Germany, then the rest of the world. Once they have gotten arms, they don't know how to put them down. They have already shown twice what they are capable of, in Rome and in Vienna."[107] Five days later, on April 6, he wrote, "Under the pretext of this [that is, imminent— S.M.] war all imaginable sorts of human riffraff will flood Germany—Jews who can't stay in Spain, villains from all over Germany who are accustomed to pillage and rob! And worse, all this herd either takes the side of the schismatics [the Reformers— S.M.] or is free of all religion whatsoever! But won't the rulers put limits to their arrogant licentiousness? We have examples here for that, Rome and all Italy, ravaged without pity. And another

example, Vienna, which suffered more from its defenders than
from its enemies the Turks (if the witnesses write truly)."[108] This
is followed by the same Erasmian formulas as are found in the
letter of April 1, that of cures worse than the ailment itself, and so
forth.

Erasmus feared that the sharpening of religious strife would
lead to real war, and the suppression of "Luther's schism" by force
of arms would, in his opinion, be a misery even more bitter than
the schism itself, because Germany would be lorded over by mercenaries without restraint or responsibility; what that would
mean they had already shown sufficiently clearly in their excesses
in Rome, seized and ravaged by Imperial troops in 1529, and in
Turk-sieged Vienna (1529). This is what most alarmed Erasmus;
although the accusations against the Spanish Jews, supposed to
have been a large part of the mercenary troops, are repeated in
both letters, they are not the nub of the matter. Further, unlike
the two earlier eruptions (of 1517 and 1518), this is not a total eruption, rather being strictly focused, so to say, on the Jewish mercenaries. Taking that into account, it may even be better to speak
not of an explosion but rather of relatively incidental information
of some type we do not have a record of, which reached Erasmus
in the context of fundamental, pressing worries, and which he
passes further along, in the same context.

The *Interpretation of Psalm 38* (from the beginning of 1532)
mentions that "even today the unhappy Jews" clutch the literal
meaning of Scripture and reject allegory,[109] as well as that both
the Jews and the pagans rejoice at seeing the impious life of Christians, or their troubles.[110]

A letter of 2 March 1532 compares the situation of Catholics in
states and cities which have accepted the Reform to that of the
Jews: "In certain towns those who could not renounce a religion
handed down from their ancestors are refused the sacraments, are
refused communion . . . they are refused the Catholic sermon,
they are refused the Church confession, and at last the doors of
the temple are locked before them, and in their own town they
live not much freer than the Jews live among Christians."[111]
Once again the position of the Jews plays the role of the standard
of misfortune.

The theme of "Jews rejoicing at the misfortune of Christians" is repeated again in that year, save that the troubles are made concrete, for Erasmus spoke of the split in the church, the Reformation.[112]

In the material from 1532 only two passages from the polemics with the Parisian theologians are important. As had Bédier (see 1526), the theological faculty (the Sorbonne) as a whole condemned Erasmus' ideas about repetition of the baptism vow as an adult, particularly the point that those who refuse to renew the vows need neither be persecuted nor punished, since God had commanded the Jews (Deuteronomy 13) to destroy without mercy all those who fall away from the Testament themselves and who will incite others to idolatry. Erasmus answered that by saying, "I spoke not of a change of the Law, but of a softening of its applications. Who does not know how gently heretics used to be treated and how slowly they resorted to punishment by death, although the right of punishment was the same? The powers of the Church over its own [sons] is no less than the synagogue had over its own, but grace has multiplied and, essentially, the severity of the former Law has weakened . . . But they will answer me, this mildness only sharpens the daring of the impious . . . However . . . fear of punishment fills the Church with false Christians . . . Fear of laws often bears hypocritical fruits and more easily binds the tongue than straightens the soul . . . And today many wonder whether it would not have been wiser to leave the Jews to live in Spain, as before, rather than to see them today in our midst, their names changed rather than their souls . . . I have no doubt that infants come under the authority of the synagogue through circumcision; I even think that simple birth to Jewish parents subordinated one to that authority. After all, during the Babylonian captivity, for example, circumcision was often not practiced."[113] Thus Erasmus not only does not renounce what he had said six years earlier but adds as well two highly significant details, condemning the expulsion of Jews from Spain and full baptism of those remaining, and affirming the right of Jewish parents to raise their children in a spirit of faithfulness to Judaism even without the fact of circumcision. It should be emphasized particularly that this approach to the problem of the Marranos was conditioned less by Erasmus' sympathies for the Jews than by the general principles of his world view and concern for the fate of the Christian world.

The Sorbonne (just as Bédier personally) condemned the interpretation of Matthew 13:29–30 (that heretics should not be destroyed, but left for the judgment of God). The theologians of the Sorbonne argued that the church authorities had the right to declare war on the Turks and Jews, or else to urge the temporal authorities to do so, which meant they had precisely the same right in dealing with obvious heretics. Erasmus thought it necessary to distinguish between Jews and Turks: "Turks not only differ from us in faith, but also seize Christian states one after another, treating us with unimaginable cruelty. If only we could pacify them by force of arms or (more desirably) attract them into Christian association! The Jews though we do not kill—save perhaps when they encroach on the laws of the rulers—even though they are the most stubborn enemies of Christ and the Christian name."[114] Again the principle of the Jews' right to the protection of the law (on the condition that they observe the law themselves) is affirmed.

This contrast of Jews to Turks appears to be contradicted by a phrase from a work of the next year, 1533 *Explanatio Symboli:* "Not only those who renounce Christ and run over to the Turks or Jews are deserters [from the service of Christ—S.M.] but so too are those who are committed whole-heartedly to the world and to worldly comforts."[115] The contradiction, however, is only apparent, since in the first instance Erasmus is speaking of a concrete political situation, while here he is reasoning in a wholly moralistic sense (it is wholly obvious, for example, that he does not mean deserters from the Christian armies fighting the Turks), in which sense for Erasmus Judaism and Islam stand approximately in one place (of which more below). It is equally clear after all the pronouncements on the numerical insignificance of Jews and their exclusion from Christian society that the attraction of Judaism is sooner allegory than a real threat.

The remaining comments in *Symboli* are not remarkable. Not seeing the Messiah in Christ, the Jews are waiting for another Messiah, a rich, powerful king who will liberate and elevate the Jewish people, who today are the outcasts and spurned of the world. "And this unhappy people comforts itself in its troubles with this empty hope."[116] The Goths and Vandals appeal to the Lord, while even today the Jews curse Him in their synagogues and serve the letter, spurning the Holy Ghost.[117] In picturing the Father as a childless loner, they do not worship God but rather some sort of idol which they have reared in their own souls.[118] (Erasmus has apparently forgotten that earlier he had affirmed, "We worship the exact same God as do the Jews.")[119]

In his answer to the "boundlessly slanderous letter of Martin Luther" (1534) Erasmus again touched on the theme of Jewish insignificance. Luther had reproached him for carelessness and inaccuracy in the formulae concerning the divine nature of Christ (in his paraphrase of Romans). Erasmus replied that he would have been more careful if he had feared in the slightest that this might serve as grounds for temptation or misunderstanding. However, "I wasn't at all afraid of the Jews," while Arianism had been eradicated and could not be revived.[120]

Thus we arrive at the very end of Erasmus' creative life, his "spiritual testament," *Ecclesiastes* (1535). There are no new ideas here, but the old ones are repeated and summarized; for us who know that this is the final word, we recognize these as the conclusions of a lifetime. Erasmus repeats that the bad habits of the Christians turn the Jews away from Christ[121]; he speaks, not surprisingly, of the "Jewish threat" (in connection with the observation that there remain many places on earth where Christianity is totally unknown): "I do not speak even of the countless multitude of Jews who live among us (*infinitam Judaeorum vim nobis admixtam*), I do not speak of the many who hide a pagan beneath the name of Christian, I do not speak of the thick ranks of schismatics and heretics."[122] It is clear that Erasmus means not Jews but "Jews," within Christianity, both from the proximity of "pagans" and because of at least two other passages in the same work. "The duty of the good shepherd," Erasmus wrote, "is to penetrate the distance with his gaze, to see into the gloom . . . so as not only to heal the ills of today but also to warn of dangers threatening from afar, the dangers of schisms, heresies, wars, paganism, Judaism."[123] The dangers of Judaism (real Judaism, without quote marks) is somewhere on the far horizons, but anyone who has studied Erasmus knows that he was incomparably more preoccupied by the close and immediate than by the distant. There is a second passage, even more significant. Origen and his followers enthusiastically discussed the struggle between Church and Synagogue, but that was apposite only for the early Church, when the struggle between Gospel and Mosaic Laws was still hot and many people were turning away from the grace of the Gospels, back to Judaism. "Even today there are Jews who insult Christ in their synagogues . . . but we have no conflict with them (*at cum his non est nobis conflictatio*). Christian meekness endures this stubborn people in the hope that someday they will come to their senses, as Paul predicted. In truth, Paul's benefaction preserves the remnants of this people! May God unstop their eyes and ears, so that they might recognize with us the true Messiah."[124] So the disparity between Christianity and Judaism, the distance of the first from the second, and the hope only for the inscrutable ways of the Lord, which will lead to the salvation of the remnants of Israel. If God's plans may be aided, it is solely with meekness and with charity. Erasmus warns that to sack and plunder the pagans (including those in places newly discovered beyond the seas) means to turn them away from Christianity.[125] In this context Erasmus poses the question, "We know how to tame wild and fearful beasts, for pleasure or for our utility, so can we not domesticate them to serve Christ? . . . I know that you can scarcely find an animal more untameable than a stubborn Jew and the inveterate heretic, but there is after all no beast, no matter how savage, who is not softened by kindness and petting."[126]

There are three other "Jewish" passages in *Ecclesiastes*, the first, that neither Jews nor heretics have Scripture, but only books, because only the Spirit permits one to understand Scripture. The Jews memorize the many volumes of the Law for nothing, since the true meaning of it they cannot know.[127] Second, he mentions, ironically, the sermons containing refutations of Judaism which the Jews in Italy were required to attend,[128] and, finally, Erasmus mentions "certain renegades who have run off to the Jews, Turks, or heretics."[129] This last mention, however, is only the device of a preacher who will show as he develops the theme that such renegades are a hundred times more criminal than the Apostle Peter, who thrice denied Christ.

Finally, from the 1535 additions to the New Testament commentary, Erasmus says, "The Jews who have settled in Germany speak not only the vulgar language but their own as well, and the same thing is true of the Jews in Spain and Italy."[130]

This survey completed, consider that phrase from a letter of 30 January 1523 (4), which often has served as the major (if not the sole) grounds for seeing Erasmus as sympathetic to Jews,[131] and which Guido Kisch eliminates from consideration entirely[132]: "I have never refused anyone friendship because the man was sympathetic to Luther or kept aloof from Luther. I have a temperament such that I could love even a Jew, if only he were well-mannered and friendly, and did not dig up blasphemy of Christ in my presence. Such decorum (*civilitatem*) I consider especially useful in ending dissent."[133] Naturally this is said with a certain facetiousness, if only because Erasmus almost certainly never encountered Jews close up and showed no desire ever to do so. Still, this entire survey demonstrates indisputably that hatred of the Jews (whether blind and rabid, as with Luther in his last years, or cold and reasoned, as with Zasius) was no less alien to Erasmus than was love for them.

In the event of a close acquaintance with one of his contemporaries among the enlightened Jews (such as, say, that unflagging lobbyist in the affairs of his persecuted fellow tribesmen, Josel von Rosheim),[134] this indifference, given Erasmus' character, would in fact most likely have become mutual regard. Once again it is important to note that his willingness to love Jews is a part of a much wider context, that differences of opinion, no matter how great, do not suppose inescapable bitterness and hatred.

Now consider certain aspects of the problem separately.

Erasmus interprets the question of the providential nature of Jewish unbelief in strict agreement with Romans 11:11–12. The blindness and stubbornness of the Jews (their "fall," in Paul's words) aroused zeal in the pagans and so led them to faith and to the Church. The pagans though were "accepted" not so the Jews would be spurned forever; just as before Christ the Jews were called to the Law, so now are the pagans called to the Gospels, and just as the example of the Jews once turned the pagans to faith, so in the future the example of the pagans will bring the Jews to faith. Thus neither Jewish blindness nor Jewish stubbornness are hopeless.[135] Further, Erasmus affirms that just as Jewish unbelief was predicted by Christ himself, so too is the eventual conversion and salvation of the Jews.[136] This conversion, however, will occur only on the last day of the world, on the eve of the Second Coming.[137]

How that will come about is not comprehensible by human minds. The concluding verses (25–36) of Romans 11 (often referred to in the preceding) were an unchanging landmark for Erasmus, in which regard the *Argumentum* which precedes Romans in Erasmus' edition of the New Testament (see Chapter 2, note 81) is instructive, as is the paraphrase of chapter 11[138] itself, where nothing is interpolated; Erasmus follows the text precisely. Erasmus insists that the entire Jewish tragedy (not solely those parts still to be played out but also those already played) is the inscrutable mystery of God. Erasmus tells his reader that when Paul used the word "mystery" in Romans 11:25 he demanded the silence of men; to bruit this secret about is license and impiety. "Divine Providence has decided why [God] spurned the Jews . . . that is, permitted them to fall away from him, even though he might have prevented it, while the pagans . . . were suddenly permitted gospel grace, when he might have left them sunk in impiety. [Providence] does not want us to be curious or search beyond what is permitted, but it does not prevent everyone from such searches, only those who reason impiously and who are unable to absorb the mystery."[139] It is precisely the mysterious unexplorability of the fate of the Jewish people, the eschatological postponement of that fate to the end of time, which provided the theological underpinnings for Erasmus' indifference to contemporary Jewry. With few exceptions (and those mostly in the letters not intended for publication), the Jews of Erasmus' day were just as much a didactic example for use in instructing Christians as had been the Old Testament and Gospel Jews. The context of the references and hints at the eleventh chapter of Romans is characteristic. In a letter to John III of Portugal (24 March 1527), Erasmus praises the rulers who concern themselves with dissemination of the Gospels. If all rulers of the Christian world were to do the same, there would be fewer wars and schisms, and we all would be further from Judaism and paganism (obviously, "Judaism" is intended). But are not our own ways at least partly to blame for the fact that "Turks, Mohammedans, Saracenes, Muscovites,

Greeks," and other semi-Christians or schismatics do not hasten
to join the fold of Christ, that the Jews are not healed of their
blindness?[140] This is followed immediately by this passage: "This
unfortunate race of people is obligated to Apostle Paul for their
survival to this day, that there exists still a seedbed from which
[new growth] can spring (*seminarium, unde possit restitui*). Truly,
in the eleventh chapter of Romans Paul gives us the fair hope that
they shall someday convert and with us confess the true Messiah,
and there shall be one shepherd and one flock. It is in this hope
that we permit them to preserve themselves."[141] Further down,
following the corresponding passages from Romans 11, the theme
of Christian imperfection comes up again; if the Jews were
spurned and we were accepted, that in our turn we might bring
them to faith and to God, then we are obligated hourly to trouble
ourselves with the Gospel purity of our lives, with the glorifica-
tion of the Gospels." Then both the Turks and the Jews, seeing
our good works, will glorify our heavenly Father and will thirst to
join such a company (*cupiantque in tale consortium asscribi*)."[142]

Only with reference to this unchanging orientation point is it
possible to interpret properly two lines from the foreword (dedication) to Erasmus' edition of the works of St. Irenaeus, written
just a half year before the letter to the Portugese king, cited above:
"The first collision of the Church was with the Jews (oh, if only
their remnants did not exist today!). Here Apostle Paul showed
himself a powerful advocate of gospel freedom."[143] The regret
here is not that centuries of persecution had not utterly destroyed
the Jewish people but that the time of conversion had still not yet
come, when "all Israel will be saved" (Romans 11:26) and there
would be "no distinction between Jew and Greek" (Romans
10:12).[144]

In speaking of the ways in which Erasmus understood and resolved the Jewish question for himself, it is equally necessary to
remember the principle of the "imitation of Christ" as observed
by the Brethren of the Common Life who (as has been mentioned) had a powerful formative influence on Erasmus' world
view. For example, *Ratio Verae Theologiae,* one of the works that
had the greatest influence on Erasmus' contemporaries and those
coming later, states, "For each mundane act we must search out a
model and example in the holy books . . . It is necessary to follow

the way Christ himself behaved . . . with his parents . . . with his persecutors, with the Jews, with pagans."[145] The example, however, of Christ and imitation of him in good conscience could not teach a Christian to hate the Jews.

Of course, Christian toleration of the Jews as Erasmus understood it was still very far from religious toleration in its modern sense, but (a fact of the greatest importance) Erasmus' willingness to put up with Jews in his environs was a private application of a general principle of toleration of foreign opinions and convictions, which is truly one of the major foundations of the Erasmian world view.[146] This has been discussed above, but a few remarks bear elaboration.

In that *Ratio Verae Theologiae* Erasmus cites the words of Apostle Peter (Acts 3:17) that "brethren, I know that you acted in ignorance," then he exclaims, "See how he softens the boundless crime of the Jews! . . . We though are blind and deaf to this lesson, to such examples. We know nothing save how to frighten and threaten; we coerce but don't teach, drag, but don't lead; we strive to turn everything to our personal glory, to our own benefit."[147] Explaining in his paraphrase the text of Matthew 12:14 ("The Pharisees went out and took counsel against him, how to destroy him. Jesus, aware of this, withdrew from there"), Erasmus declared, "He withdrew . . . in order . . . to show that the philosophy of the Gospels is defended against attack not by threats, curses, or squabbling, but by meekness."[148] In his paraphrase of Luke he poses the question of how the true disciples of Christ have treated the Pharisees and scribes today, since they could not cause another person evil. His answer was that if the enemies of Christ's glory would not listen to reason, and thus are incurable, there is no need to traffic with them at all. They will meet the punishment of the Eternal Judge.[149]

Erasmus' consideration of the Reformation, expressed almost fifteen years after it began, is remarkable: "First of all, there was no need to have paid any attention to Luther and his pronouncements about indulgences, no need to pour oil on the fire. Further, the matter should have been conducted not by monks, detested by almost the entire world, no bursting into impotent squeals in front of people, no burning of books and people, but rather everything should have been shut into books addressed from scholar to scholar. Finally, we should have pretended for a time that we simply did not notice these [rebels] and endured them just as we endure the Bohemian brothers and the Jews. Time itself often brings good medicine for incurable ailments."[150] This parallel (of the Lutherans, the Bohemian brothers, and the Jews) permits an excellent, clear view of both the tactic and the strategy of Erasmian toleration.

It has already been noted (in Chapter 2) that when speaking of Erasmian anti-Mosaism it is necessary to correct for his individualism, which is true in application both the Jewry of Gospel times[151] and to contemporary Jewry. Thus in *Hyperaspistes II* Erasmus takes up the meaning of the Old Testament "topos" of Esau subordinated to Jacob (an allegory of Jews and pagans), noting, "Today the Jews are subordinate to the Christian, the older people serves the younger, but not all Jews are doomed and not all Christians are saved."[152] It is also instructive to juxtapose two general conclusions, the first from the beginning of Erasmus' career, and the second from the end, but both from celebrated works which were dear to the author himself. In *Enchiridion militis Christiani* (1504) Erasmus wrote, "The Christian must not nurse hatred for any man . . . He is an enemy only to vices. The heavier the ailment, the greater troubles let pure charity exhibit. Here is a fornicator, here a blasphemer, here a Turk; let the Christian curse the fornicator, but not the man, hate the blasphemer, but not the man, defeat the Turk, but not the man."[153] (It should not be forgotten that Turkish expansion was in full heat, that the Turks were a more serious threat to all of Europe, and that war with them was a necessity, a question of life and death.) In *Ecclesiastes* (1535) Erasmus affirms that one may not revile and defame as an entity an entire group of people, whether the group be social, professional, or national. "One should take caution and not attack an entire people or state or estate. How would it be if someone accused all Germany of drunkenness, when this is the vice of a few, and from the other side, there is no people who does not contain a few without restraint. Italy is cursed for . . . lasciviousness, when there is a great multitude of people there who are untouched by this infection." Not all the monks are bad, or the courtiers, or merchants, or even mercenary soldiers. "And since there is nothing which does not mix good with bad, if

Chapter V

someone curses everybody then his speeches will contain more
hatred than sound reasoning, and thus he will not encounter belief but will evoke more enmity among good people than among
those whom he attacks."[154]

The beginning of this chapter remarked that even after baptism
Jews remained Jews in Erasmus' eyes. In other words, the word
Iudaeus for him means national membership, not religious affiliation. In reality though the same word also served to signify the
religion, giving rise to a terminological confusion. Joseph Flavius
wrote in Greek, although he was a Jew by birth (*Iudaeus
natus*)[155]; the Law was addressed only to Jews, the Gospels to all
peoples of the earth (*Judaeis—omnibus mundi nationibus*)[156];
"neither the Jew nor man of other nation" (*neque Judaeo, neque
alterius nationis*)[157]; Paul attacks the false apostles as "Jew upon
Jews, Christian upon Christians" (*Iudaeus in Iudaeos, Christianus
in Christianos*)[158]; Christ reconciled all nations of earth with God,
the Jews, Greeks, Latins, Scythians, Hindis[159]; Christ distinguished the Jews from the other peoples.[160] In all these cases
and in many others Erasmus absolutely uniformly speaks of Jews
as a people, but then in a close parallel to the first example above
he writes, "Joseph, by religion a Jew" (*professione Iudaeus*).[161]
This is far from an exception; a woman mentioned in Mark 7:26
"was not a Jewess by religion" (*Judaeam religione*)[162]; the proselyte was from Antioch, a Jew by religion (*religione Judaeum*)[163];
"Jew was the name of the religion, while Hebrew (*Hebraei*)
means more the people (*gentem et nationem*)."[164] In this last example (from the commentary to Acts 6:1) Erasmus is attempting
to delimit terminologically national and religious affiliation. Another distinction is offered in another instance, *Judaeus* and *homo
Judaicus,* the first to mean the people, the second the religion.[165]
Finally, it is not hard to find instances where *Iudaeus* encompasses
both meanings. Acts 13:6 mentions a false prophet, a Jew
(*Iudaeus*); in the paraphrase Erasmus writes "a Jew by birth and
by religion (*natione et religionis professione Judaeum*)."[166] Commenting on Acts 2:10 he speaks of "Jews by origin" (*Judaei genere*), and "adoptive Jews" (*adoptione Judaei*), meaning proselytes
who are "pagans by birth, become Jews by religion."[167] Here too
Erasmus distinguishes the Jews of Israel from the Jews of the Diaspora (*Judaei ex gente* versus *Judaei ex religione et origine*). This

distinction is occasioned by the text of Acts itself (2:5): "Now there were dwelling in Jerusalem Jews, devout men from every nation under heaven." It is this verse from Acts Erasmus has in mind when he writes of the "Jewish people, fused of various nations (*populum Judaicum, ex variis nationibus conflatum*) who then . . . were gathered in Jerusalem."[168]

Still, with all the imprecision of terminology and the fruitless attempts to resolve the imprecision, nevertheless Erasmus inarguably meant when speaking of Jews first and foremost a people, a national affiliation. As was seen (this chapter, note 11), Matthias Adrian is called "*genere Hebraes,*" following the rule Erasmus formulated in his commentary on the New Testament (see note 164). In other instances, however, this rule is not followed, for Adrian is regularly called "*Hebraeus.*"[169] It is possible that what affects the circumstances here is that Adrian taught Hebrew (see Chapter 3, note 116); parenthetically Erasmus referred to the famous and not converted Hebraicist Elijah Levita as *Iudaeus.*[170] It is something else though that is of significance, that whether a Jewish contemporary is called *Hebraeus* or *Iudaeus,* either name means first common nationality and only then—and not always—religion.

Common nationality, however, had no value in Erasmus' eyes; he was a confirmed and thorough cosmopolitan. To him the bonds of common national origin were nothing in comparison to individual qualities or common allegiance to the international fraternity of scholars, the "*respublica bonarum litterarum.*"[171] He does not deny national differences, national character, national vices and virtues,[172] but he holds them insignificant in comparison with spiritual wealth (or poverty), with the fact of allegiance to the faith and Church of Christ. For this reason Erasmus condemns nationalism as something alien and inimical to the spirit of Christianity.[173] There is no doubt as to the main source of this condemnation, the various statements of the Apostle Paul, of which the most famous is Colossians 3:11: "Here there cannot be Greek and Jew, circumcised and uncircumcised, barbarian, Scythian, slave, free man, but Christ is all, and in all." Still, it is not just this Erasmian "return to sources" that defines the antinationalist position, for it is strengthened by individualism as well, distrust of and revulsion for mass psychology in general (na-

Chapter V

tionalism is but part of the phenomenon of mass psychology). "Nowadays the noble spurn the lowborn; the rich man does not seem to consider the poor man a man; the scholar despises the layman; the priest curses the worldly man; the monk scarcely even considers the worldly as Christians; the Italian is condescending with all other peoples, as though they were barbarians, almost cattle, and he fears them; the German hates the Frenchman; the Englishman the Scot. And it is just these and others of man's foolest passions like them that cause wars and strife."[174]

This quotation is particularly remarkable since it comes from a period which was peaceful and happy for Erasmus, and so is born not of the heat of the moment or the evil of the day, but is sprung rather from the depths of his world understanding.

Erasmus steadfastly rejects the attacks of his opponents who scorned him for his Dutch origins. What if he was Dutch (*Batavus*)? There is no shame in being born even Bactrian or Sogdian, so no one has the right to despise Holland. Such feelings are particularly reprehensible in a theologian, who is obligated to know that for a Christian philosopher there can be no such thing as a Spaniard, a Frenchman, a German, a Sarmatian, but rather only the new man, the new creation of God.[175] Whether Erasmus is French or German has no import whatever for the matter of faith, nor is he interested in the origins of his critics, who is Norse, who Cenomanus (Spanish). Following the example of the Apostle Paul, the theologian ought to be interested in the essence of dispute, not the genealogy of the disputants.[176] There is no exception for Jews. Commenting on Matthew 23:30 Erasmus wrote that Christ promised the Jews misfortunes neither because they built tombs for the prophets nor because they are the descendants of the murderers of prophets, since the first is their duty and the second, of whom we are born into this world, is not within our powers to affect (*alterum non sit in manu nostra unde nascamur*).[177]

However, in the practice of daily literary warfare Erasmus often, even too often, departed from his own principles and general rules. Following the ancient Catholic tradition[178] (from at least the seventh century), he never fails to let pass an opportunity to accuse his enemies of Jewish origins, even if at times he has to invent an accusation. It has already been shown how he chided

104

Lopez Zuñiga for un-Christian and untheological feelings when Zuñiga accused the Dutch of stupidity (saying they floated in fat from overuse of butter and beer).[179] Erasmus though answered this un-Christian accusation with an insinuation of no greater Christianity, since in almost all his polemical exchanges with Zuñiga Erasmus hints at Zuñiga's Jewish origins, as though explaining Zuñiga's particular "caviling" at the mistakes in the Hebrew material in Erasmus' commentaries on the New Testament, just as Zuñiga's origins were implied to explain his interest in the Hebrew originals of Scripture.[180] The author of a study of the first two Erasmian editions of the New Testament wrote of these hints, which were contemptible not only from a present-day point of view but also from the viewpoint of true Erasmism. He said, "In the squabbles of those days they dragged out all the most intimate relations, even parents and relatives, and placed them on public view in the most laughable or shameful light."[181] Although the spirit of the times is no excuse for Erasmus, who in so much had surpassed his own era, still it is important to understand that "common anti-Semitism" is here combined with another form of mass psychology (in this case, with an educated mass).

Girolamo Aleandro, a high-ranking official of the Roman curia who had reached the cloth of cardinal, was another target of Erasmus' anti-Semitic insinuations. The two at first had been friends, until Erasmus began to suspect Aleandro of slyness and intrigues, and so stuck with the label "Jew," without, it appears, the slightest basis for doing so.[182] At first he did so in an anonymous pamphlet, "Acts of the Louvain Academy Against Luther" (1520), which said that Aleandro's native tongue (*vernacula*) was Hebrew, that he himself had been born in Judaism but had imperceptibly hidden himself among Christians in order to magnify his Moses and to diminish Christ's glory, which had only just begun to flower again, while the prejudices and fatal rituals made by men had begun to fade.[183] (This pamphlet was written in defense of Luther, who at that time seemed to Erasmus to be destroying the new Judaism of the church; it was Aleandro who had brought the anti-Luther *Exsurge Domine* to Germany.) There was more; general rumors as well as Aleandro's whole appearance and manner of speaking revealed him as a Jew, and the Jews themselves accepted him as one of theirs. "The Christians are condemned to suffer from the Jews. So it was a Jew who goaded Pope Julian [II] to destroy the universe. It was Pfefferkorn in Cologne who stirred up the Christian world. And now it is Aleandro, the cousin of Judas, who is surpassing his ancestors, ready to sell the cause of the Gospels even for three drachma."[184] Erasmus put similar rumors out verbally too, as was exposed both by Aleandro himself and by Ulrich von Hutten.[185] However, when appearing in print and under his own name, Erasmus was much more reserved, not even calling Aleandro by name, limiting himself to transparent hints.[186]

Finally, a third target of such "criticism" was the Spanish Franciscan Lodovico Caravajal, who had condemned Erasmus for his attacks on monasticism. The coarseness of tone in Erasmus' two replies to Caravajal's statements is remarkable[187]; Caravajal is a raving lunatic, the emperor should have sent him to the gallows, while the authorities of the Franciscan order should whip him with rods and incarcerate him for life. Parenthetically, the man is not even a Franciscan at all, or even a Christian, but a Jew who is hiding behind an assumed name, for "there is a great quantity of such muck" which meddle in today's church turmoil.[188]

Some of these phrases recall the judeophobic explosions mentioned above in virulence of tone, but solely in tone, not in fact; this is not total judeophobia, a hysterical explosion of hate and fear. Rather this is an incidental dig, a low and common polemical device, on the level of an argument on a city bus.

The hint at Luther's Jewishness in a letter of 2 March 1532 stands alone. Erasmus wished leaders to be above reproach, so that there could be no rumors about them, even false rumors, among which was that said of Luther in the beginning, that his father was a Jew and his mother a Czech. Erasmus gave no credence to the old rumor, adding, "In addition no one may be accused because of the fault of the birth."[189] The cheap and petty guile of this addition is clear.

Accusations of sympathy for Judaism are not worth particular attention, since in such cases what is meant is new Judaism, or the predominance of rituals "made by man."[190]

It has already been mentioned (as well as shown by some of the quotations) that Erasmus had no interest in Talmudic and cabalistic works. He repudiated the Jewish medieval literature without knowing anything about it at all (see also the following chapter, on Erasmus' attitude toward Hebrew commentaries on Scripture). This *a priori* flat rejection continues to the very end of his career. In the scholia to Jerome (1516) Erasmus wrote that heretics fooled and frightened the great unwashed with magic words, purportedly gleaned from the Hebrew scriptures and the Talmudic and cabalistic books.[191] The *Ratio Verae Theologia* (1518) condemns those attracted to numerology, who used Hebrew wisdom on Greek and Latin numbers (that is, using the number value of the words). "It is not that I completely reject the mystery hidden in numbers" but that its interpretation is often distorted or even senseless, yet we use such clumsy calculations as the basis for serious discussions.[192] Clearly present here is the same distrust of Hebrew studies, the conviction that such studies are wholly superfluous and unnecessary for a Christian, as can be seen in Colet's letter to Erasmus (as quoted at note 34, this chapter).

The letters of 1519 state categorically Erasmus' dislike of the Cabala and Talmud. A letter to Thomas Wolsey, Archbishop of Canterbury, of 18 May, says, "They confound the cause of the humanities (*bonarum literarum causam*) with the business of Reuchlin and Luther, though there is no connection between them. Personally I have never felt the attraction of Cabala or Talmud. I have met Reuchlin only once, in Frankfurt, and there is nothing between us except friendship and courtesy such as exist between almost all scholars."[193] The letter to Hoogstraten of 11 August, analyzed in detail above, says there is no reason to mix Erasmus up in a matter which is totally alien to him: "May Christ be as well disposed to me as I am poorly disposed to the Cabala."[194] A letter to Albert of Brandenburg on 19 October says, "The Cabala and Talmud, whatever they may be, never attracted me."[195] The 1527 edition of the commentaries on the New Testament states that the Talmudic and cabalistic mysteries of the Jews of the day can be compared to the wiles and tricks of the false apostles.[196] The book *De Conscribendis Epistolis* (1522) again warns against the attraction to the Jewish mystical works, saying that they should not be touched without fundamental knowledge of the antiquities, which practically none of the new cabalists possessed.[197] Finally, in *Ecclesiastes* (1535), referring to 2 Timothy 4:13, Erasmus explains that "Paul asks that he be sent books . . . I doubt this was Plato or Pythagoras, or Talmud and cabalistic books, but rather the Old Testament."[198]

Only once in his life did Erasmus speak of the Cabala without obvious hostility. Paulus Ricius (mentioned in the beginning of this chapter) had written an apologetic speech in reply to Hoogstraten's *The Cabala Refuted*; Erasmus wrote Ricius in November 1520: "Your booklet, most learned Ricius, forced me to treat the Cabala a little more justly; incidentally, even before that I was not wholly against it. I consider it a forgivable human failing if someone is taken with such activities, wasting great amounts of time on it . . . And on the other hand, who can bear people who viciously and stubbornly hate all that they cannot understand?"[199] This, however, is neither a concession to the Cabala nor a new understanding of it[200] but rather simple personal courtesy toward Ricius, a Christian cabalist and old friend whom Erasmus, by all appearances, loved.[201] The phrase aimed at Hoogstraten (about those who hate without understanding) hits Erasmus on the rebound, with the qualification (a decisive one, from present viewpoints and for present purposes) that the Inquisitor of Cologne (and millions of "dark people" and hundreds of "worthy" enlightened ones along with him) did not understand the Cabala and so wanted to trample it down and pull it out by the roots, while Erasmus, neither understanding it nor wishing to, also did not wish to persecute it, and instead simply kept his distance.

It is interesting to note the place Jews occupied in the ranks of the other enemies of Christianity. The most common combination (in a simple enumeration) is heretics, Jews, pagans (or, a variant, philosophers). This is occasionally enlarged to include schismatics.[202] Almost as often Jews and heretics are linked, without the pagans; they also can be joined by bad Christians (a tradition going back to Augustine),[203] those who profess Christ in words but deny him in their deeds.[204] From time to time the rank includes rulers (or tyrants), meaning the persecutors of the early Church. For example, Jews, philosophers, rulers[205]; Jews, tyrants, philosophers, heretics[206]; and rulers, Jews, heretics.[207] On occasion this list grows unexpectedly curious, such as Jews and morosophes (lovers of stupidity) rather than philosophers (lovers of wisdom), and the unhappy spawn of Eve.[208] Sometimes too the list is unjustifiably and illogically detailed, as in Jews, philosophers, Sophists, rhetoricians, tyrants, kings, deputies, magistrates, magicians, and charlatans, demons.[209]

The grouping of the Jews with the other contemporary enemies of Christendom, the Turks, deserves particular attention. Here too there are variations on the same theme: the enemies of faith, Jews and Turks[210]; the Turks, Jews, and all other enemies of the Church, Christ's bride[211]; the Jewish people, the pagans or Turks or Mohammedans or any other kind of people who are alien to Christ, schismatics or heretics[212]; Jews, Turks, and the rest, who either know You not or envy You your glory[213]; Turks, pagans, Jews, and heretics.[214] Erasmus' concept of the insignificance of Jewry on a practical plane has already been shown (as compared with the Turkish threat), but in a purely theological way Judaism was more of a threat than Islam, since the Turk's religion "is a mixture of Judaism, Christianity, paganism, and Arianism. The Turks recognize Christ and some of the prophets. The Jews do too, but they say that Christ was only a man, which is worse than the Arian doctrine."[215] Hopes for the conversion of the Turks and other barbarians are also greater than for the conversion of the Jews "since as far as I know they do not worship idols, but their religion is half Christian (*dimidiatum habent Christianismum*)."[216]

Comparison of the Jews (here the Jews of the Gospel period) with the pagans is naturally not favorable to the Jews. In Erasmus' opinion those who have set out on the pathway to salvation but who then fall back into their former impiety are worthy of far harsher condemnation than those who were always sunk in the gloom of sins. The Law had set Jews apart from the pagan idolators, but they returned to their former vices, even going so far as to conspire against Christ and his disciples.[217] Thus it was no accident that when the light of gospel truth dawned the pagans turned out to have greater piety and sounder reason than the Jews.[218] On the other hand, and more originally, Erasmus saw the pagans and Jews as equal in error and sins,[219] in means of worship (sacrifice),[220] and in responsibility for deafness to the message of the Gospels,[221] but in morals and daily life, Jews occasionally seemed superior. Thus the Romans forbade the slaves who turned the stones in mills to eat the grain, putting yokes on their necks to prevent their hands reaching their mouths. Comparing this cruel treatment with the Old Testament injunction, "You shall not muzzle an ox when it treads out grain" (Deuteronomy 25:4), Erasmus exclaims, "What Jews would not do with an ox, they did with people!"[222]

In *Ecclesiastes* Erasmus gave this definition of heresy: "I call heresy not some error, but an inveterate perversion (*pervicacem malitiam*) which distorts the dogma to disrupt the peace of the Church for some sort of gain."[223] Clearly Jews do not fall under that definition, and so Erasmus refuses the ancient Catholic tradition that equated Jews with heretics and Judaism with heresy.[224] In fact, after recounting the intrigues of the heretics against Athanasius of Alexandria, Erasmus exclaims, "Did the Jews dream up anything of the like against Christ?"[225] There are other instances, however, where he openly terms the Jews heretics and even worse than heretics (*plusquam Haeritici*).[226]

Erasmus drew no overt parallels between the Jews and the reformationists, and his isolated attempts to imply links between Judaism and the Reformation (and thus compromise it) have already been noted in this systematic survey. In one curious passage, however, Lutherans are accused of a Jewish failing: "Is this really the example of the Gospels, to use tricks and force to drag all who pass by into your nets? . . . This was how the Jews ransacked sea and land to bring even a single proselyte before the Law, while the Apostles took no one by human means."[227]

On the other hand, Erasmus countless times called his enemies in the conservative camp (the leaders of the new Judaism, first and foremost the theologians) "rabbis," sometimes explaining the word (already found in Greek transcription in the New Testament) seriously,[228] sometimes ironically: "For respect they are called 'theologians' in Greek, 'rabbis' in Hebrew, and in Latin it is 'our masters.'"[229] However, the explanation aside, and even out of context, it is plain that by calling the theologians "rabbis" he was paying them no bigger compliment than if he had called them "pharisees." In fact, the two terms converge: "Our age too has its pharisees and rabbis"[230]; "I call the theologians who are like scribes and pharisees 'rabbis.'"[231] The abusive metaphor sprouts:

the synagogues of theologians[232]; the mysti of the Old Synagogue.[233] Usually "rabbis" may be distinguished from rabbis by
hints in the text. "Rabbis love to preside in schools and at luxurious banquets, love to be greeted well . . . They darken and
smother the spark of Gospel love with their petty rituals . . . They
rush to force, as though the human mind could be made to believe other than as it feels. If only Christ . . . would finally spare
his people from this Judaism and this tyranny!"[234] It happens too
though that the guiding words are absent; when Erasmus paraphrases Luke 14:7 (about the first and last when invited to a wedding feast) he writes, "Christ wished to condemn the arrogance of
those who were invited by the Pharisitical superior; having come
to the feast they solicit places as high as possible and rejoice at
getting an honored place, mourning if the place is not so honored. Such too now are the triumphal parades of the rabbis when
they leave the synagogues for a feast. In the synagogue they sit on
a dais, looking down on everyone else . . ."; this continues for
many lines, depicting the haughtiness and smugness of "the rabbis."[235] Naturally even an inexperienced reader of today would
doubt that Erasmus meant Jewish clergy, while his contemporaries would readily guess whom Erasmus is satirizing. The "rabbis" themselves also guessed, and complained publicly about this
blasphemous lack of respect for their rank and calling.[236]

VI

The Hebrew Language

*E*rasmus' general attitude to the Hebrew language is pithily and precisely defined by his position as a humanist or, more exactly, a Christian humanist; the accomplishments and principles of humanist philology, which was revitalizing the ancient learning, must be put to the service of theology. This new theology (though in Erasmus' mind a restored theology of the early Church) had as its object of study the text of the Scriptures, with its goal the true, authentic understanding of the text, freed of the weight of later mistakes and additions. The most important means for achieving this goal was a real knowledge of the languages of Scripture and the Church Fathers.

This general position would suppose wholly equal evaluation of all three "holy tongues"—Hebrew, Greek, and Latin—and in fact Erasmus valued them the same, in principle. The equivalence in principle of Hebrew to Latin and Greek is a thesis of primary, decisive importance; any attempt to argue with it or refute it would mean to break with the Erasmian tradition.

The first declaration of the necessity to study all three languages appear as early as 1501. Erasmus refers to the famous Constitutio Clementina, promulgated at the Council of Vienne in 1311–1312: "I am supported by the holy authority of the pontifical

Note: Because this chapter has a more specialized character than the others, parts of the quotations are given in the original.—S.M.

council [which specified] . . . that the leading universities . . . should engage persons capable of giving complete instruction in the Hebrew [note: in first position—S.M.], Greek, and Latin languages and literatures, because Scripture cannot be understood, much less discussed, without knowledge of them."[1] Just before that,[2] however, the same letter says that only a madman could reason about the mysteries of theology without knowing Greek, as an example of which Erasmus cites the text of one of the psalms which is unclear in the Vulgate and clear in the Septuagint; it seems never to have occurred to him that in such a case one ought to have referred to the *veritas Hebraica*. This contradiction illustrates the other extraordinarily important aspect of Erasmus' attitude toward Hebrew.

Only in one of his most important pedagogical works, *De Ratione Studii* (1511), did Erasmus consciously exclude Hebrew from the program of study, which his modern publisher Professor Margolin felt obliged to point out.[3]

What might be termed Erasmus' fundamental programmatic statements on the role and significance of Hebrew in the education of a Christian in general and a theologian in particular (though it is well-known that Erasmus insistently blurred the boundary between the professional theologian and the pious Christian)[4] come in *Ratio Verae Theologiae* (1518) and *Ecclesiastes* (1535), meaning near the apogee, the *akmē (ἀκμή)* of Erasmus' life and career, and near their epilogue. The agreement, the consonance of these two statements is wholly significant. However, before taking up the first of these, a short survey is necessary of Erasmus' chance words and passages written in passing in the years 1511–1518.

To take up theology without knowing all three holy tongues is not only stupid, it is impious. "Quas qui ignorat, non theologus est, sed sacrae Theologiae violator."[5] Only a scoundrel would dare call himself a theologian if he knows nothing of Greek and Hebrew.[6] In the *Apologia* preceding the first edition of the New Testament (1516), Erasmus writes in invocation, "First of all . . . I urge again and again that all theologians, whom age and affairs permit, to taste of Greek literature and, if there is the possibility, of Hebrew as well."[7] He goes even farther in the commentaries: "These three holy tongues should be studied by each and every one in Christendom," because of all the languages on earth, only these three were inscribed on the cross of Jesus Christ.[8]

If Erasmus preferred the theology of St. Jerome to that of St. Augustine, it was precisely because the former had the great advantage of familiarity with Greek and Hebrew literature.[9] Knowing absolutely no Hebrew, Augustine had condemned Jerome for correcting the Latin translation of Scripture by comparing it to the Hebrew original, even though Augustine himself was not slow to point out mistakes in the Latin text of the Old Testament books.[10] Meanwhile, "vide quid est alienis cernere oculis, alienis ambulare pedibus."[11] St. Hilarius, "vir alioqui et eloquens et eruditus, Graeci pariter et Latini sermonis gnarus,"[12] but who had absolutely no Hebrew, interpreted the Hebrew word *osanna* to mean "redemptio domus David," although the absurdity of the interpretation is obvious. (No doubt he had asked a Jew who decided to make fun of the naive Christian and so gave him the first answer that sprang to mind.)[13] "At idem [St. Hilarius] non probat ullam interpretationem Veteris Instrumenti, praeter eam que fertur esse Septuaginta, propterea quod Bresith BRESHITH (בְּרֵאשִׁת) quae prima vox est libri Geneseos apud Hebraeos tria significet, in principio, in filio, et in capite."[14] This Erasmian irony is typical.

The decline of Hebrew and the aversion to it were signs of general decline and acculturation.[15] The scoffers and enemies of Hebrew were know-nothings and fools, more stupid than pigs, though they consider themselves luminaries of wisdom.[16] (Erasmus made no attempt to hide whom he was addressing this criticism to, the theologians of the old school)[17]; after all, Hebrew was the language of the Savior himself, and if his speeches had but been preserved in the same form as that in which they were spoken, "cui non cordi foret . . . non solum verborum vim ac proprietatem, verum singulos etiam apices excutere?"[18] Already then Hebrew had become a constituent element in the ideal picture of the world, in Erasmus' Utopia, or perhaps Thélème. In October 1515, he wrote of his circle of new friends in Basel: "In truth it seems as though I have chanced on some wonderful temple of Muses! So many scholars here, and such rare scholars! Every last one of them knows Latin and Greek, and the majority also know Hebrew. This one surpasses the others in knowledge of history, while that one is a first-class theologian. One is versed in mathematics, while another has studied antiquity, a third has penetrated the depths of law . . . Never before have I been able to circulate in such remarkable society, surely!"[19]

The basic points of the program outlined in *Ratio Verae Theologiae* are that, in order to acquire the knowledge which lead to true theology, it is necessary first of all to learn the three languages—Latin, Greek, and Hebrew—as even Augustine admitted (who knew Greek poorly and Hebrew not at all, with no hopes of learning it); just as one who does not know the letters cannot read, so one who does not know the languages cannot understand what he is reading. Besides the desire to learn, good teachers are also necessary, whence the extraordinarily great significance of the Collegium Trilingue in Louvain (as is known, Erasmus took an active part in the organization of this school).[20]

It was not necessary to seek full mastery of Greek and Hebrew; it was enough to achieve a middle level, sufficient to allow one to form one's own judgment of the text. This though required work; the frivolous laggard could scarcely have the right to rely on the apostolic "gift of tongues."[21]

The Vulgate alone would have been insufficient, even had the translation been beyond reproach. "Quid quod quaedam ob sermonum idiomata ne possunt quidem ita transfundi in alienam linguam, ut eamdem lucem, ut nativam gratiam, ut parem obtineat emphasin? Quid quod quaedam minutiora sunt, quam quod omnino reddi posint? id quod passim queritur, clamitatque divus Hieronymus."[22] The text of the Vulgate though was far from ideal, as well as considerably corrupted by scribes, which had been the cause of many obvious and shameful errors by the most famous theologians, including St. Augustine and Thomas Aquinas.

If you are already too old, you must submit to fate and so use, so far as is possible, the fruits of another man's industry; the main thing is not to remove the hopes and zeal of the young, to whom these lines are primarily dedicated. (The addressee here is not in doubt, the same moss-bound scholastics of whom Erasmus spoke in the letter to VanDorp.) Incidentally, age is no excuse; "Rodolphus Agricola, unicum Germaniae nostrae lumen et ornamentum," began to study Hebrew when he was past forty. "Even

I myself, though in the fifty-third year of life will nevertheless return, when the opportunity arises, to Hebrew literature, which I once nibbled."[23]

In conclusion, Erasmus returns once again to Augustine, who was inconsistent in his attitude to Hebrew, to make the sound psychological observation: "It is a peculiarity of human nature that each approves [of the actions of others] only so far as one feels able to accomplish them one's self. Augustine compared the Old Testament with the translation of the Septuagint, but he would have compared it with even greater enthusiasm to the Hebrew original, if he had had Hebrew."[24] The observation is even more curious for its occasional applicability to Erasmus himself as well.

Ecclesiastes was composed over ten years, which gives even greater foundation for considering the work to be (as has been said) the summary of a lifetime, Erasmus' spiritual legacy,[25] so it is particularly important that the work does not omit Hebrew. The future preacher "must study three languages—Greek, Latin, and Hebrew—which are important . . . so that we might more truly understand the holy books, while if something unclear is encountered in the divine books, it would be possible to attain it in the sources. The first sources of the Scriptures are the Hebrew language and its relatives, Chaldean and Syriac. The doctrine of true religion has been passed down from the Jewish people . . . These three languages [Hebrew, Greek, and Latin] once were in common use. Today, however, the decay has gone so far that the Jews (with the exception of scholars) do not understand the holy books written in Hebrew; the Greeks do not understand those translated or written in Greek; and the Italians and Spanish, the French and Africans do not understand the translations into Latin. Among those languages the highest dignity belongs to Hebrew, but its use is limited to the very narrowest bounds. Use of Greek is extraordinarily broad, not only because the Old Testament was first translated into Greek and the New Testament written in it, but also because almost all sciences, all philosophy come to us through the Greeks, and in Greek. Thus knowledge of all three languages is important for acquiring one's own ability to judge."[26]

This long quotation deserves very close attention, for while affirming the immutability of Erasmus' viewpoint in principle, it introduces a refinement which was not immediately evident as of great importance, namely, that while the worth of all three holy tongues is identical, and in value, weight, and authority Hebrew stands even higher than the other two, the practical utility of Hebrew, the sphere of its use, is insignificant in comparison with Greek. The main reason for this refinement is not so much the "Augustinian complex" mentioned above, which Erasmus could not fail to develop in old age after so many attacks on his New Testament commentary that exposed his lack of Hebrew, as much as the hidden polemic with the reformationists, who persecuted and destroyed (or so Erasmus thought) *bonarum litterarum* and who moved Hebrew to first place, at the expense of Greek. Of this, more later.

Thus the only purpose of Hebrew is to resolve difficulties and doubts which arise while reading the books of the Old Testament in Latin translation (it should be remembered that Erasmus is speaking of preachers here, meaning practical theologians). Erasmus demonstrated the practical side of matters in detailed examples,[27] showing how errors arise in translation and reproduction, and he proposed four means of correcting them: collation of the doubtful passage with the original, in Greek or in Hebrew; a close study of the translation with the goal of discovering the source of the error; the collation of various translations; and study of the commentaries, particularly the ancient ones.[28] In other words, a wholly scientific device could be replaced by a philologically doubtful and wholly unreliable device; this is that "antiphilology" mentioned in connection with the first quotation, possible with Erasmus only in the case of Hebrew (never Greek!), and which plays a particular role in Erasmian exegesis.

The fundamental agreement of positions in *Ratio Verae Theologiae* on the one hand and *Ecclesiastes* on the other permits the supposition that the intermediate statements are made in the same spirit. In fact, in 1519 Erasmus condemned Augustine for interpreting the Old Testament books without knowing the language. "Certe non sine lapsus periculo versatur in enarrandis divinis Libris, qui linguarum ignarus id agit." Even supposing Augustine had made no mistakes in doing this, how many mistakes had other renowned theologians made precisely through lack of knowledge of the languages![29] Erasmus could hardly have forgotten that four years before he had written and published a paraphrase of Psalm I; apparently he felt that no matter how modest his knowledge of Hebrew, it was enough to justify his working on Old Testament texts. It is useful to juxtapose this with words from a letter to Jacopo Sadoleto, dated 14 May 1530: "Non semel rogatus sum quum ab aliis, tum ab Anglorum rege, ut in omnes Psalmos aederem commentarios; sed deterrebant me quum alia multa, tum illa duo potissimum, quod viderem hoc argumentum vix posse pro dignitate tractari, nisi quis calleat Hebraeorum litteras atque etiam antiquitates, partim quod verebar ne turba commentariorum obscuraretur sermo propheticus."[30] The true scope of Erasmus' Hebrew knowledge is a separate question, to be taken up below, as far as it is possible to do so.

At that time (1519) Erasmus still accorded Hebrew and Chaldean a broader role than later, in *Ecclesiastes:* "non solum hunc habent usum, ut apud barbaros nationes praedicetur Christus, verum etiam ut de Scripturis judicemus."[31] It is particularly curious that Erasmus uses the same word in *Ecclesiastes:* "Ad judicium igitur parandum valet harum linguarum peritia." Here though "judgment about Scripture" is put only in second place.

Also, later, on various occasions, Erasmus many times praised the three holy tongues, approved the study of Hebrew, and spoke of the importance of Hebrew for the theologian.[32] Two other details seem worthy of mention.

In the dialogue *Antibarbari* (second version, 1518–1520) the decline of Hebrew studies in the Middle Ages is not only correlated to the same decline in pagan studies (in other words, the loss of the classical heritage), but also is included in the very widest possible conception of the cultural development of the Christian world.[33] In this regard it is very important to emphasize the lack of isolation, the asingularity of the problem, which is subordinate to general principles of world view. Just as with the problem of Erasmus' attitude to Judaism as a whole, the problem of his attitude to Hebrew can be properly understood only in the makeup of the entire Erasmian "world model," in relation to the other major elements of the model.

The second detail is that Erasmus refutes the suspicion that the study of Hebrew is fraught with the danger of Judaism, for this is the suspicion of ignoramuses and the enemies of science. "With equal basis one might fear acquiring paganism from Homer, Demosthenes, Virgil, and Cicero."[34] The same idea repeats in *Adagia* (Ne bos quidem pereat, 1526), with an interesting addition, that not long before rumors had gone through the princes' courts that supposedly "both Lutheranism and peasant revolts had come from languages and literacy. If someone who knows Hebrew and Greek risks an accusation of heresy because Luther is not ignorant of the three languages," Erasmus then asks, why not also remember that around the pillars of today's Church, who are perfectly versed in all three holy tongues?[35]

Skeptical, hateful, and even inimical statements sound dissonant against this background; they are not many, but there is no sense in ignoring them, since each statement is easily explained within the context of Erasmian heritage without contradicting the general picture; rather this broadens, even enriches, the whole.

Five times Erasmus calls Hebrew a "barbaric" language; as Erasmus himself points out, the source of this expression was St. Jerome, who knew Hebrew and studied it industriously (and, in addition, "quasi Plautus non vocarit et Romanam sermonem barbaram").[36] Since Erasmus finished his many years of preparatory labor for the publication of St. Jerome's works in 1516, it is scarcely a coincidence that all five instances date from 1516 to 1522. Three of the uses of "barbaric" appear defamatory.

In opposition, "publica Ecclesiarum omnium consuetudounius Hieronymi ex ignota barbaraque lingua annotamentum"[37] (though here Erasmus is also angry with his idol Jerome).

Second, "Equidem non arbitror operae pretium de barbarica vocula vehementius contendere, et magis libet Latinorum et Graecorum in hoc consensum sequi."[38] This is polemic with the critics of the first edition of the New Testament commentary over the word *Golgotha,* and, as all Erasmus scholars know, in a polemic Erasmus observed neither restraints nor rules.[39]

Finally, "Verum in his barbari sermonis Labyrinthus non est animus distorqueri"[40] (referring to the meaning of the word *bar* in Syriac and Hebrew).

This last bilious observation was provoked by the lack of agreement among the commentators on whom Erasmus ultimately was wholly dependent. In any Hebrew discussion of the slightest seriousness Erasmus could not have an opinion of his own. His position must have been the more unpleasant and degrading since Erasmus was (according to Ludwig Geiger) the only one of the important humanists of the day who did not know Hebrew.[41] Taking into account Erasmus' acute sensitivity and anxiety, it is astonishing that his "Augustinian complex" appears so infrequently.

Here are three typical statements about the difficulty and "ambiguity" of Hebrew:

"Atque ego sane vix unqam duos vidi, qui in re Hebraica consentirent, sive hoc linguae, sive hominum est vitium."[42]

"Nulla enim est lingua, quae plus habet ambiguitatem, aut in qua facilior sit lapsus, aut in qua magis varient interpretes."[43]

". . . sermonem Hebraicam et Graecam plus habere ambiguitatem, quam Latinam. Apud Hebraeos partim in causa est, quorundam elementorum similitudo, quae parum attentis praebet erroris occasionem, partim puncta, quae subnotantur litteris: ea in priscis illorum codicibus non apponebantur, et tamen ex his mutatis varius nascitur sensus."[44]

This last quotation is from *Ecclesiastes;* the tone is calm, wholly academic. Probably in old age, at death's door, Erasmus' anguish at his sense of personal helplessness in Hebrew problems had subsided and died away.

Erasmus' sharpest anti-Hebrew statement comes in the letter to Wolfgang Fabricius Capito of 13 March 1518, quoted in Chapters 3 and 5, where the psychological reality, the psychological mechanism of the "eruption," are examined in some detail. It should be added though that immediately after the first, anti-Pfefferkorn, eruption Erasmus was once again praising the study of Hebrew. On 30 November 1517, he wrote Count von Neuenahr: "I hear you are giving public lectures in your part of the world in Greek and Hebrew. Happy indeed are those studies, if such men have started to take them in hand."[45] These words come only fifteen days after the last of the anti-Pfefferkorn series.

Chapter 5 has already noted Erasmus' reproof to Capito for excessive interest in Hebrew studies sounds the same notes as John Colet's letter to Erasmus. Those same thoughts and feelings also play a certain role in the polemic with the reformationists, as already mentioned (a "certain role" because the main driving force for the polemic was the humanist's concern for the fate of the reviving classical studies).

In 1524 Erasmus wrote to Melanchthon: "Argentorati, nec ibi tantum, publice docuerunt nec ullas disciplinas, nec linguas esse discendas, praeter unam Hebraicam. Adversus hos acerrime scripsit Lutherus."[46] He makes almost the same accusation of Luther himself in *Hyperaspistes I* (1526): "Hic [sc. Basileae] tui discipuli palam docebant, disciplinas humanas esse venenum pietatis, non esse discendas linguas, nisi Hebraicam et Graecam ex aliquantula parte, Latinam prorsus negligendam."[47] And in at least two places in *Hyperaspistes II* (1527) Erasmus seems to condemn Luther for "using Hebrew arguments."[48]

Erasmus' general attitude to Hebrew is also characterized by his attitude to the influence of Hebrew on the style of the New Testament, on the Latin and Greek texts of the Old Testament, and on the Latin and Greek that both the Eastern and Western Churches had used throughout their history. These attitudes are sound, objective, and strictly scientific, in the modern sense of the word.

Christ spoke with his disciples and to the people in a Hebrew different from that in which the Pentateuch was written and in which the prophets prophesized: "ipse Christus, ut multis colligi potest conjecturis, vulgatissimo maximeque populari sermone est usus, Syriace loquens, et fortasse aliquando Chaldaice, et haud scio an Graece nonnunquam."[49]

No matter what language the apostles used among themselves and with their countrymen, they wrote (or those who wrote in their names wrote) in Greek, as did the evangelists,[50] although they knew the language poorly and so often made mistakes, expressing their ideas in Hebrew style, just as today people of incomplete education mix into their Latin words and phrases taken from the common speech ("ex sermone vernaculo").[51] This is true even of the most educated of the apostles, Paul, who spoke Greek such that "ut nihilo secius interim Hebraeum agnoscas."[52] The New Testament Hebraisms are so justified, so "correct," that their small number makes Erasmus doubt the text is genuine or truly attributed. Thus in his final comment on the Epistle to the

Apostle Jacob Erasmus remarks: "Nec Hebraismi tantum, quantum a Jacobo, qui fuit episcopus Hierosolymitanus, exspectaretur."[53]

However, the poor Greek of the New Testament and the Epistles is not solely and simply the natural result of the apostles' "simplicity," of men who "learned Greek not from Demosthenes' speeches but from the speech of daily life."[54] The Gospels were addressed not to scholars but to cobblers and sailors, even to pimps and harlots, and hence were written in a style accessible to them, a "coarse," "mixed" style with an abundance of solecisms and barbarisms. "So too the Latin translator (he whom I consider the first) translated into the language which at that time was in general use among men, children, women, and people of the very lowest station, though it was also comprehensible to educated people, since everybody used it. If at that time Latin had been as corrupted as it is today among the French, Spanish, and Italians, probably the translator would have used that folk tongue, even though it is corrupted. Precisely in the same way the preachers of today speak [to their audiences in] French or Spanish or Italian, languages which are extremely corrupted in comparison to Latin. This means then there is nothing to be astonished at if the translator, in the opinion of elegant speakers, sprinkles the text with solecisms, since he desires more to be understood by the simple people than by the scholars, who vehemently opposed the Gospels."[55]

This is a remarkable observation, for it places the style of the New Testament into direct dependence upon its social address. The various constituent elements of this style (including, in first order, the Hebrew element) which seemed to strict defenders of linguistic purity to be senseless and destructive here acquire a stylistic function of primary significance; it is precisely these elements that give the gospel message its dynamism, penetrating force, and energy, the elements that brought "the good news" to everyone, excepting neither wise men nor simple. Equally, therefore, the person who translates Scripture into any language is committing an irremediable error if he fails to follow the example of the first Latin translator in attempting to preserve these stylistic peculiarities. (This practical conclusion was important not only then, when the Reformation had posed a pressing need to translate the

Bible into the national languages, but it is also important today. Translations age and die much faster than original works, and the majority of "national Bibles" are hopelessly antiquated, acquiring a thick patina of archaism which gives the text a ceremonial sound, elevated to the bombastic, which gravely distorts the stylistic intent of the "fishers of men".)

This defense of the New Testament Hebraisms is fully understandable, coming a year after *Ciceronianus* (1528), in which Erasmus attacked the "Ciceronian apes" who were heading for a "new paganism" beneath a banner of linguistic purity. Each profession and art (*ars*), each epoch, has its style and vocabulary, so what is surprising in "our expressing the mysteries of our religion in its own words? Some Hebrew expressions and many Greek ones were brought in along with the heart of things, since the Christian philosophy came to us first from Palestine, Asia Minor, and Greece."[56] So too there is no cause to be upset and sniff haughtily if a Christian from time to time decorates his speech with expressions drawn from Solomon, not Socrates, from David the psalmist, not from Pindar or Horace, even if such decorations are not of the coinage or assay to which the ears of the Ciceronians are accustomed.[57]

Long before *Ciceronianus* Erasmus also had pointed out the elements of Hebrew origin in "living Latin," the universal language of Church and science as well as in the language of Scripture, either pointing out their necessity or fittingness, or at least not rejecting them in any way. Thus in *Adagia* (1508) he says that the Greeks had gotten expressions of the type "extreme extremorum" from the Jews.[58] In the commentaries to the New Testament he says, "Divus Hieronymous putat vocem [sc. eudokēsamen] (εὐδοκήσαμεν) esse novam a Septuaginta confictam ad explicandam proprietatem Hebraei sermonis."[59] That the linguistic peculiarities of the Old Testament should be reflected in the translations is here proposed as self-evident. The second (or third) edition of the commentaries states the idea unequivocally (commenting on John 16:23, *In nomine meo*): "Hebraeis in nomine alicujus fieri dicitur, quod auctoritate ac virtute cujuspiam fit. Id non video quomodo Latine possit exprimi. Siquidem in nomine meo non est elegantiae Romanae. Sub nomine meo non prorsus idem exprimit. Nomine meo certe ambiguum. Proinde fortassis praestiterit hunc sermonem inter eos numerare, quos oporteat peculiari sacrarum scripturarum linguae condonare."[60] Even the term "peculiar language of the holy Scripture" appears, and this peculiar language acquires particular rights, connected to the Hebrew original of Scripture.[61] In the *Apologia* preceding his edition of the New Testament Erasmus speaks of the influence of simple Greek and Latin speech on the formation of the Gospel tradition. Why does Hebrew pronunciation of the name Jesus differ so sharply from the Greek, which we find in the New Testament texts? Erasmus answers that he supposes "sic Graecos et Latinos sonuisse nomen illud et Apostolos usurpasse receptam vocem, non sollicitos de elementis et apicibus"[62] (that is, about the original Hebrew form; the assumption that mutual influence is possible in a mixed linguistic setting is very likely, despite being purely speculative).

However, in granting particular rights to the "Hebrew element," Erasmus sees it precisely as a stylistic device, to be used consciously and, most important, *in measure*. If the peculiarities of the Hebrew original were not refined in the majority of cases, as Jerome had done in translating and editing the old translations, "quid esset eo sermone prodigiosius?"[63] Erasmus particularly sharply rejected calques of Hebrew grammatical phrasing.[64] He saw Jerome's superiority over the Septuagint in the fact that Jerome "sustulit Hebraismum et sermonis peregrinitatem, quam habent Septuaginta et hos secuta prisca illa translatio"[65] (the subject is Jerome's editorial work on the so-called old Latin versions).

Concrete analysis of Erasmus' Hebrew knowledge, its depth, breadth, usability and sources, is beyond the scope of this study, save for some general conclusions and points.

The Hebrew material is most abundant in the New Testament commentaries (meaning only linguistic material, philological material in the narrow sense). Among the other works (of which none can compare in this regard with the New Testament) are the scholia to Jerome, the New Testament paraphrases, and the interpretations of the Psalms. There are insignificant Hebrew commentaries in various apologiae, in *Ecclesiastes, Vidua Christiana, Enchiridion,* and some few others.

All this material might be divided into three large groups: interpretations of individual words (lexical material), explanations of properties of the Hebrew language (grammatical material), and comparisons against the Hebrew original. The largest group is the first, while the other two are about equal.

The greater part of the first group consists of the translation of significant names, a tradition going back to the Bible itself, which was energetically supported by the literatures of the Church Fathers and the Middle Ages. (The ancient interpretations often had the most blatant errors imaginable and the most fantastic etymologies; in repeating these interpretations Erasmus naturally also repeated the mistakes.) Of course Hebrew words taken into Christian culture are also explained, such as "satan," "Nazarene," "messiah," "hosanna," "amen," and so on; also explained are the words left untranslated in the Greek and Latin texts of Scripture which Christianity did not assimilate, such as "Raca" (Matthew 5:22) or "Selah" (the concluding exclamation in many psalms).

Some words are, as it were, translated from Greek to Hebrew, in order to explain, clarify, or amplify the meaning of the Greek text. How can Christ have the "brothers" of which the New Testament speaks? Because "Mater Jesu cum aliquot illius cognatis, quos Hebraei fratres appellant."[66] How can the word *testamentum* (legacy) also mean the union of God with man? Erasmus understood; commenting on the text "Testamentum confirmatum a Deo" (Galatians 3:17), he wrote, "Admonet hoc loco divus Hieronymus, si quis diligenter expendat Hebraea volumina, quoties Septuaginta verterunt *diathēkēn* (διαθήκην), id est *testamentum*, Hebraeis esse *BRITH* (בְּרִת) quod *pactum* sonat potius quam *testamentum*."[67]

Finally, Erasmus on occasion comments on the spelling (transliteration) of Biblical texts and interpretations (or translations), including Luke 3:28 (*Salathiel*): "Rectius, ni fallor, dicendus *SHALTHAL* (שְׁאַלְתִּאֵל) *Shealthiel*, si modo vocem Hebraicam reddere volumus."[68] Or on Mark 14:36 (*Abba Pater*): "Euangelista vocem Syriacam posuit eamque velut interpretatur."[69]

In explaining the grammatical properties of Hebrew Erasmus shows the sources of that specific style of Church Latin (and Greek) mentioned above, and names the reasons for which the ancient authors (and translators) fractured the linguistic and stylistic norms. Writing of Matthew 6:21 (*Domine, Domine*): "expressit sermonis Hebraici proprietatem: quae quod exaggerat, congeminatione auget."[70] Of 1 John 5:6 (*Quoniam Christus est veritas*): "*Veritas est,* Hebraice dixit, pro *verax est.*"[71]

The reasons for addressing the Hebrew original can vary. One reason is to comment on an Old Testament quotation or allusion in a New Testament text; the types of such commentary are wholly various, but first among them is explanation of the accuracy of translation, since the Latin text upon which Erasmus was commenting was already a translation twice removed (Hebrew to Greek to Latin), in which process losses may also be doubled. Further, the translation in the New Testament text (in Greek) very often differs from the Septuagint. How Erasmus reconciled two, three, and even four contradictory texts, each of them holy and untouchable, is a question more of exegesis than philology.

A second reason was to introduce an Old Testament parallel for a New Testament text. This though is quite rare; as a rule the original is not used for parallels.

A third reason is to argue a commentary on a lexical or grammatical basis, such as: "Similiter et Angeli dicuntur Dii ut in Psalmo [8:6]: *Minuisti eum paululum ab Angelis:* Hebraice est *Eloim.*"

A fourth reason was to go beyond the translation because of the Old Testament text itself, in search of its real meaning. This occurs most often in the interpretations of the psalms, but it also occurs in the scholia to Jerome as well as in the various Apologiae and certain other works (such as *Ecclesiastes, De Magnitudine Misericordiarum Domini Concio,* and *De Libres Arbitrio*).

It is important to recall that in most cases "veritas Hebraica" for Erasmus meant Jerome's translation: "juxta veritatem Hebraicam, juxta quam ita legis interprete Hieronymo . . . I . . . Hebraea sic habent interprete Hieronymo . . . Hieronymus juxta veritatem ita vertir . . ." These and similar formulas accompany nearly every rationalization connected to problems of Hebrew philology, not disappearing even when the Old Testament word or phrase is in fact given in Hebrew.

It is scarcely necessary to point out that the boundaries between these groups and subgroups are flexible and conditional. Certain remarks of a different order stand outside these groups, in which Erasmus speaks of the similarities and differences of

Hebrew, Syrian, Chaldean, and Phoenician, of details of Hebrew phonetics, both ancient and modern, of Hebrew dialects, of the Latinization of the endings of Hebrew proper names, and so forth, comments which might be termed general philology.

Here are some examples of commentary, both successful and unsuccessful:

Of John 18:1 (Trans torrentem Cedron): "*tōn Kedrōn* (τῶν Κέδρων) Articulus additus indicat *Cedron* non esse nomen Hebraicum sed *Cedrorum* . . . Divus Hieronymus meminit hujus nominis in *Locis Hebraicis*, indicans torrentem ac vallem esse ejus nominis ad orientalem plagam urbis Hierosolymitanae. Atque haud scio an a situ loci vocabulum loco sit inditum, quum idem inibi testetur KDM (קָדָם), quod est apud Ezechielem, ab Aquila et Symmacho versum fuisse *Orientem*. Etiamsi Capnion noster putat ab obscuritate dictum Hebraeis, et vocem *Cedron* Hebraicam esse, non Graecam, quum Hebraei cedros AKHNIM (אֲכָנִם) appellant. Fit autem hujus torrentis mentio libro Regum secundo capite decimo quinto . . . libro Regum tertio capite decimo quinto . . . libro Regum quarto capite vigesimo tertio . . . Atque ex primo loco non satis liquet, quid senserit interpres de *Cedron*. Sic enim legimus *kai ho basileus diebē ton kheimarroun Kedrōn*. (καὶ ὁ βασιλεὺς διέβη τόν χειμάρρουν Κέδρων) In secundo loco videmus additum articulum . . . Rursus tertio loco bis ponitur *Kedrōn* (Κέδρων) absque articulo . . . Nec secus legitur libri Regum tertii capite secundo . . . Neque tamen negarim haec omnia committi potuisse culpa Librariorum Graece scientium, Hebraice nescientium. Proinde non invitus subscribo sententiae Capnionis."[73]

This commentary seems almost a model, not in subject of course but in method, in principle, since Erasmus remains within the bounds of his own abilities and does not "make himself a crow in peacock's feathers," as he was often criticized (and not unjustly) for doing.

The comments on Luke 2:15 (Verbum hoc quod factum est) are extraordinarily important methodologically: "Nihil obsto quo minus hic filosophetur, qui volet, de *verbo facto*, modo sciat juxta proprietatem Hebraei sermonis *verbum* dici rem novam quae rumore divulgetur: et ita esse deprehendet, quisquis observare voluerit."[74] In placing science in service to theology[75] Erasmus demanded that the philological foundation of theological constructs be sound and solid, or they would collapse at the first blow, as some of Augustine's allegories collapsed, based as they were on incorrectly understood first meanings in Scripture.[76] Using his "antiphilology" (already mentioned) Erasmus discredited and rejected his own method; "antiphilology" begins by ignoring the original just when it ought to be be crucial and ends by stating something that, to put it mildly, is just as illogical as Augustine's doubtful allegories. Unfortunately for Erasmus, more than enough examples of this exist; here are but two:

Of Psalm 33:11: "Pro eo quod nos [sc. in Psalterio Romano] legimus *divites,* Hieronymus reddidit *leones,* alius *catuli leonum.* Haec vocum varietas nihil officit sensui, sed explicat magis. Non enim . . . sentit [sc. Propheta] de quibuslibet opulentibus, sed divitibus in hoc saeculo, qui tument ac ferociunt."[77]

Such manipulations, which avoid the most obvious solution of reference to the original, scandalized even Erasmus' contemporaries, as can be seen in his polemic with Augustine Steuchus (Guido Steuch). In 1523, paraphrasing the Gospel According to Luke, and again in 1525, in *Lingua,* analyzing a verse from Genesis (37:2), Erasmus preferred the Septuagint reading to that of Jerome. In the Septuagint Joseph's brothers informed Israel against Joseph, while in the Vulgate it was the other way about. Erasmus' main argument was that the former reading seemed closer to Christ, the "perfected Joseph" (Joseph as *typus Christi* is a common idea from early Christianity on). In addition he referred to the context and authorities[78] without mentioning the original at all. In 1529 Steuchus published *Recognitio Veteris Testamenti . . .*[79] which showed the Septuagint translation was mistaken and which accused Erasmus of credulity and thoughtlessness. In defending himself Erasmus repeated his earlier arguments: "Certe hoc loco quod verterunt interpretes Septuaginta rectius quadrat at typum Christi."[80] Steuchus replied with fatal accuracy that not only the Vulgate was against the Septuagint but so too were the original, all the Greek commentators, and Jerome, which Erasmus, Steuchus said, either did not know or pretended not to know; as for the original, it is absolutely certain Erasmus did not know it: "Sensus autem typicus a litera pendeat necesse est: typus autem esse non potest, ubi perperam litera legitur. Nemo praeferret, opinor, LXX Hebraicae veritati. Ego si quando praefero LXX Hieronymo, ex Hebraico facio, non contra ipsum fontem."81

In this exchange of letters (or more precisely, in this argument over the verse from Genesis, since on the whole Steuchus was also no example of scholarly honesty), Erasmus' opponent appears in the role of defender of humanistic, Erasmian philology, while Erasmus himself appears as its direct opponent, accusing Steuchus of lack of respect for the Church Fathers and for the Septuagint, which the Fathers had considered to be divinely inspired: "qui crediderunt Septuaginta divini Spiritus afflatu nobis eam prodidisse versionem."82 In addition, he said that there was no need to choose between the Septuagint and Jerome, since Jerome could follow one reading of the original and the Septuagint could translate another: "One was changed by the ignorant, while the other was added by someone's diligent hand, a third differs in words but agrees in essence, while a fourth *may differ, but has a pious meaning*" (italics mine—S.M.).83

Erasmus' antiphilological tendency, which emerges in evaluating the role of the Septuagint (alongside the Hebrew original or in spite of it), appears in Erasmus' earliest works (as has already been said), but grows stronger with time. In his scholia to Jerome and the New Testament commentaries Erasmus was generally inclined skeptically to the Septuagint translation; Origen did not trust the Septuagint and referred to the Hebrew original (which Erasmus noted sympathetically).84 For no known reason the Seventy had added three words to the original and thrown out one. St. Jerome points out an obvious error in the Septuagint. Also Erasmus notes ironically that the Ethiopian eunuch of Acts 8:32–33 read his scripture not in the Hebrew books but in the Septuagint translation.85 However, as early as 1516 the commentaries show attempts to reconcile the contradictions between the Septuagint and other translations by forcing the Hebrew original,86 while in 1517, in the very first polemic caused by criticism of the New Testament commentary, Erasmus comes out in defense of the Septuagint. In fact, though he was defending not the Seventy but himself, Lefevre d'Etaples chided him for repeating the Septuagint error in the translation of Psalm 8:6 (cited in Hebrews 2:7); to defend his own reputation Erasmus claimed that "the translation of the Seventy always enjoyed the greatest authority among all," that no Christian may reject the Septuagint with mockery, and that the Holy Ghost itself could correct the original text through the medium of the seventy sages.[87] However, in 1520 he just as decisively said the opposite, criticizing Augustine, who considered the Septuagint holy and unchangeable solely because it was accepted by the Church, and praising Jerome, who avoided general opinion and judged things on their merits, with reference to the Hebrew and Chaldean originals.[88] Here he rejected the legend of the miracle supposed to have accompanied the work of the Seventy (who were said to have worked scattered about and alone, but to have translated the Old Testament absolutely identically, each the same, word for word). Augustine believed the legend, which for him, just as for many theologians after him, was one of the major proofs of the divine inspiration of the Septuagint. Jerome though ridiculed the legend, considering it an invention, a fable.[89] In 1525, while defending his translation of the New Testament, Erasmus referred to the fact that the Church accepted both the Septuagint and Jerome's translation despite the many differences between them, for "what danger threatens the Church if it keeps both translations in its treasuries? . . . As long as it sees that variant readings do not lead to serious disagreements [nihil oriri dispendii] it can ignore them."[90] Two years later he approved of a new Latin translation of the Old Testament done from the Greek, comparing this work with his own translation of the New Testament, precisely as though he had forgotten that the Old Testament too had an original, in Hebrew, not in Greek.[91] In 1531, as has been seen, Erasmus defended his right to a pious mistake. A year later, in a concluding passage in the interpretation of Psalm 38, after saying that holy and learned men had beaten their heads over the meaning of the Psalter and so had turned to the original, he announced that "I have no mind to reproach these pious men, but I preferred to follow that which seems simpler and more in agreement with the mood and order of the entire psalm (ad totius Psalmi tenorem ac seriem accomodatius)."[92] This is an open confession of helplessness before the Hebrew original, strengthened by a sanctimonius *malui*, a variation on the eternal situation of the fox and the grapes.

The formula "ad totius Psalmi tenorem ac seriem accomodatius" is fairly ill-defined (even though able to serve as the basis for such confusions as that over Joseph, who is transformed from an informant into a victim of informing), while what Erasmus says in *Ecclesiastes* is less ambiguous. Moving from the difficulties caused by the polysemanticism (*ambiguitas*) of the Hebrew lexicon and by the lack of clarity of Old Testament onomastics, Erasmus passed to the Hebrew system of writing without vowels, which permits variant readings of a single text and hence permits various interpretations. In such a situation, Erasmus states, "first of all, every idea which contradicts the unshakeable dogmas of faith must be rejected."[93]

In his later years, Erasmus understood that, if clear bounds were not put to this antiphilological piety, it could easily jump from the sphere of Hebrew philology to Greek and Latin studies. Interpreting Psalm 83 (1533), Erasmus remarked on the sharply differing readings of verse 12 to be found in Jerome and the Septuagint: "What Jerome and some others translated from the Hebrew here so strongly differs from the translation of the Seventy that clearly there can be no talk of the usual variants which arise when the same thought is conveyed by different means or because different translators get different meanings out of the exact same words, but apparently the Hebrew scripture [itself] varied from copy to copy . . . Nam quod ex Hebraeo reddunt, sic habet: Quia sol et scutum Dominus Deus, gratiam et gloriam habet Dominus."[94] Thus the scholar who is both theologian and philologist must establish which of the two supposed variants of the Hebrew original should be accepted as the first and true text and which to ascribe to the later error of a copyist. Although Erasmus himself did not draw that conclusion, it is inescapable (for no other one is possible) and corresponds to the actual practices of Erasmus as textologist. Finally, in the foreword to the fourth and fifth editions of the New Testament, Erasmus speaks of Jerome's proper skepticism for the Septuagint[95] and objects sharply to those "qui post receptam Hieronymi translationem negant quicquam esse tribuendum vel Hebraeis, vel Graecis voluminibus."[96]

The question of the sources of the Hebrew commentaries and remarks is the more interesting as it leads to an *objective* evaluation of Erasmus' own knowledge of Hebrew. "Sources" means, first, the books Erasmus used or could use more or less on his own (though the degree of independence in usage must be defined in each case), and, second, the consultants who helped him with advice. It is essential too to know whether Erasmus accepted the advice blindly and uncritically or tried to check the information and, if so, how much he was able to do so.

It is understandable that of the Church Fathers Erasmus refers most often to Jerome, the exegetical works and epistles. The greatest number of such references is to the guide *Liber de nominibus Hebraicis* (Erasmus was virtually certain that the work was mistakenly attributed to Jerome), then to a similar reference work, *Liber de situ et nominibus locorum Hebraicorum,* then the commentaries on various Old and New Testament books, and others. It is equally unsurprising that Erasmus refers to the authority of St. John Chrysostum, Ambrose, and Origen; what is surprising though are the very common appeals to Augustine, whom Erasmus several times (as has been shown) called a total ignoramus in knowledge of Hebrew.[97]

Of all the medieval authors, Erasmus showed a particular preference for Bede and Theophylactus of Ochrida; this latter was one of the four most important Erasmian authorities, along with Jerome, Origen, and John Chrysostum.[98] Of his contemporaries or scholars of the recent past, Erasmus mentions Lira, Valla, Reuchlin, Elio Antonio de Nehrija, and Lefevre d'Etaples.

Listing and explaining the entire collection of Erasmus' written sources should be the subject of another work and one wholly different than this one, but one detail is of too great a significance to this book and so cannot suffer delay, that of Erasmus' attitude to the Jewish scholarly tradition, to the rabbinical and still earlier sources.

First of all, the value of the Hebrew original of Scripture (in the form in which the Jew of Erasmus' day preserved it) cannot be doubted, although the possibility of "Jewish falsification" is recognized as real. Had the Jews deformed their own books after the coming of Christ, then Jerome would have been mad to correct the Latin text of the Old Testament against the Hebrew original, and the Church would never have sanctioned such correlations with its authority. Although Jerome did complain of some Jewish falsification, this still did not hold him back from searching the ancient and reliable copies for help in establishing the true sense, which the Septuagint translation had corrupted.[99] In one of the Apologias of 1525, Erasmus gives several remarkable examples of how poorly understood or corrupted passages in the Latin text of Scriptures can be clarified or corrected only with the help of the Hebrew original, since the Greek intermediate text is insufficient.[100] That Apologia though also says of Genesis 27:2: "Fieri potuit ut Hebraeus aliquis corrupit eum locum, qui putavit non convenire in sanctissimum et innocentissimum puerum crimen pessimum, haudquaquam intelligens ejus loci mysterium."[101]

Further, the ancient authorities on whom Jerome had relied were seen as useful and of good quality.[102] Erasmus defended Philon of Alexandria particularly warmly; "That Philon was a Jew cannot be denied, but this is a quality he shared with Peter the Apostle . . . If the books of such Jews could not be trusted at all, then why, pray tell, did Jerome quote so many Jewish attestations? Where did he get information about the customs of the Jews if not from their commentaries? . . . It is impossible to believe the Jews in the same way that we believe the canonical writings, but it does not follow that we should refuse to listen to them if they impart something believable; after all, much in the books of the Old Testament we are unable to understand because of our ignorance of the antiquities of this people. From whom ought such information to be sought if not from Jews?"[103] Another: "It cannot be refuted that [Philon] was a man of uncommon learning and knew everything having to do with Jews as no other man did. Also, we are speaking here not of the faith of the gospels—where it would not be wholly safe to trust Philon—but of Old Testament narrative."[104] This latter is a precise definition of the boundaries within which the Jewish authorities may and must be trusted and so is of particular importance.

Erasmus himself refers to Hebrew tradition, generally anonymously, since such information is gleaned from other commentators, the Church Fathers, and Doctors (first and foremost from Jerome), and from medieval and contemporary scholars. In such cases Erasmus writes, "Judaei referunt" or "juxta Hebraeorum interpretationem" or "quaestio videtur ex Hebraeorum commentis nata," and so on.[105]

As for Erasmus' attitude to the rabbinical philological tradition, Erasmus clearly was ambiguous. He did not trust the medieval Jewish commentators (it doesn't bear pointing out that all his knowledge in this sphere was secondhand). Citing Rashi's interpretation of one of the verses of Psalm 2 Erasmus adds: "Ego ut non in totum damno . . . quid adferant Hebraeorum Interpretes, praesertim antiqui, ita non arbitror, illis esse multum tribuendum, quum animadvertam horum commentarios fere fumis ac fabulis anilibus refertas, ne quid interim dicam de studio falsandi nostra odioque Christi"[106] (Erasmus is speaking here of theological exegesis, but that is closely interwoven with real and purely linguistic commentaries.) This reaction is far from an exception,[107] but if this and other statements like it were to be juxtaposed to what Luther said of rabbinical literature,[108] Erasmus would appear an ardent admirer of such literature. Not that the device of comparison is overly convincing; better to look at Erasmus' own remarks, which reveal the ambiguity mentioned above. In the Explanation of Psalm 85 (1528), he says, " . . . hujus Psalmi argumentum esse Saulis persecutionem . . . Haec ut recte conjectent Hebraeorum Rabbini nihil officiunt interpretationi nostrae [sc. sensui mystico] . . . Non itaque certabimus cum Hebraeorum divinationibus, sed Ecclesiasticorum Doctorum auctoritatem secuti adferemus pro incertis certa . . ."[109] This sounds not only neutral, but even conciliatory.

In *Hyperaspites I* (1526), Erasmus energetically refutes Luther's thesis that nothing is necessary for the understanding of Scripture save grammar and common sense,[110] and in passing refers with obvious approval to Oecolampadius, who in the foreword to his commentary on Isaiah "adeo non profitetur se nihil non explicuisse, ut fateatur se frustra conaturum fuisse, ni commentariis Hebraeorum fuisset adjutus."[111] Already this is not a hypothetical comparison but a direct polemic with Luther over the question of the Hebrew authorities. The Christian theologian and moralist categorically refuses all compromise whatever with Judaism, but the knowledge-hungry humanist-philologist cannot agree, *a priori*, to do without even those books he is not in a condition to read: "Et Averroes blasphemus utiliter legi potest, et Homerus pie legebatur ab iis, qui scribebant adversus paganos, et hodie Judaeroum impii libri possunt pie legi."[112]

If among the printed sources there are books Erasmus *could* have used but of which use there is no direct proof, the analogous possibility is far richer in the case of oral sources. Erasmus met and corresponded with a countless number of citizens of the invisible *rei publicae litterarum,* and there were many Hebraicists among his acquaintances and friends, both professionals, who were teaching the language of the Bible, and amateurs, who sometimes surpassed the majority of the professionals. So, for example, Nicolas Winman, who taught Greek and Hebrew in Ingolstadt; he visited Erasmus in Basel somewhere between 1526 and 1529.[113] Did they discuss "Hebrew topics"? Not only do there seem to be no direct or even indirect bases, however faint, for such a possibility, but even the date of their meeting is not established. Still, no matter how small the likelihood of Hebrew consultations in this encounter, the possibility still cannot be entirely ruled out. There are also no direct bases for the idea that Erasmus consulted with Wolfgang Fabricius Capito, but there are indirect ones of some substance. Erasmus several times referred to Capito as a very great scholar of Hebrew and even put Capito much higher than Reuchlin.[114] They met often while Erasmus was working on the New Testament, and Capito energetically supported the efforts of Erasmus and his publisher, Froben.[115] It is thus possible to suppose, with all due caution, that Oecolampadius, Erasmus' "Theseus," was the primary but not the sole Hebrew consultant on the New Testament commentaries (1516).

Still, no matter how attractive a prospect it is for a scholar to find and precisely define the "Jewish influence" on Erasmus, such as the influence of convert Paulus Ricius, a doctor and a humanist (and hence fully possible), or that of Gerhard Lister (extremely unlikely), or to establish the identities of the two Hebrew informants to whom Erasmus refers in passing in his New Testament commentaries (after the first edition),[116] one ought not lose sight of the primary figures, those men whom Erasmus openly calls his helpers, first among whom are Oecolampadius and Matthias Adrian. Although the history of the collaboration on the first two editions of the New Testament commentaries is not exhaustively documented, the correspondence and many apologias, as well as a collation of all five editions (published in Erasmus' lifetime), still permit that history to be reasonably well detailed.[117] One extremely important fact bears remarking here, that of the change in

Erasmus' view of his own role in the Hebrew part of the commentary.

The formal recognition of Oecolampadius as Theseus sounds grand but somewhat diffuse: "Testimonia Veteris Instrumenti . . . vel ex interpretatione Septuaginta, vel ex ipsis Hebraeorum fontibus, si quando illorum editio cum Hebraica dissentit origine, contulimus et excussimus: quamquam id quidem *ouk aneu Thēseōs* (οὐκ ἄνευ Θησέως) ut Graecorum habet proverbium . . . Hac igitur in parte cum primum hoc Opus ederemus, nonnihil adiuti sumus opera subsidiaria viri non solum pietate, verum etiam trium peritia linguarum eminentis, hoc est veri Theologi, Ioannis Oecolampadii Vinimontani."[118] Erasmus speaks of Oecolampadius just as vaguely but without ceremony in a letter of 23 December 1515: "Adest qui in Hebraicis nonnihil succurrat."[119] However, in June of the following year, 1516, Erasmus clearly defines Oecolampadius' function as that of corrector and nothing more: "Ad haec [sc. codices castigandos] conducti fuerant duo probe docti, alter iureconsultus, alter theologus etiam Hebraice peritus, qui formis praeessent; at hi quoniam eius laboris erant rudes, quod susceperant praestare non poterant: proinde necesse fuit extremam formarum, quas vocant, recognitionem in me recipere."[120] Oecolampadius himself confirms this in his epistle "To The Pious Reader," a panegyric to Erasmus and his work which, after the custom of the day, was attached to the 1516 edition: "Erasmus suarum etiam laudum partem in alios reiicit. Quale et illud exemplum, cum subsidiarum solum in castigandis formulis operam accersitum a Frobenio . . . Thesea etiam suum vocare dignatus sit; plane tanto heroi mea alioqui ne tantillum quidem vel opus fuerit, vel profuerim, quamquam non minus taedii dispendiique libenter suscepimus facileque decoximus, ne quatenus possimus, tam pio deessemus operi"[121] (In fact, the opposite is more believable, that Erasmus took advantage of the modesty of his younger collaborator and his formulas, which he repeated in a letter to Budé.)

As soon as the Hebrew parts of the commentary came under the fire of critics, however, Erasmus hastened to hide himself behind Oecolampadius' back. A letter to Oecolampadius from 13 March 1518 leaves the wording wholly vague: "Hebraica quae te fretus asscripsi."[122] The apologias against Edward Lee of 1520 makes the wording clearer: "Jam quod discrepat [sc. Leus] de vocibus Hebraicis, quae sunt in prophetia, respondeat Joannes Oecolampadius, quo auctore hoc admiscui meis commentariis . . . Neque est quod clamitet, me mihi vindicare laudem alienam, quum ingenue testatus sim, hac in parte me Theseo usum, etiamsi in posteriore Editione pleraque amputavimus. Et quod in priore fuit admixtum, magis additum est in gratiam typographi, quam ex animi mei sententia. Nam hoc agebatur illic, ne quis facile posset aemulari, quod tum perpaucis essent Hebraicae formulae."[123] In defending his interpretation of two Hebrew (Aramaic) words in Mark 5:41, Erasmus concludes that "et tamen quod illic addidimus de Hebraea voce, addidimus ex consilio Joannis Oecolampadii, cui plus tribuendum in his litteris, quam Leis aliquot."[124]

The first apologia against Lee (of March 1520), which is not included in the Leiden edition, contains another general but very important wording: "Adfuit, immo praefuit, aeditioni priori Ioannes Oecolampadius . . . Rogatus est a me moneret, praesertim si quid ad fidei sinceritatem attineret."[125] The apologia against Lopez de Zuñiga explains this function of "supervisor": "In Hebraeis fere sequebamur auctoritatem Hieronymi. Et loco commonstrato Hebraea asscripsit Oecolampadius, tum voces admodum paucas admiscuit . . . Oecolampadius satis idoneus est ut sua tueatur adversus Stunicam; et tamen si quid forte lapsus fuisset, iniquum fuerat alienos lapsus mihi impingere."[126] Farther on in the same apologia, referring to two concrete objections by Zuñiga, Erasmus writes that "non dubito, quin scripserim admonitu Oecolampadii[127] . . . Sic me docuerat Liber interpres nominum Hebraicorum . . . Oecolampadius non dissentiebat."[128]

Erasmus thus moves from partial confession of authorship to denial of it as a whole and in many parts, to categorical refusal to "answer for the mistakes of others" and persistent attempts to bring Oecolampadius into the discussion.[129] Oecolampadius, however, remained deaf[130] to all challenges and invocations, and the argument about the mistakes of others[131] was not convincing.

It bears repeating that this process is remarkable not in and of itself, not for its psychological qualities, but rather as a sort of indicator to aid in getting closer to the true scope of Erasmus' knowledge of Hebrew, in order to evaluate it objectively. Another such indicator is the Hebrew texts in the New Testament commentaries and the paraphrases of the psalms. As has been shown, Erasmus frankly admitted that these texts had been included in the commentaries at the printer's request, since he wished to protect himself from the danger of pirated editions. In what way do the number of such texts decline from one Froben edition to the next? Is there a regularity to this decline? Hebrew texts occur only five times in the commentaries to the Psalms, all of them in the interpretation of Psalm 1,[132] the very earliest of Erasmus' paraphrases of the psalter (finished in April 1515, published in September of the same year). How might this be explained, since after all Erasmus used the services of a consultant (or consultants) later as well: "Whoever is too busy to study Hebrew, let him at least follow my example: in preparing to write about the psalms I consulted with scholars of Hebrew, while on matters which I cannot judge I say nothing at all."[133] (These words were written in the summer of 1525, after the apperance of the paraphrases of three more psalms.) All questions of this sort must be left for a special study of Erasmus as Hebraicist.

For the time being, another question might be answered, one already touched upon in the beginning of this chapter: how did Erasmus evaluate his own knowledge? In part this question is answered by the quotation immediately preceding, where Erasmus numbers himself among those who did not have the time to master Hebrew. At the same time it is quite obvious that he considered his own knowledge much more than nothing. Erasmus' first attempts to master Hebrew date back to 1504: "I also took up Hebrew, but the strangeness of the language frightened me; in addition, neither my age nor human reason can contain many things [at the same time] with equal success, so I let it drop."[134] This was to Colet, after informing him that he was wholly burdened with Greek studies. Eleven years later the situation had not changed much: "I dare make no judgment about Hebrew literature, for I scarcely set my lips to it."[135] The naming of Oecolampadius as Theseus in December of the same year (1515) ends, "For I myself had not yet made enough progress in Hebrew literature to take upon myself the authority to decide."[136] That "not yet" shows that Erasmus had not abandoned hopes for achieving mastery of Hebrew, while a letter from Colet to Erasmus on 20 June

1516 directly suggests that Erasmus was at that time again studying Hebrew[137] (a new attempt unquestionably provoked by the work on Jerome and the New Testament). This attempt, however, proved scarcely more successful. On March 27, 1517, Oecolampadius wrote to Erasmus, "Vale, optime Erasme, *ATRTH ROSHI* (אֲטֶרֶת רֹשִׁי) hoc est corona capitis mei,"[138] meaning that Erasmus was unable to understand two Hebrew words, even when the vowels were marked. (This is the more noticeable since in his correspondence with the humanists Oecolampadius generally left Hebrew quotations and expressions untranslated.) Erasmus did not conceal this melancholy blight on his erudition, but he still placed himself no lower than Lefevre d'Etaples: "Ingenue fateor me in hisce litteris judicem esse non posse, neque te puto eo progressum, ut postules nos hac in re auctoritati tuae cedere . . . ."[139] This self-evaluation by comparison supplies one benchmark (though not especially reliable), while the refusal to judge (just as eighteen months before, in the foreword to the New Testament commentaries!) in this context means that in complex instances Erasmus will not try, but in relatively simple ones he will, relying on trustworthy authorities, to judge without fear or embarrassment.

Erasmus' own judgments or, in any event, part of them, can be filtered out with precision, since they are indicated either by the general context, as in the apologia addressed to Lefevre, or by the "microcontext," as in this example: "Non sic loquuntur Latini, fateor: sed probabile est, sic fuisse loquutos Hebraeos, quorum idiomata frequenter exprimit Apostolus[140] . . . Haud scio, an juxta proprietatem sermonis Hebraei dicatur alicui esse, quod ad illum pertinet et illius bono destinatum est."[141]

It might be assumed too that here also should be included all the commentaries and observations which do not indicate their source.

The degree of complexity or simplicity of such judgments varies within fairly wide boundaries. A preliminary guess would be that the apologia defending against Lefevre's criticism could scarcely have been written without help, for it is too skilled, showing for example that the word *MET* (מְעָט) (meaning few in number) often denotes time, with a number of citations from the psalter, each time with a transliteration of the Hebrew original.

Erasmus concludes: "Nec dubito quin triginta loca possint colligi, si cui vestigandi non desit otium, quando haec e Psalmis duntaxat occurrerunt; nam is liber Hebraice excusus mihi tum aderat."[142] This is absolutely irreconciliable with the Oecolampadius letter mentioned above, with two Hebrew words followed by their translation, especially since Erasmus received that letter just before starting work on that apologia against Lefevre. The assured tone of that polemic with Lefevre differs strikingly from the modesty, almost caution, which is sensible in the works from the last fifteen years of Erasmus' life, especially in the paraphrases of the psalter: "In Hebraeis vocibus, ajunt, esse minimum discriminis, ut appareat";[143] "Annotavit enim hoc Hieronymus aliique litterarum Hebraicarum periti";[144] "Qui tractant Hebraicae linguae proprietatem, indicant";[145] "qui callent Hebraice, vertunt."[146] Or to move beyond these paraphrases, "qui periti sunt sermonis Hebraici, demonstrant";[147] "qui tenent litteras Hebraicas, docent nos in Genesi."[148]

Another comparison is also useful, that of the self-evaluation in the apologia against Lefevre, on the one hand, and the replies to Lee and Zuñiga, on the other.

Lee directly accuses Erasmus of "Hebraice nescis,"[149] with which Erasmus *doesn't even attempt to argue,* instead arguing on the primitive grounds that "you're a fool too," to show that Lee knows nothing of Hebrew himself.[150] In addition, Erasmus often refuses Lee's Hebrew arguments at the door, without a glance, on the grounds that, supposedly, they are without significance, that everything is clear without them.[151]

In the argument with Zuñiga Erasmus cannot conceal his helplessness and timidity: "Ait me *Solomonem* vertisse, quum Hebraeis recte dicatur etiam *Salomon,* quod ego non ignorabam, nec inficiatus sum usquam. Atqui si paiculum est quod *Solomon* verterim, quemadmodum constanter pronuntiant Graeci, quur non reprehenditur Latinus interpres, quod *Jesu* nomen vertit juxta Graecorum, non juxta Hebraeorum pronuntiationem . . . ? Sed mox civilor est Stunica, ac mihi propemodum ignoscit, quod in Annotationibus *Bersabee* scriptum est, non *Bethsabee,* et Oecolampadium, Theseum meum, in ius vocandum arbitratur. Atque ex hoc tanto argumento deprehendit homo nasutus neque me neque Oecolampadium scire linguam Hebraicam. Si quid frontis haberet Stunica, typographis hoc imputasset . . . Certe videt hoc esse correctum proxima aeditione, etiam sine Theseo, ne me putet usque adeo alienum a litteris Hebraicis, ut hoc scire non queam."[152]

This is followed by praise for Oecolampadius' erudition and piety and with a threat to Zuñiga (watch out that Oecolampadius doesn't make it hot for you), but there is not a single word in defense of his own knowledge.

These preliminary observations suggest clearly enough how useful and suggestive a detailed study of Erasmus as Hebraicist might prove.

Conclusion

Thus it seems incontrovertible, and obvious, that it is just as unfounded to speak of Erasmus' hatred for Jews as it is to speak of his sympathy for them. While struggling tirelessly against "Judaism," which for him was the antithesis of the "philosophy of Christ," endlessly employing the idea and image of the Jew in abstract moralistic lessons and atemporal, ahistoric allegories, Erasmus was indifferent to the living "remnant of Israel," to its troubles, its culture, and its spiritual property. Erasmus simply had no interest in Jews—let them swarm in their dens; we Christians have no business with them, and their future is in the hands of Providence, as Apostle Paul predicted.

The living, flesh-and-blood Jew is simply not within Erasmus' field of vision. The several arguments *ad silentium* that have been offered here would seem especially convincing, showing as they do the deep psychological foundation of Erasmus' reaction to Jewish problems. The same types of arguments can be found in *De Copia*, in *Adagiae*, in *Colloquia*, in *Ecclesiastes*. While cataloguing examples or listing the qualities and manners of various peoples, Erasmus almost never refers to contemporary Jewry, and at times even forgets about the Jews of antiquity (as in, for example, LB II, 859E–860A: *Lex et regio*). It has been shown that Erasmus had no reaction to the news in 1521 that the religious schism among the Czechs was being complicated by the presence of Jews; he also had no reaction to news of the circumcised Moravian Sabbatarians (LB V, 505D–506A, 1038B) or to the "Judaiz-ing" of the Anabaptists (see the letters of 1534–1535). This indifference contrasts vividly with Luther's passionate outcries. As for the small number (two, really) of judeophobic eruptions and the many anti-Semitic petty jibes, these are incidental, reflect-ing not Erasmus' worldview but rather common, "folk" anti-Semitism, a mass psychology alien to and despised by Erasmism.

If one were to use the terminology of newer times, Erasmus' attitude toward the Jews would have to be called *a-Semitism,* an indifferent alienation from all things Jewish. Vladimir (Ze'ev) Zhabotinsky, one of the great figures of modern Jewish history and one of those who helped lay the foundations of modern Isra-el, considered that a-Semitism could become a first step toward anti-Semitism,[1] but what could have been true of the Russian intelligentsia of the twentieth century is certainly not applicable to the sixteenth century. The sixteenth century was a time of cata-strophic schism in the Western Church, accompanied by an equal-ly catastrophic sharpening of religious and national fanaticism, a time when it was extremely important to learn to look calmly at those who were different, unlike oneself, without hatred or tears of regret for lost souls who were condemned to eternal flames. This was a necessary initial step toward true toleration; as he did in many other things, Erasmus took the first steps along this new path, the end of which we have not reached even today.

An Afterword by
Arthur A. Cohen

I

The Austrian Catholic intellectual historian, Friedrich Heer, writing in his remarkable study *God's First Love,* observed flatly that "Erasmus was in fact no more anti-Semitic than Goethe, who also made some sarcastic comments on the Jews."[1] Heer was prompted to this comment by his citation of a letter from Erasmus to Sir Thomas More, in which Erasmus stated that he had no intention of accepting the invitation extended to him by Cardinal Francisco Ximenez de Cisneros to come to Spain and assist him in the work of establishing a center for biblical studies that would ultimately result in a Polyglot Bible,[2] since he regarded Spain as "strange, sinister, and Jew-ridden." It was the last that impelled Heer to his parenthetic temporizing on Erasmus's behalf, since Erasmus's rhetorical dismissal of Spain as "Jew-ridden" signifies in Heer's view little more than sarcasm.

Arthur A. Cohen is the author of *The Natural and the Supernatural Jew: An Historical and Theological Introduction, The Myth of the Judeo-Christian Tradition, The Tremendum: A Theological Interpretation of the Holocaust.* He is completing with Paul Mendes-Flohr the editing of *Contemporary Jewish Religious Thought,* to be published in 1986.

virtually all of his contemporaries
Thomas More who never in all his
spondence directed his hostility
day),[3] was locked by a formulaic
and Judaism, for the Jews of the
ws contemporaneous to the events of the
ws of history and tradition including his own
...ntemporaries with whom he had no contact. Heer is
much too gentle with Erasmus. He is probably correct about
Goethe who is rude about Jews rather than vicious. Unlike
Goethe, however, whose irritation with Jews is more often social
annoyance and intellectual snobbism, Erasmus's attitude derives
from a long and unbroken tradition of anti-Judaism.

II

It is the considerable achievement of Shimon Markish, that remarkable son of a remarkable parentage, non-Yiddish-speaking
heir to the most eminent Yiddish poet of the Soviet Union, Per-
etz Markish, to undertake after nearly a generation during which
the passion of his Jewish loyalties lay dormant while he acquired
the immense scholarship that made him one of the foremost clas-
sicists of the Soviet Union, the first translator of works by Erasmus into Russian, author of numerous critical translations from
the literatures of ancient Greece and Rome, to turn to an estima-
tion of the writings of Erasmus on the Jews. Markish asserts that
at the time of the composition of this book he was possessed of
two great interests: Erasmus, and the Jews.[4] Moreover, he announces that his care for the Jews is the greater of the two,[5] this
despite the fact that he has given vastly more of his intellectual
gifts to the interpretation of Erasmus[6] than to his explication of
Judaism. He will not object surely if we utilize here his Erasmian
erudition to conclude from the evidence differently than he.
Whereas Markish undertakes more completely than any predeces-
sor to gather together and interpret the considerable variety of
remarks, asides, outbursts and expostulations, exegeses and interpretations, excursuses and scholarly exhumations whereby

An Afterword by Arthur A. Cohen

Erasmus employs the Jew as the marker and index of failure, he succeeds to our mind in demonstrating rath than he wishes. Markish believes that he has proved that E is no commonplace anti-Semitic vulgarian. He succeeds, ho er, in demonstrating that Erasmus is thoroughly anti-Jewish though he knew no believing Jews, against Jewish traditi although he knew hardly anything of Jews beyond the era of th Gospels, that he was anti-Jewish in all the familiar typological and exegetical modes that transcribe the Christian reading of pre-Christian Jewish sources, and that finally his anti-Judaism was frequently gratuitous, crude, malicious, intemperate, lacking in all that grace and charity with which he otherwise pursued his return to the sources of Christian civilization in the ancient world. Erasmus was a master of Latin and Latinity and a scholar of Greece and the Greek New Testament; however his knowledge of Hebrew—despite his avowal of its value—is scant and ambivalent.

In all things Jewish, Erasmus was of two minds: the Jews are bearers of the Holy Word, their tradition is sacred, their literature divine speech, and yet, by reason of their unbelief in Jesus Christ, they are a sinful nation, and, even if not cursed with deicide, they might as well have done the murder of a god for all the mercy, kindness, and goodwill their exculpation does them. Erasmus was never bloodthirsty, but when it comes to Jews he is as bloody-minded, obtuse, and unyielding as his age.

III

It may seem to Shimon Markish that Erasmus is no anti-Semite, no judeophobe, because the only styles of anti-Semitism that Markish authenticates are those that grow up out of the mob, the anti-Semitism of the streets that instigated the Crusader depredations of the Jewish communities of the Rhine and the massacres of countless Jewish communities of Eastern Europe by Russian and Soviet armies and marauders before and after the Revolution of 1917. But such a view is to make ideological vulgarization and brutality of means the sufficient signs of anti-Semitism, separating such extremity from the more intellectually locked and narrow-band hostility that derives wholly from theological sources. It may be the case that Markish can free Erasmus of the charge of anti-Semitism leveled against him by Guido Kisch in his *Erasmus' Stellung zu Juden und Judentum*[7]—apparently the occasion and point of departure for Markish's study[8]—but is his reasoning convincing? His book, *Erasmus and the Jews,* is eminently convincing. Erasmus maintains a consistency of animosity and bile against the Jews which is for the most part couched in elevated language, only on few occasions descending to the streets where blood could flow. But does the absence of explicit invitation to cruelty and violence which distinguishes Erasmus from Martin Luther's *Concerning the Jews and Their Lies*[9] where the burning of synagogues, the driving out and pauperization of the Jews, the prohibition of their teaching and destruction of Jewish books is advocated, mean that Erasmus is no anti-Semite? Surely Erasmus is no anti-Semite like Martin Luther, but is he really different than the benign Johannes Reuchlin who advocated the dissemination of Hebrew studies among Christians for the twofold purpose of sophisticating knowledge of the Hebrew sources of Christian faith and to facilitate the conversion of the Jews? Prior to modern times, did the Jews ever enjoy the right to exist among Christians for their own sake, because they were human beings, albeit human beings who had transmitted a sacred tradition that bore the Word of God up to the Gospels and beyond into history? The natural Jew—he of flesh and secular dimension, he with habits and affections of ordinary creatures—might be allowed to conclude his days in peace, but as supernatural Jew, that is, as one bonded to a different vision, a different revelation, an alternative estate of grace and salvation, he, surely, that supernatural Jew, remained as damned by sixteenth-century Erasmus as he had been damned in the first.[10] The sixteenth-century Jew was for the sixteenth-century Christian always and everywhere defective, incomplete, willfully ignorant, and therefore by consequence always blasphemer and sinner against Jesus Christ and His Church.[11]

Shimon Markish has made his case in *Erasmus and the Jews* and made it profoundly, discriminating the thought and works of Erasmus as they deal with the Jews from the documents of contempt and reprobation clearly marked out by Jules Isaac in his *Jesus and Israel, The Teaching of Contempt,* and *Génèse de l'anti-sémitisme,*[12] but has he made his point catch hold in the broader arena of argumentation, where the issue is not the evaluation of historical context alone but the assessment of the theological underpinning that describes the historical context during its formation?

The argument that I wish to set alongside Markish's inquiry is this: the fact that it was commonplace and unexceptionable for Christians of northern Europe to be anti-Semitic during the fifteenth and sixteenth centuries makes it difficult, if not impossible, to exclude anyone from the judgment of being anti-Semitic. To tergiversate and moderate the anti-Semitism of one humanist sage, Desiderius Erasmus of Rotterdam, is to protect him from a charge that was without uniqueness. If we were to contend that Erasmus favored cruel treatment of heretics as advocated by Thomas More, it would be important to protect him from our misreading; or if one felt him slandered by reference to his superficially homoerotic affections, it would be just to protect him. But why protect him from the charge of anti-Semitism if every thinker of the northern Renaissance were to a more or less significant degree anti-Semitic. It matters little whether such anti-Semites attacked the Jews wisely or ignorantly, whether they were informed about Jewish literature or wholly uninformed about it, whether they were curious about the habits and doctrines of Jews or content to retail rumor and unsubstantiated hearsay, whether they were aware of Jews as neighbors and acquaintances or wholly unfamiliar with living Jews and conscious of them only to the extent that they had converted to Christianity and wished to supplement native Christian anti-Semitism with contributions of their own. It has struck me throughout my close inspection of Markish's exhaustive and clear appraisal of Erasmus's language that what is at work in Erasmus is something that needs identification in even a broader context than a general search of Erasmian writings allows: namely, the formulaic language of anti-Judaism.

To speak of the carnality and materialism of Jewish law as does Erasmus has a long and unbroken tradition that runs from the Gospels through Augustine of Hippo to Erasmus and down to the present day where the use of such language in Leon Bloy and

Jacques Maritain brought me to personal confrontation with the latter during the early 1950s.[13] The "carnality" of the Jews, of Jewish practice and observance, is a convenient trope with which to belabor Jews, since carnality is so evidently contrastable with the spirituality that is the magnetic pull of Christian grace. And yet what is missed in all such polemical polarization is that no Jew imagines that there is a symmetric correlation between fulfilling the commandments and the granting of redemption. Nowhere is it believed—certainly not by any Jew who cares for the complexity and paradox of the believing life—that doing the commandments guarantees salvation. Hence to call the observances and rituals of the tradition of Jews "carnal"—despite its subtle structure of *kavvanot* (intentions and scruples), its care for inwardness and concentration, its mystical as well as its literal structure—is to succumb to a formulaic employment of demeaning language as ordinary and pedestrian for Erasmus as would be the insistence of those whose anti-Semitism is nourished by *The Protocols of the Elders of Zion* to think of Jews as conspirators, secretly meeting in cabal to plan the conquest of the world.

Anti-Semitism depends upon formula, that is, upon language which is a settled constellation of tropes whose meaning need no longer be examined, whose employment immediately generates anger, whose intention is to consolidate rage and enlarge the irrational grounds of contempt and repudiation. Of course we are aware of formulaic language in the Homeric epics and formulaic language in the Bible where structural tropes and stylistic conventions supply the narrative with devices of transition, with means of alluding shifts of place or passage of time, with modes of elevation and enhancement; however, in such great epic literatures the formula is often a means of coping with unresolved metaphysical problems which need to be addressed surreptitiously in order to press the narrative forward without distracting the hearer of the epic (and latterly its reader) from the central progress of the hero or the divinity and his human instruments. Formula in Homer supplies context and narrative relief so that the real detail of action and characterization can unfold unimpeded by stylistic variora or alterations of mood. No less, although differently intended in the biblical narrative.[14] The fact, however, that formulaic language served beneficently the uses of ancient epic and the exposition of revelation does not make all its uses splendid. The formula of hatred remains exemplary. Formulaic anti-Semitism conditions and triggers the psyche, its images and conventions are so well established and defined that the literary anti-Semite has only to allude and suggest for the whole machinery of anti-Semitic logic to be set into motion.

The extreme difficulty therefore of ridding human thought and speech of the formulaic tropes of anti-Semitism is that its linguistic devices are settled into the culture as a means of assuring the vulnerable and threatened that their universe is intact and unassailable. Richard Marius is certainly right in observing that anti-Semitism had a tendency to intensify during those periods of Christian history when Christian uncertainty and anxiety was magnified by the suddenly glaring appearance of the Jew who had not been converted to the superior truth of Christianity.[15] Among such periods was the Age of Humanism and the German Reformation when it was believed by the young Luther, among others, that the reform of the Catholic Church would compel Jews to flock to his banner only to discover and be obliged to recognize that Jewish indifference to Christianity did not arise from Jewish hostility to a corrupt Catholicism but to a doctrinal chasm as wide in the sixteenth century as it had been at the beginning. Indeed, more ignominious was the apparent fact that for most Jews the spiritual life of Christianity was never a source of curiosity or temptation but a matter of almost excessive indifference. For the Christian, on the other hand, the living Jew was hardly a reality; he was for the most part (excepting of course those who were sought out to give instruction to the Christian Hebraists during the Italian Renaissance)[16] a frozen remembrance, a memento, a pallid reflection (not even an iconic image) of the ancient Jews who were declared superseded by the events of the life and death of Jesus Christ and hence in living beyond that ominous epoch were to be counted among the living dead and hence of no consequence. It was easy for a formulaic tradition of Christian anti-Judaism to be continually elaborated and further ornamented with new filigree and tracery since the presence of the odd Jew—the peddlar, beggar, banker, *Hofjude*— who occasionally abraded the unobstructed Christian view of salvation was a rude reminder that such recusant people still existed, that the whole world, despite being fallen into sin, was imaged in the nature of things by the Jew who continued to exist and worship at the margins of Christian life.

Indeed, it is precisely here that Erasmus makes an original contribution to the tropes of anti-Judaism by insisting that wherever the monastery is false and corrupt, wherever Christians are greedy and materialistic, wherever the Church and its officers are devious and deceiving, they are merely falling into "a new kind of Judaism."[17] Erasmus can settle a brilliant polemic upon the failed Christian by accusing him of being a renovated Jew, of having revived and restored to eminence all the materiality and antispiritual grossness of the ancient Jew who, in Erasmus's reading, expects God to be literally obedient to the promises of Scripture, mathematically faithful to the rewards granted for observance of the Law which, in Erasmus's code language, means that such debased believers repudiate the spirit of Christ, betray the Gospels, and fall into the sin of imagining that Christ and His grace are superficially visible and manifest. The hypostatic Jew—never a living Jew, never an observant Jew, never a Jew of historical presence and manifestation—is always a metaphor whose mere mention connotes a congerie of carnalities, denials, and refusals. The Jews are always a sign and index of what is wrong in the Christianity of Erasmus's day—wrong when Christians attack Erasmus's scholarship or his interpretation of Scripture or criticize his attacks upon the clergy and the monastery. When Erasmus is criticized he replies by suspecting that the corruption of the Jew has been infectious or that his opponent is a covert Jew or worse—as in the case of Johannes Pfefferkorn—by recognizing that he is a converted Jew. But what is this—this ready appeal to Jew and Judaism as the palimpest through which can be read the failure and debasement of the Christian other than the formulaic usage of anti-Semitism? Agreed that Erasmus does not have his heart in the murder of the Jews (he would never like Stalin have shot Shimon Markish's father), but it is hardly believable that if a Jew were burned by someone else that Erasmus would protest loudly, much less offer himself in the stead of the innocent. Which, of course, raises another point: the clear and irrefutable cowardice of Erasmus—genial, charming, energetic, passionate, always on the attack when he is not on the defense, but never, ever courageous—not courageous toward his erstwhile friend Thomas More whom he virtually deserts during More's last terrifying years, not courageous toward Luther whom he initially supports and then repudiates, nor courageous to many and generally minor critics and friends to whom Erasmus may have once been generous but whom he chooses at other times to attack or to leave to other wolves. Erasmus, of course, paid a considerable price for being a loner, an itinerant genius, a vagabond intellectual, attaching himself to whatever patron seemed most succorous and promising, inditing dedications of his works to anyone whose power, position, or bursaries might be dispensed upon the cause of *bonae literae* and upon its most spirited advocate, Desiderius Erasmus.

But having said all this about Erasmus's employment of the whole armamentarium of formulaic anti-Judaism—and Markish's marshaling of texts confirms all of it, documenting as he does with splendid calm and geniality the anti-Jewish usage that Erasmus installs in his interpretation of Hebrew Scripture, the Jews of Gospel times, the Jews of history and his own contemporaneity, it must still be wondered along with Markish whether Erasmus is *really* anti-Semitic. Surely he is not anti-Semitic as we have come to know anti-Semitism in this century. His is always an anti-Semitism of letters and literatures, of sources and origins, of languages and texts, and never an anti-Semitism of policy. This is the crucial charge from which Markish wishes to defend his Erasmus and to mark him out and gird him with interpretations and qualifications which distinguish him from the anti-Semitism of Luther, for instance. Erasmus never advocates or sponsors violence, never employs his judgments to embroider a case for expulsion of Jews or theft of their belongings, never interprets the Jews as Marrano or *converso* as forming part of a conspiracy of infiltration and corruption. In other words Erasmus is not—except rarely and exceptionally—marked by the paranoid style so characteristic of those masters and monsters of anti-Semitism from Luther to Marx to Hitler and Stalin. The anti-Jewish formulas are never woven by Erasmus into a litany of conspiratorial policy and hence never move from ideology to politics. The move from ideology to politics—recognized and characterized by Markish in his discussion—is never undertaken by Erasmus, and hence to regard

Erasmus as an anti-Semite in the formidable European tradition of anti-Semitism never occurs.

In short, Erasmus is no paranoid hater of Jews *in principle,* hence he is not regarded as anti-Semite. He is more placid, only occasionally exploding into judeophobic formula. By and large his is a reasonable and calm defense of Christian faith and piety against the misrepresentation of fools and ignorants, powerful princes and potentates, illiterate and impious burghers and bourgeoisie. Erasmus uses the Jews as did every polemicist of his generation to represent what was defective in Christian civilization, but the Jew was no more loathed than the Turk or Muslim, than the pagan or the heretic. The Jew was among the worst, but not the worst by far, protected as he is by being at least the conduit of sacred tradition and the conserver of the Word of God into the time of Jesus Christ and His Apostles.

The incredible achievement of Shimon Markish's *Erasmus and the Jews* lies in the fact that Markish has for the first time examined all the Erasmian literature, the whole vast body of his work, in order to organize the gray tapestry of Erasmian anti-Judaism. He does prove—against the argument of Guido Kisch who had based his attack on Erasmus solely on the volumes of his correspondence (which, to be sure, has a kind of justice, since one is less guarded in language when there is at least uncertainty whether a given letter will be published and widely disseminated)—that Erasmus's anti-Judaism, however fierce, is not corrupted by the crudities of vulgar anti-Semitism. But one wonders whether this is enough? It is perhaps the case that for Shimon Markish, grown up in the Soviet Union where Jews have not enjoyed freedom of conscience, where Jewish life has been virtually destroyed and Jewish knowledge and culture all but suppressed, the only anti-Semite who truly qualifies as anti-Semite is the one who will readily pull the trigger because he has already pulled the trigger and knows how. We, in this remarkably tolerant Anglo-Saxon culture, where traditions of anti-Semitism are no more distinguished and publicly endorsed than any other mode of ethnic contempt and considerably less virulent than some that are directed against race, can look at the Erasmian literature assembled by Professor Markish and be justly horrified. If this as-

sembled document of eloquent contempt and reprobation is the
work of that exquisite humanist, that scholar of Greek and Latin,
respecter of ancient traditions and hoary sources, then let him be
cursed for what he is, one more European Christian who imagines that his hatred of Jews, Jewish faith and practice, Jewish history and institutions will be forgiven because God no longer cares
for the Jews nor hears their prayers. Markish proves his case, but
only in part: Erasmus is no street anti-Semite such as a Soviet
Jew knows with intimacy from his childhood, but he is surely
within a grand tradition of contempt and supersession that leads
if not to the crude fulminations of Julius Streicher, then surely
through the permutations of secular diabolism straight to the
death camps.

Notes

The most commonly used sources are abbreviated as follows:

LB: *Desiderii Erasmi Roterodami Opera Omnia emendatiora et auctiora,* edidit Joannes Clericus, 10 vols. (Lugduni Batavorum, 1703–1706).

ASD: *Opera Omnia Desiderii Erasmi Roterodami recognita et adnotatione critica instructa notisque illustrata* (Amsterdam, 1969–1983) (13 volumes published to date).

OE: *Opus Epistolarum Desiderii Erasmi Roterodami denuo recognitum et auctum,* per P. S. Allen et a., 12 vols. (Oxonii, 1906–1958).

(In addition, the translator has used the translations offered in *The Collected Works of Erasmus,* University of Toronto Press, in such instances as this was possible; this is abbreviated CWE and follows the author's note.)

CHAPTER I

1. Kisch, G., *Erasmus' Stellung zu Juden und Judentum* (Tübingen, 1969). On Erasmus and Luther, see p. 38. The bibliography (or, more precisely, a short survey of what has *not* been written about Erasmus and the Jews) is on pp. 5–6.

Unfortunately, when working on the book I did not know

about a 1970 article, G. B. Winkler, "Erasmus und die Juden," in *Festschrift Franz Loidl zum 65 Geburtstag* herausgegeben von V. Flieder, vol. 2 (Sammlung "Aus Christentum und Kultur," Sonderband 2) (Wien, 1970), pp. 381–392. Winkler's evaluation of Erasmus' position is close to my own conclusions, but his material is as limited as Kisch's (see below).

In 1980 there appeared the article by Dr. C. Augustijn, "Erasmus und die Juden," in *Nederlands Archief voor Kerkengeschiedenis* 60, no. 1 (1980), pp. 22–38. In great and in small, and, more important, in method and approach to the material, Dr. Augustijn and I travel the same paths, which in part was noted by Heiko A. Oberman in his book *Wurzeln des Antisemismus: Christenangst und Judenplage im Zeitalter von Humanismus und Reformation* (Berlin, 1981), p. 74. Dr. Augustijn did not know of my book's existence and so of course made no reference to it. Mr. Oberman's observation though seems less reasonable: "In comparison with Augustijn, Shimon Markish offers no new points of view." A simple comparison of the two publication dates will show the lack of substance (not to say giddiness) of this scornful remark.

2. On the "Luther theme" in Streicher and his newspaper, see the remarkable book by Johannes Brosseder, *Luthers Stellung zu den Juden im spiegel seiner Interpreten* (München, 1972), pp. 182–192.

3. *Christen und Juden, Ihr Gegenüber vom Apostelkonzil bis heute,* Hrsgb. von W. D. Marsch und K. Thieme (Mainz and Gottigen, 1961), p. 146.

4. In this sense the inflammatory speeches and writing of renegades like Pfefferkorn, or "Black Hundred intellectuals" like Arnold of Tongres, or even the stern pronouncements of jurists like Ulrich Zasius, or from the other side the infrequent defenses of Jews and their literature such as those of Andreas Osiander—all have equally little weight; they disappear without a trace, meaning nothing for the future.

5. *Kirche und Synagoge, Handbuch zur Geschichte der Christen und Juden,* Hrsgb. von K. H. Rengstorf und S. v.Kortzfleish, 2 vols. (Stuttgart, 1968–1970), 1:443–445.

6. *Christen und Juden,* p. 141. See also Salo V. Baron's long article about Calvin in the *Encyclopaedia Judaica,* 16 vols. (Jerusalem, 1971), 5:66–68. It is wholly characteristic that this newest and most complete of Jewish encyclopedias has no article whatever about Erasmus.

7. *Christen und Juden,* p. 284. Compare *Kirche und Synagoge,* p.

16: "The murderous totalitarianism of the newest nationalist ide-
ologies, including the national-socialist one, was in a certain sense
anticipated structurally . . . by the totalitarian unity of the Christian Church and State."

8. B. Blumenkranz writes of this very delicately and with ut-
most generality in the foreword to his dissertation *Juifs et chrétiens
dans le monde Occidental, 430–1096* (Paris: The Hague, 1960), p. ix:
"Any minority is subject to alarm; this alarm forces the minority
to ponder its relations with those who simply surround it—the
majority—and with those who actively and inimically oppose it.
This occurs not only at the present moment; the mind eagerly
plunges into the past with the secret hope of finding an answer in
history to the questions of the present day. Jews have suffered the
lot of the minority for almost two thousand years, and alarming
thoughts have not left them for even a moment. Belonging myself
to this minority, I could not evade this tendency of its cast of
mind." On the other hand, it is impossible to believe Kisch, who
in his foreword to *Zasius und Reuchlin* avers that he set himself no
other goals than to create "a sketch from the history of the spiritual life and, primarily, from the history of law in the 16th century." This even comes just a few lines after Kisch has announced
that "this work permits a glance at the still-unwritten prehistory
of the anti-Semitism of most recent times, the anti-Semitism
which would not have found such ready ground in Germany were
it not for the entire ages of ideological preparation." G. Kisch,
Zasius und Reuchlin (Konstanz-Stuttgart, 1961), p. vii.

9. J. Lecler, *Histoire de la tolerance au siecle de la Reforme,* 2 vols.
(Aubier, 1955), 1:125–126, 133–149, 157, 188 ff., 237–242, 259 ff.

10. R. Lewin, *Luthers Stellung zu den Juden* (Berlin, 1911).

11. For the polemic with Kisch, see my article "Erasmus és a
zsidóság," *Filologiai közlöny* (Budapest, 1973), pp. 90 ff. nn. 1–2.

12. Lewin, p. x.

13. Kisch, *Erasmus' Stellung* . . . , pp. 30 ff.

14. L. Poliakov, *Histoire de l'antisemitisme,* vol. 1 *Du Christ aux
Juifs de Cours* (Paris, 1955), pp. 229 ff.; L. Geiger, *Das Studium der
hebräischen Sprache in Deutschland vom Ende des XV. bis zum Mitte
des XVI. Jahrhunderts* (Breslau, 1870), pp. 2, 14–15.

15. Kisch, *Zasius und Reuchlin,* p. 71.

16. L. Geiger, *Johann Reuchlin, sein Leben und seine Werke,*
(Leipzig, 1871), p. 162, Poliakov, pp. 231, 234.

17. Kisch, *Zasius und Reuchlin,* pp. 32 ff.; Kisch, *Erasmus'
Stellung,* pp. 32–34.

18. Geiger, *Johann Reuchlin,* p. 164.
19. Ibidem.
20. Ibidem, passim E. gr., p. 426.
21. *Kirche und Synagoge,* passim.
22. E. Telle, *Erasme de Rotterdam et le septième sacrement* (Geneva, 1954), p. 458: "As long as the anti-Mosaism of the end of the Middle Ages and the beginning of the 16th century remains uninvestigated it is impossible to judge properly the hostility to monasticism of that era, as well as to evaluate the intensity of this hostility in Erasmus by comparison with that of others. The anti-Mosaism which existed in northern Europe at the end of the Middle Ages seems to me to be the basis on which antimonastic opinions developed."

CHAPTER II

1. LB V, 537 E–F (Enarr. Psalmi 85, 1528). Compare ibidem, 413 A (Enarr. Psalmi 33, 1530).
2. LB VI, 502 D (Annotationes in Novum Testamentum, 1527). Compare ibidem, 637 A–B (1535).
3. ASD I-1, 109, 111–112, 116–118 (Antibarbari, 1518–1520, 2d rev. ed.). Compare: "Hoc erat maximum mandatum in lege Mosaica, hoc iterat et perficit in Euangelio Christus," LB V, 35 E (Enchiridion, 1504).
4. LB X, 1529 F–1530 D (Hyperaspistes II).
5. LB V, 1075 F (Ecclesiastes). Compare also ibidem, 941 B": "Exordium humani generis fuit in Paradiso: incrementum, sub triplici lege, Naturae, Mosis et Euangelica."
6. LB VII, 1046 A–B (Paraphr. in 1 Tim., 1519). See M. Simon, *Verus Israel* (Paris, 1964), pp. 101–102. See also B. Blumenkranz, *Die Judenpredigt Augustins* (Basel 1946), pp. 10, 28, 131. These two works served as my major guides in the question of the New Testament and Holy Father sources of Erasmus' anti-Mosaism.
7. ". . . sublata funditus Judaeorum religione," LB VII, 439 D–E (Paraphr. in Luc., 1523). Compare ibidem, 464 A.
8. Ibidem, 295 A.
9. Ibidem, 962 C (Paraphr. in Gal., 1519). Compare the no less categorical demand in such an important work as *Ratio verae theologiae:* "Neque enim quidquid Judaeis vel imperatum est, vel interdictum, vel permissum, ad Christianorum vitam est

accommodandum." LB V, 86 F (1518). Compare also LB VII, 1000 D (Paraphr. in Phil., 1519). Of the New Testament texts to which this thesis may be dated, the first must be Galatians 5:4.

10. LB IX, 827 D–E (Declar, ad cens. Lutetiae, 1532). This in part was also the viewpoint of John Chrysostum, the most bitter and most passionate anti-Judaic polemicist among the Church Fathers (Simon, pp. 109, 256 ff.). Erasmus even refers directly to Chrysostum in the context which in effect concretizes the thesis above. Referring to the transfer of "Sabbath rest" to Sunday, Erasmus explains, "Apostolorum auctoritate factum esse. Mutatus est dies, ne in hoc convenientes cum Judaeis videremur et in reliquis consentire, quemadmodum Chrysostomus, nec is tamen solus, miro studio deterret christianos, ne iisdem diebus ieiunarent, quibus Judaei solenniter ieiunabant." ASD V-1, 309 (Symbolum, 1533).

11. LB V, 1051 B (Ecclesiastes, 1535).

12. LB X, 1347 A–1348 F (Hyperaspistes II, 1527).

13. LB VI, 799–800 (Annotationes, 1519).

14. This opposition has an important place in the formula "the difference between Old and New Law" which is offered in the dialogue *Ichthyophagia:* "That was given to one people, while this teaches salvation to all peoples. That announced marvelous and extraordinary spiritual grace to only a few prophets and chosen men, while this has poured bounteously over people of all ages, sex, and tribe gifts of every sort." ASD I-3, 521 (Colloquia: Ichthyophagia, 1526).

15. LB VI, 996 F (Annotationes, 1519).

16. Ibidem, 342 D (1519). Compare Simon, p. 101.

17. LB V, 181 A (Enarr. Psalmi I, 1515); ibidem, 342 A (Enarr. Psalmi 22, 1530); LB VII, 369 B (Paraphr. in Luc. 1523); LB V, 1078 A (Ecclesiastes, 1535).

18. LB VII, 164 B (Paraphr. in Marc., 1523); LB IX, 472 A (Divinat. ad not. per Beddam, 1526).

19. "Ob hoc potissimum natus ac mortuus est Christus, ut nos doceret non Judaizare, sed amare . . ." LB V, 35 E sq. (Enchiridion, 1504).

20. LB VII, 1036 F (Paraphr. in 1 Tim., 1519); LB IX, 691 B (Supput. errorum Beddae, 1527). It is particularly interesting that just before this above phrase in *Enchiridion* Erasmus recalls this "highest commandment of the Law of Moses," which Christ repeated and fulfilled, while the discussion which follows seems to efface the recollection. Of course the theologian can resolve this

contradiction by referring to the tradition (going back to the New Testament texts) of seeing in Judaism the incomplete fulfillment of the true meaning of God's commandments. See Simon, pp. 106–108. See also E.-W. Kohls, *Die Theologie des Erasmus,* 2 vols. (Basel 1966), 1:144; Blumenkranz, *Judenpedigt . . . ,* p. 126.

21. Particularly since in the final analysis even this opposition can also be derived from a New Testament text. See Matthew 5:43–47.

22. LB V, 32 F (Enchiridion, 1504). Compare: ". . . Judaici cultus, qui fere totus aestimabatur corporalibus observatiunculis . . ." LB VII, 212 E (Paraphr. in Marc., 1523).

23. See my book *Znakomstvo s Erazmom iz Rotterdama* (Moscow, 1971), pp. 77, 151–153, 176.

24. For example: LB VI, 1061 F (Annotationes, 1516); ibidem, 1041 F (1519); LB V 372 E (Enarr. Psalmi 33, 1530); ibidem, 797 F–798 A (Ecclesiastes, 1535); ibidem, 308 C–D (Enarr. Psalmi 14, 1536). Since this opposition is the basic one in the Pauline epistles, choice of citations is complicated by the wealth of New Testament texts. I refer for example to Romans 7 and 8. See also Simon, p. 97.

25. ASD I-3, 501 (Colloquia: Ichthyophagia, 1526).

26. Ibidem, 234 (Colloquia: Convivium religiosum, 1522).

27. LB V, 835 D (Ecclesiastes, 1535).

28. LB VII, 334 D–E (Paraphr. in Luc., 1523); LB IX, 610 E (Supput. errorum Beddae, 1527). Romans is also in the foreground here, particularly chapters 3–5 and 10.

29. For example: LB X, 1525 F–1526 A (Hyperaspistes II, 1527); LB IX, 1192 A–B (Apologia adv. rhapsodias Al. Pii, 1531); LB V, 308 C–D (Enarr. Psalmi 14, 1536). The first of these texts contains a curious definition of Jewish hopes for eternal life: "Judaei . . . non aliter sibi pro operibus externis existimabant deberi vitam aeternam, quam fabro lignario pro opere absoluto debetur merces, quae ni reddatur, sit ex lege debiti actio." See Simon, p. 99.

30. For example: LB V, 34 C–D (Enchiridion, 1504: ". . . ne Judaico more certis quibusdam observationibus, tamquam Magicis ceremoniis Deum demereri velimus . . ."); LB VII, 1042 A (Paraphr. in 1 Tim., 1519); ibidem, 209 E (Paraphr. in Marc., 1523: ". . . ceremoniarum superstitio, unde fere nascitur omnis inter homines calumnia"); ibidem, 70 D (Paraphr. in Matt., 1522).

31. Ceremoniae humanae. LB VII, 146 B (Paraphr. in Matt., 1522).

32. Ceremoniae pharisaicae. Ibidem, 209 F–210 A (Paraphr. in
Marc., 1523); 615 D–E (Paraphr. in Ioan., 1523).
33. LB VII, 144 F, 146 C (Paraphr. in Matt., 1522).
34. LB VI, 629 D–E (Annotationes, 1535). Compare Acts 7:41–
50. See also Simon, pp. 112–113.
35. LB V, 208 E–209 F (Enarr. Psalmi 2, 1522). Compare Galatians 3:24. The theme of "Law as pedagogue" is developed in
particular detail by John Chrysostum, to a somewhat lesser degree
by Clement of Alexandria. See Simon, pp. 96–97.
36. LB VII, 352 C (Paraphr. in Luc., 1523); LB V, 828 B (Ecclesiastes, 1535). Compare also: "Miserat [sc. Pater] Mosen et Proph-
etas; per hos curata est Judaeorum natio, sed non est sanata . . .
Multa [sc. pharmaca] miscuit Moses, praescribens varias religionis
ceremonias, multa Prophetae; sed invalescentibus morbis nihil
profuit medicina, nisi quod auxit morbum et prodidit . . . Mosi
praescriptis superstitiosiores reddebantur, non meliores." OE V,
316 (N. 1381, 142–158), 29/VIII–1523. See Romans 10:4.
37. Kohls, 1:139.
38. ASD I-3, 501–502. Compare LB VII, 570 C, 797 E (Paraphr.
in Ioan., 1523; in Rom., 1517), which speaks of how Christ alone
freed the Jews from slavery.
39. ASD I-3, 502.
40. Ibidem, 503. Compare Romans 2:14–15, where Paul talks
directly about the coincidence of the Decalogue with natural law.
The same occurs, in greater detail, in Clement of Alexandria (see
Encyclopdaedia Judaica, 5:602).
41. ". . . Legis ceremoniae per se malae non erant nec ciborum
delectus, nec Deus voluit suam Legem subito reiici, ne videretur
fuisse impia, cum abolendae quoque ceremoniae typum haberent
Christi, sed paulatim antiquari." ASD IX-1, 366 (Epistola ad
fratres Germaniae, 1530).
42. ASD I-3, 247 (Colloquia: Convivium religiosum, 1522).
43. Ibidem. It is especially important to note that these words
were written before the start of the open polemic with Luther.
See also ASD I-3, 510–513 (on commandment-laws and com-
mandment-advice) and, particularly, 519–520 (the description of
divine and human laws, from which it follows that a part of "the
Moses works" must all the same be ascribed to the latter!) (Colloquia: Ichthyophagia, 1526). See also ASD V-1, 309–310 (Symbolum, 1533).
44. Compare Vidua Christiana (about Ruth gathering wheat
in the field of Boaz): "Id enim Mosaicae legis humanitas indulsit

pauperibus." LB V, 747 B (Vidua Christiana, 1529). No matter how infrequent and restrained these praises of the Law, they are important in principle; Erasmus does not deprive Moses' lawgiving of the quality Erasmus thought most valuable, humanity.

45. Ibidem, 1076 A–1077 A. See Blumenkranz, *Judenpredigt . . . ,* pp. 138–139.

46. "In plerisque non res, sed animus nos discernit a Iudaeis. Illi manum abstinebant a certis cibis, velut ab immundis et animum inquinaturis. Nos, quum intelligamus omnia munda esse mundis, tamen carni lascivienti velut equo ferocienti pabulum subducimus, quo magis dicto sit audiens spiritui." ASD I-3, 227 (Colloquia: Convivium profanum, 1522). Compare LB I, 907 D–E (De utilitate Colloquiorum, 1526). Compare also LB V, 830 F–831 A (Ecclesiastes, 1535).

47. OE IV, 181–182 (N. 1062, 45–52), 5/II-1519 [1520] (Paraphr. in Eph., Praefatio). The conclusion of the citation is, "Sic olim Euangelicae doctrinae mustum aversabantur Iudaei, veteri vino Mosaicae legis assueti . . . ac novitatem habebant invisam, cum potius ad priscam vetustatem revocarentur." This thesis, developed in detail by Eusebius, is based primarily on Galatians 3:6 and 3:17, as well as on Romans 4:9 and 4:20. See Simon, pp. 106–108.

48. See particularly Galatians 4:1–9, 21–31, and 5:1. For the role of this opposition in Erasmian spiritualism, see J. Étienne, *Spiritualisme érasmienne et theologiens louvanistes* (Louvain 1956), passim, particularly pp. 17, 35 ff., 57. See also A. Renaudet, *Erasme et l'Italie* (Geneva, 1954), p. 37.

49. For example (some examples almost at random): LB VI, 888 F (Annotationes, 1516); ibidem, 799–800 (1518), 821 C–D (1535); LB VII, 921 A (Paraphr. in 2 Cor., 1519); ibidem, 318 A (Paraphr. in Luc., 1523); ibidem, 615 F–616 B (paraphr. in Ioan., 1523); ASD I-3, 520–521 (Colloquia: Ichthyophagia, 1526); LB IX, 645 B (Supput. errorum Beddae, 1527). In medieval literature this variant of the opposition under discussion, that is, "fear (of the Law) versus love," was widely distributed during the epoch of the so-called "first pre-Renaissance" (ninth century). See B. Blumenkranz, *Les auteurs chrétiens latins du Moyen âge sur les Juifs et le judaisme* (Paris: The Hague, 1963), p. 194.

50. LB V, 1070 C–D Ecclesiastes, 1535).

51. "In his quae corporis sunt et ad Legis accedunt ceremonias, lenior est nostra institutio: sed in his quae sunt animi, longe severior est." LB VII, 342 E (Paraphr. in Luc., 1523). Compare also ibidem, 55 B–C (Paraphr. in Matt., 1522); LB IX 838 B–F, 842 B

Notes to Pages 13–15

(Declar. ad cens. Lutetiae, 1532). Among the Church Fathers this is particularly clear in Clement of Alexandria (Simon, p. 100).

52. LB IX, 711 C (Responsio ad notulas Beddae, 1527).

53. *S. Hieronymi lucubrationes omnes . . . per Erasmum Roterodamum emendatae* . . . (Basileae 1516), 1:34. See also LB VII, 158 B, 177 B (Paraphr, in Marc., 1523); LB IX, 644 B (Supput. errorum Beddae, 1527); ibidem, 826 B–C (Declar. ad cens. Lutetiae, 1532); ASD V-1, 310 (Symbolum, 1533).

54. Ibidem, 73–76 (De contemptu mundi, ⟨c. 1498⟩); LB I, 882–890 (Colloquia: Epicureus, 1533).

55. See, for example, LB VI, 637 A–B (Annotationes, 1535). It is interesting to juxtapose this image with the dialogue *Diluculum* ("Dawn"-1529), which condemns the torpid; the spiritual (allegorical) and real planes correspond clearly, as happens very often with Erasmus.

56. See Hebrews 10:1 and Corinthians 2:17.

57. *Hieronymi lucubrationes* IV, 27 B (1516). This is mentioned in connection with 2 Corinthians 3, which contains the famous aphorism (verse 6): "the written code kills, but the Spirit gives life."

58. LB VII, 1035 E (Paraphr. in 1 Tim., 1519).

59. Ibidem, 953 D–E (1519).

60. See, for example, LB IX, 460 A–C (Divinat. ad not. per Beddam, 1526); ASD V-1, 238 (Symbolum, 1533). See also the particularly expressive formulations in LB VII, 911 D (Paraphr. in 1 Cor., 1519), 920 A (Paraphr. in 2 Cor., 1519). See also Simon, p. 98.

61. LB IX, 859 D (Declar. ad cens. Lutetiae, 1532).

62. For example, *Hieronymi lucubrationes* I, 30–31 (1516); OE V, 339 (n. 1390, li. 66–73), ⟨X⟩ 1523; LB X, 1488 B (Hyperaspistes II, 1527); LB V 293 F (Enarr. Psalmi 14, 1536).

63. LB VII, 1012 D (Paraphr. in Col., 1519). This by the way is Origen's viewpoint (Contra Celsum 4, 8); Erasmus had almost as much love for Origen as for Jerome.

64. OE I, 566 (n. 296, 42–43), 8 July 1514; LB VII, 326 A (Paraphr. in Luc., 1523); ibidem, 620 F, 551 F–552 A (Paraphr. in Ioan., 1523); ibidem, 345 B (Paraphr. in Luc.); ibidem, 536 A, 640 C–D (Paraphr. in Ioan.); ibidem, 715 B–C (Paraphr. in Acts, 1524); OE V, 168 (n. 1333, 224), 1 May 1523; ibidem, 339 (n. 1390, 67–68), ⟨November⟩ 1523; *Hieronymi lucubrationes* I, 192 (1516); LB VII, 634 C (Querela Pacis, 1517).

65. LB IX, 862 B–F (Declar. ad cens. Lutetiae, 1532).

66. LB V, 203 D (Enarr. Psalmi 2, 1522).

67. Ibidem, 901 C (Ecclesiastes, 1535).
68. OE V, 94 (note to letter 1301) ⟨c. 14 July 1522⟩; OE VI, 389 (n. 1379, 223–227, 234–237), 27 August 1526.
69. LB VII, 755 A–B (Paraphr. in Acts, 1524).
70. LB IX, 590 E–F (Supput. errorum Beddae, 1527).
71. LB V, 297 D–E (Enarr. Psalmi 14, 1536); about the decalogue in greatest detail, ASD V-1, 302–318 (Symbolum, 1533).
72. ". . . Deum mutilum . . ." LB V, 535 A (Enarr. Psalmi 85, 1528). Compare: The Jews are blasphemers, since their abuse of the Son falls also on the Father. LB VI, 611 E (Annotationes, 1535); LB VII, 525 A (Paraphr. in Ioan., 1523).
73. Markish, *Znakomstvo s Erazmom*, pp. 81–82, 203, 205–207.
74. LB V, 118 D (Ratio verae theologiae, 1518).
75. LB IX, 687 F, 688 C (Supput. errorum Beddae, 1527). Compare also LB VII, 251 B–C (Paraphr. in Marc., 1523).
76. ". . . apud Judaeos multi fuerint . . ." LB IX, 833 A–B (Declar. ad cens. Lutetiae, 1532).
77. LB V, 40 A–D (Enchiridion, 1504).
78. Kohls, pp. 143–152. See particularly pp. 144, 147, 149, 151.
79. Ibidem, p. 143.
80. Ibidem, pp. 98 ff.
81. LB VI, 549–550 (1516).
82. Ibidem, 553 D–E (1516).
83. Simon, pp. 97–99.
84. Ibidem, p. 100.
85. Ibidem, pp. 103–104.
86. Ibidem, p. 123.
87. Kohls, pp. 27–28. This is the typical (one might say classic) medieval conception of time. See A. Ya. Gurevich, *Kategorii srednevekovoi kul'tury* (Moscow, 1972), pp. 99 ff.
88. J. Huizinga, *Erasmus and the Age of Reformation* (New York, Evanston, and London, 1957), p. 102.
89. LB V, 400 B sq. (Enarr. Psalmi 33, 1530).
90. Ibidem, 542 D (Enarr. Psalmi 85, 1528). Mr. Jacques Chomarat, author of a review of my book which was printed in *La Bibliothèque d'Humanisme et Renaissance* 5, no. 43 (1981), pp. 197–202, calls this assertion of mine monstrous and without any relationship to Erasmus whatsoever, as proof of which he gives, in French translation, a somewhat larger context (C–D) taken from the interpretation of Psalm 85. I also would like to quote that excerpt, but in the original and without ellipsis:

Nunc contemplemur velut unam personam capitis aut
corporis, et juxta mysticam rationem, ut unam omnium
carnem, ita omnium piorum unam esse animam, quam
magna misericordia liberavit a tot inferis, dum gratis con-
donavit nobis peccata, redemit a servitute Satanae, non
sinit nos obrui tentationibus, dat vincere in cruciatibus,
et si mori patitur, non patitur mortem esse perpetuam,
etiam haec mortalia corpora revocaturus ad immoralitatis
gloriam. Sentit anima Christi beneficium, quod singulis
animabus impendit, quemadmodum et adhuc quodam-
modo pascitur ac refocillatur in membris suis. Quam
longe Gentes erant a Deo, dum vel nullum crederent esse
Deum, vel Bestias ac muta Signa colebant pro Deo, tam
contaminate viventes, quam erat illorum impia religio. At
non tum in profundo tartaro versabamur? Judaei, qui
videbantur Deo propiores, nonne in profundissimum
barathrum devenerant, quum occiderant Filium Dei? Et
tamen tanta fuit misericordia Domini, ut ab his inferis tot
animarum millia liberaret.

Since the subject here is the Son of God, the Perfect Man who
died a real death, whose soul then descends into Hell to free and
save from there the souls of sinners, the meaning of the excerpt
cannot be interpreted in any other way. Both pagans and Jews
who found themselves in Hell were there *before* the saving death
of the Savior.

91. Ibidem, 332 A–C (Enarr. Psalmi 22, 1530). See also 322 F–
323 A.

92. LB VII, 725 F–726 A (Paraphr. in Acts, 1524).

93. For example, LB V, 96 F, 138 C (Ratio verae theologiae,
1518); 211 B (Enarr. Psalmi I, 1515); 542 E, 545 A–C (Enarr. Psalmi
85, 1528); 815 D–E (Ecclesiastes, 1535); LB VII, 435 A, 443 E (Paraphr. in Luc., 1523). Compare Blumenkranz, *Les auteurs chrétiens . . .*, p. 86, 134. Christians once again crucifying Christ with
their sins was discussed by Pope Gregory the Great and later by
the Venerable Bede (Erasmus had deep respect for each of them;
Bede was one of the few medieval authors whom Erasmus cited
frequently and enthusiastically).

94. LB V, 836 D (Ecclesiastes).

95. LB VI, 117 F–118 F (Annotationes, after 1516), 416 E (1516).

96. ASD V-1, 280 (Symbolum, 1533).

97. LB V, 842 E (Ecclesiastes, 1535).
98. Ibidem, 843 A.
99. LB VI, 33 F (Annotationes, 1516).
100. LB V, 306 C (Enarr. Psalmi 14, 1536).
101. OE I, 374 (n. 164, 25–28) [CWE, 2:52—A.O.]
102. OE I, 405 (n. 181, 46–49), ⟨December⟩ 1504 [CWE 2:87—A.O.].
103. LB V, 32 E–F.
104. Ibidem, 33 A.
105. LB VI, 518 E–F (Annotationes, 1516). Erasmus refers to Augustine, who (Ep. 55, §35) lamented the fate of the Church, which was so crushed under "slavish burdens" that in that regard even the Jews had it better; they at least were subordinate to the Law, not human prejudices. OE III, 486–487 (n. 916, 234–243), 5 February 1519; LB VI, 64 B–D (Annotationes, 1519). However, the search for the sources of Erasmus' hatred of rituals in the writings of the Church Fathers ought more properly to address Jerome, who was much nearer to Erasmus than was Augustine, and who had the greater intolerance of Jewish ritual. See *Encyclopaedia Judaica*, 9:1378; Blumenkranz, *Judenpredigt . . .* , pp. 135–137.
106. For example: "Qui Judaismum sapiunt, religionis laudem constituunt in palliis ac phylacteriis, in delectu ciborum, in lotionibus, in prolixis precibus, caeterisque ceremoniis, quae sic aliqoties adspernandae non sunt, si per haec veluti signa commonefiamus eorum, quae sunt propria pietatis: perniciosa vero, si quis arbitretur per haec hominem fieri religiosum . . . Ponunt pietatem in rebus visibilibus, quae signa sunt fortasse pietatis, non causa . . ." LB VII, 1124 E–F (Paraphr. in Iac., 1520); so, in Erasmus' mind, would the holy apostle James have spoken, had he thought to enlarge upon chapter 1, verse 26 of his epistle in greater detail.
107. LB VII, 75 B (1522). See also ibidem, 211 C (Paraphr. in Marc., 1523), 375 B–C (Paraphr. in Luc., 1523).
108. Ibidem, 1081–1100 (1520).
109. Ibidem, 1101–1110 (1520).
110. Ibidem, 1141–1160 (1521).
111. Ibidem, 1005–1016 (1519).
112. Ibidem, 1165–1198 (1521).
113. P. Smith, *Erasmus: A Study of His Life, Ideals, and Place in History* (New York, 1962), p. 187.
114. OE IV, 514 (n. 1211, 238–240), 13 June 1521; ASD IX-1, 46

(De interdicto esu carnum, 1522); LB IX, 1143 E (Apologia adv. rhapsodias Alb. Pii, 1531).

115. Ibidem, 889 D (Declar. ad cens. Lutetiae, 1532). Compare Ibidem, 473 A (Divinat. ad not. per Beddam, 1526).

116. Ibidem, 889 D–E.

117. ASD IX-1, 259 (Detectio praestigiarum cujusdam libelli . . .). Compare the same year, 1526: ASD I-3, 518 (Colloquia: Ichthyophagia, 1526).

118. OE VIII, 226 (n. 2193, 125–128), 7 July 1529. For more detail on Erasmus' allegiance to old "anti-Jewish" slogans in the last years of his life, see Markish, *Znakomstvo s Erazmom*, pp. 194 ff.

119. LB VI, 638 F–639 B (Annotationes, 1516).

120. OE V, 263 (n. 1353, 34–36), [23 March] 1523. Almost exactly the same thing appears in LB IX, 827 E (Declar. ad cens. Lutetiae, 1532).

121. Some examples: LB V, 36 A–D (Enchiridion, 1504); OE I, 567–568 (n. 296, 81–84), 8 July 1514 ("Iam ad laudatus religiones si te conferas, imo ad laudatissimas, praeter frigidas quasdam et Iudaicas ceremonias, haud scio quam Christi reperias imaginem"): *Hieronymi lucubrationes* I, 53 (1516); LB VI, 82 C–D, 258 F (Annotationes, 1519); LB V, 109 F–110 A (Ratio verae theologiae, 1518); LB IX, 614 B–D, 615 F, 647 A–648 C (Supput. errorum Beddae, 1527). For detail see Telle, passim, especially pp. 86–88, 194, 457.

122. LB II, 655 B.

123. ASD IX-1, 46 (De interdicto esu carnium, 1522).

124. OE IV, 439 (n. 1183, 35–40), 28 January 1521. Points 2 and 3 of this "program" are repeated in a letter of 13 August, in the same year; ibidem, 560–561 (n. 1225, 219–225).

125. OE VI, 208 (n. 1891, 183–195), [17 October 1527].

126. OE X, 236 (n. 2817, 32–36), 9 June 1533.

127. Compare Telle, p. 85.

128. It must be remarked that this is not the only confirmation Erasmus gives for Huizinga's famous thesis, that "the Renaissance was the autumn of the Middle Ages." See, for example, Markish, *Znakomstvo s Erazmom*, p. 40.

129. This is proven in part by the reaction of the conservative theologians; often they understood Erasmus' criticism of Judaism as blasphemous insult to the Church and to God Himself, and as a heretical attack on the foundations of the Christian religion. See, for example, LB IX, 382 A–B (Apologia ad conclusiones Jac. Stunicae, 1524); ibid., 470 D, 479 E, 480 A, 508 E, 510 C–F, 512

A–B, 639 B–641 A, 678 D–679 A (various apologiae against Noel
Beda, 1526–1527); 829 B–830 E, 832 E–834 C, 840 D–843 B, 847
A–848 B, 853 B–863 C, 893 C–894 D (Declar. ad cens. Lutetiae,
1532). Thus the Parisian theologians held Erasmus responsible for
militant rejection of the laws about food and fasting, for the assertion that the Old Testament encourages war while the New Testament forbids it, for the rejection of "works," for defining the Law
of Moses as "coarse religion or prejudice," and so on. Of course
there is no question here of any defense of Judaism; the orthodox
were simply trying to prove Erasmus guilty of supporting the
Lutheran doctrine of justification through faith alone. Erasmus
did everything he could to deflect the accusation, referring first of
all to the fact that he meant only "the fleshy part of the Law," then
openly distancing himself from Luther and total condemnation of
"works." For example: "Perspicuum est me non damnare bona
opera neque docere leges divinas aut constitutiones Ecclesiae non
esse servandas. Sed fortasse tale quiddam docet Lutherus. Quid
hoc mea? . . . Scylla est dicere nullum esse bonum opus hominis,
fateor, sed Charibdis est docere viribus humanis fretos homines
pervenire ad aeternam felicitatem." LB IX, 568 B–C (Supput. errorum Beddae, 1527). See also ibidem, 620 E–621 B, 645 D sq.
This type of justification is far from a tactical maneuver, and it is
entirely natural that in the polemic with Luther (particularly in
Hyperaspistes II) Erasmus assumes the role of defender of the Law,
the exact same role played by the orthodox in their polemic with
Erasmus himself, and along the exact same lines, not because his
anti-Mosaism had in any way weakened or softened but rather to
expose "Luther's heresy." He categorically rejects Luther's accusation of having ridiculed the sacred history and sacred books of the
Jews (LB X, 1333 A–F), then, moving to the counterattack, he
shows Luther's extremes in his views of the Law (1351 D sq.),
reminding his opponent that "externa Legis opera . . . non fac-
iunt impium, nisi adsit perversus animus" (1495 B); further, he
even finds positive arguments in favor of the Law of Moses: ". . .
Lex etiam fidem praecipit et caritatem, quam homo non asse-
quitur puris naturae viribus, sec auxiliante gratia: nec ea defuit
olim Judaeis in lege viventibus" (1498 D). This detail of a battle
on two fronts (the biplanarity of the polemic about the Law) is
very interesting, but, as far as I am able to judge, it has not yet
become the object of special attention for historians or religious
thought nor for students of Erasmus' work.

130. Telle, p. 86.

131. Ibidem, p. 457.
132. Ibidem, p. 194.
133. I find an example of this sort of madness (as well as igno-rance) in the theses of a talk by Harry S. May, presented at the Sixth World Congress of Jewish Studies in Jerusalem, in August 1973. This paper, titled "Erasmus and the Jews—a Psychohistoric Reevaluation" (more detailed bibliographical information is not available), claimed that Erasmus' anti-Semitism went far beyond the general medieval norms, that Erasmus was syphilitic (a "fact" supposedly established by medicine), that he blamed all the trou-bles of the world on the Jews, that he demanded their expulsion from Western Europe, that he accused them of conspiracy against Christianity, of poisoning air and food, of instigating peasant up-risings, that he abused anyone who called for humane treatment of the Jews, and possibly, like Hitler, even suspected that he owed his illegitimate arrival in the world to a Jew, so making him in-fected with Jewish blood. All of this nonsense could be viewed as a nasty hoax, save that it was offered at an international congress.
134. LB IX, 1103 F (Responsio ad. Alb. Pium, 1529).
135. Ibidem, 911 B (Declar. ad cens. Lutetiae, 1532).

CHAPTER III

1. For example, A. Renaudet, *Humanisme et Renaissance* (Gen-eva, 1958), p. 167; J. W. Aldridge, *The Hermeneutic of Erasmus* (Winterthur, Del., 1966), p. 44–49; Kisch, *Erasmus' Stellung . . . ,* p. 7; G. Faludy, *Erasmus of Rotterdam* (London, 1970), pp. 82–83; Ch. Béné, *Erasme et Saint Augustin* (Geneva, 1969), p. 367.
2. OE III, 127 (n. 701, 33–38), 253 (n. 798. 19–28).
3. LB V, 744 E–F (Vidua Christiana, 1529, said about "Judith").
4. Ibidem, 744 B.
5. Ibidem, 790 F (Ecclesiastes, 1535).
6. Ibidem, 870 C.
7. LB VI, 644 E–F (Annotationes, 1535).
8. LB V, 568 A–B (De misericordia Dom., 1524).
9. Ibidem, 1062 D. Here is another remarkable instance: ". . . De figuris veteris Testamenti, quae tametsi jam cessarunt velut umbrae exorta luce, tamen propter nos olim scriptis prodita sunt, quibus praefacta mysteria ministrant salutarem doctrinam, etiam

ex illis quae videbantur supervacanea . . . Quae scripta sunt in veteri Testamento, per Euangelium vel exhiberi, vel aperiri, ne Gentes crederent illa ad se non pertinere." LB VI, 644 D–E (Annotationes, 1535).

10. LB V, 29 C–E.

11. Ibidem, 869 E-870 A.

12. Ibidem, 30 B (Enchiridion); LB IV, 588 F–589 A (Instit. princ. Christ., 1516).

13. See Markish, *Znakomstvo s Erazmom*, pp. 101 ff.

14. ASD II-5, 168 (n. 2201: Syleni Alcibiadis, 1515).

15. For example, LB V, 142 B (Paraclesis, 1516).

16. ASD I-1, 645 (Ciceronianus, 1528).

17. ASD I-5, 236.

18. OE X, 171 (n. 2774, 80–83).

19. LB V, 91 C–D (Ratio verae theologiae, 1518).

20. LB VII, 224 C (Paraphr. in Marc., 1523).

21. LB V, 372 A–B (Enarr. Psalmi 33, 1530). Compare Blumenkranz, *Judenpredigt* . . . , p. 120.

22. LB V, 829 D–830 A (Ecclesiastes, 1535).

23. Ibidem, 30 B (1504).

24. ASD IV-2, 75.

25. LB VII, 82 A (Paraphr. in Matt., 1522).

26. Ibidem, 205 E (Paraphr. in Marc., 1523).

27. LB V, 575 A (De misericordia Dom., 1524).

28. ASD V-1, 208; see also 230; compare Blumenkranz, *Les auteurs chrétiens* . . . , p. 96.

29. ASD V-i, 388 (De praepar. ad mortem, 1533).

30. LB VI, f⁰ *4 (r.)—*5.

31. Ibidem, f⁹ *5.

32. LB V, 578 B–C. Compare Simon, pp. 104–105.

33. Ibidem, 427 C (Enarr. Psalmi 38).

34. ASD IV-1, 182. Compare LB V, 1008 B–C (Ecclesiastes, 1535).

35. Ibidem, 1028 E–1029 B.

36. Compare also: ". . . Scriptura Veteris Instrumenti sermonem suum ad populi rudis affectus attemperat, modo minitans externa incommoda, modo pollicens hujus saeculi commoda . . ." Ibid., 781 F–782 A.

37. Ibidem, 132 B.

38. LB VI, 926 C.

39. OE III, 127 (n. 701, 35–36) [CWE, 5:181—A.O.].

40. Ibidem, nn. 694, 697, 700, 701, 703, 713 (2 November–15 November 1517).
41. Ibidem, 58–59 (n. 636, 1–11, 28–34), 25 July 1517. See also ASD IX-1, 136, 138, 140 (Spongia, 1523).
42. ASD I-3, 267 sq. (Colloquia: Apotheosis Capnionis, 1522).
43. OE IV, 43 sq. (n. 1006).
44. Allen, ibidem, 42 (introduction to n. 1006).
45. Allen, OE III, 122n.
46. Ibidem, 122 (n. 697, 11–13). Erasmus ordered a Latin translation of Pfefferkorn's book and sent it to some of his friends: Allen, ibidem (note).
47. See, for example, Huizinga, *Erasmus*, pp. 128–129, 131–133.
48. OE III, 128 (n. 703, 1–7), 4 November [1517].
49. Ibidem, 358 (n. 856, 20–21).
50. Ibidem, 253 (n. 798, 19–28).
51. Ibidem, 252 (n. 797, 3–4).
52. See Chapter 4.
53. Allen, OE III, 109n. This is obliquely confirmed by letters nn. 707 and 722 (OE III, 134, 151), from November 1517, where news of successful work on the re-edition of the New Testament is accompanied by praise for Adrian.
54. Ibidem, 259 (n. 797, 3–4).
55. ASD I-3, 333 sq. (Colloquia: Diversoria).
56. OE V, 434 (n. 1437, 98–99).
57. LB VII, 34 C, 1135 A (Paraphr. in Matt., Paraphr, in Jac., 1522, 1520).
58. LB IX, 577 A–578 C, 856 D–857 F (Supput. errorum Beddae, 1527; Declar. ad cens. Lutetiae, 1532).
59. I cite for comparison the work by G. Marc'Hadour, *The Bible in the Works of St. Thomas More*, 5 vols. (Niewcoop, 1969–1972).
60. *Hieronymi lucubrationes* II, 6.
61. Ibidem, 11. See also *Hieronymi lucubrationes I*, 311 (in "Catalogum scriptorum ecclesiasticorum"); IV, 12 B (in "In Danielem praefatio").
62. LB V, 92 C.
63. LB VI, 926 C.
64. ". . . quid illos [sc. Hebraeos] moverit, facile divinet, qui libros eos attentius legerit." LB IX, 1221 B.
65. LB V, 427 D (Enarr. Psalmi 38, 1532).
66. ASD V-1, 278 (Symbolum).

67. LB V, 1049 E.

68. "Quod si quis meo velit uti consilio, statim a tradita loquendi ratione proponet Proverbia Solomonis, Ecclesiasticum et Librum Sapientiae . . ." ASD IV-1, 180. See also praise of Proverbs: ASD I-3, 242 (Colloquia: Convivium religiosum, 1522), ASD V-1, 169 (Modus orandi, 1535).

69. OE V, 109 (n. 1304, 395–397).

70. LB V, 313 D–F (Enarr. Psalmi 22, 1530).

71. Ibidem, 429 E (Enarr. Psalmi 38, 1532).

72. Ibidem, 466 F–467 A.

73. Kisch, *Erasmus' Stellung* . . . , p. 35.

74. OE VIII, 433 (n. 2315, 171–176), [c. 14 May 1530]. On the "various people" who approached Erasmus with a request of this sort, see OE VI, 69 (n. 1571, 46–48), 28 April 1525; 94, 102 (n. 1581, 291–294, 672–675), 15 June 1525; OE VIII, 12 (n. 2083, 16–21), 6 January 1529. As for the motivation of refusing the request, its second half had been given, in almost the exact same words, seven years earlier: "Scripsimus et in Psalmos duos commentarium . . . Verum hic non solum deterret operis tum magnitudo tum difficultas, verum etiam turba commentariorum, ut periculum sit, ne prophetiam obruant citius, quam explanent." OE I, 21, 11–15 (n. 1), 30 January 1523, [4]. It is very interesting and important that for all the formal distinction between "explication" (enarratio), as Erasmus names the majority of his interpretations of the psalms, and paraphrase, in essence this is one and the same genre. Erasmus recognized this himself; he calls his interpretation of Psalm 3 a "paraphrase" and announces in the introduction that people want a paraphrase of the entire Psalter from him, on the model of his New Testament paraphrases, but he says that the task is not possible to complete. (LB V, 233 A–234 A). See also D. Harth, *Philologie und praktische Philosophie. Untersuchung zum Sprach- und Traditionsverständnis des Erasmus von Rotterdam* (München, 1970), pp. 155 ff.

75. See, for example, Aldridge; Bludau; G. Chantraine, "Erasme, lecteur des psaumes" (*Colloquia Erasmiana Turonensia* [Toronto and Buffalo, 1972], vol. 2); J. Etienne, "La meditation des Ecritures selon Erasme" (*Scrinium Erasmianum*, [Leyde, 1969] vol. 2); J. B. Payne, "Toward the Hermeneutics of Erasmus" (ibidem); H. Schlingensiepen, "Erasmus als Exeget" (*Zeitschrift für Kirchengeschichte* 48, N.F., 11, 1929). The article by Chantraine has a particular place in this highly selective list, since it is the only

one of which I am aware that is dedicated exactly to Erasmus' Old Testament exegesis. The best general article, in my opinion, is that of Payne.

76. For example, Aldridge, pp. 30–35. Erasmus' attitude to the allegorical method is examined not only in specialized works (such as those cited in the preceding note) but also in nearly all general monographs.

77. For more detail see Harth, pp. 163 ff.

78. For example, LB V, 124 E–125 A, 1038 E, 174 A–B, 372 E.

79. For example, ibidem, 1027 A–1028 A, 1028 D–1029 D, 1030 F–1031 C–D, 1033 A–B.

80. For example, ibidem, 825 B–C, 1038 E, 1043 C–D, 1044 D–E.

81. Ibidem, 1045 E–1046 A.

82. In Erasmus' opinion, this was how it was called by the Doctors of the Church. The division of a single spiritual sense into the tropological, allegorical, and anagogical was the work of most recent theologians (neoterici); incidentally, Erasmus not only did not reject such a classification, he even found it useful. LB V, 1034 D–1035 A (Ecclesiastes).

83. Ibidem, 1038 E, 1043 C–D.

84. Ibidem, 825 B–C. Compare Simon, p. 95.

85. LB V, 1044 D.

86. Ibidem, 540 F (Enarr. Psalmi 85, 1528).

87. See E. Schneider, *Das Bild der Frau im Werk des Erasmus von Rotterdam* (Basel, 1955), pp. 72 ff.

88. LB VI, 580 D (Annotationes, 1516–1519–1522–1535).

89. LB VII, 569 A (Paraphr. in Ioan., 1523); LB VI, 709 F (Annotationes, 1527); ASD IV-1, 303 (Lingua, 1525).

90. LB VII, 469 D–470 B (Paraphr. in Luc., 1523).

91. Ibidem, 560 B (Paraphr. in Iona., 1523).

92. Ibidem, 788 E–F (Paraphr. in Rom., 1517).

93. LB V, 8 C–E (Enchiridion, 1504).

94. ASD IV-1, 79 (Paneg. ad Philippum, 1514).

95. LB VII, 569 A (Paraphr. in Ioan., 1523).

96. LB V, 313 A–B (Enarr. Psalmi 22, 1530).

97. Ibidem, 200 A–201 C (Enarr. Psalmi 2, 1522); *Hieronymi lucubrationes* III, 58 A (in "Ep. adv Vigilianum", 1516); LB VI, 486 F (Annotationes, 1516); LB V, 197 E–200 A (Enarr. Psalmi 2).

98. Ibidem, 977 F–978 A (Ecclesiastes, 1535). Parenthetically it should be noted that Lev Tolstoy considered the scene of Joseph

Notes to Pages 45–49

meeting with his brothers to be one of the peaks of world literature and always cried when he read it.

99. ASD V-1, 165 (Modus orandi, 1535).
100. LB IX, 154 A (Apologia ad notat. Lei, 1520).
101. LB V, 86 D–E (Ratio verae theologiae, 1518).
102. Ibidem, 993 B (Ecclesiastes).
103. ASD IV-1, 294–300.
104. Ibidem, 336–369.
105. Erasmus confuses not only chapters but even books. For example: "Apud Hieremiam indignatur Dominus his, qui . . . convictia iaciebant in montes Israel . . ." (ASD IV-1, 302, Lingua). In fact, this is not Jeremiah but Ezekiel (36:1–7). The commentary to ASD gives an incorrect reference to Jeremiah 20:10.
106. LB IX, 393 C (Epist. adv. Stunicam, 1529).

CHAPTER IV

1. For example, LB V, 591 A (Virg. et mart. comparatio, 1523), 273 D–F (Enarr. Psalmi 4, 1525); LB VII, 287 B (Paraphr. in Luc., 1523).
2. LB V, 33 A (Enchiridion, 1504).
3. LB X, 1507 D (Hyperaspistes II, 1527). Compare LB VI, 558 B–C (Annotationes, 1516).
4. Ibidem, 553 F–554 A (Annotationes, 1516). Compare also LB VI, 616 F (Annotationes, 1527); LB V, 231 B (Enarr. Psalmi 2, 1522); LB X, 1518 F–1519 A (Hyperaspistes II).
5. LB VII, 547 B–C (Paraphr. in Ioan., 1523).
6. LB V, 410 E (Enarr. Psalmi 33, 1530). Compare the very significant passage from the paraphrase of Luke: "Habent autem proprium illud ac genuinum ceremoniae Pharisaicae, quae rebus corporalibus constant, ut gignant obtrectationes, suspiciones malas, perversa judicia, dissidium, odium et rixas. Jesus igitur intelligens, hanc esse praecipuam pestem Euangelicae pietatis, acriter coarguit Pharisaicam superstitionem" LB VII, 835 C–D.
7. Ibidem, 113 A–B (Paraphr. in Matt., 1522).
8. LB V, 235 F (Enarr. Psalmi 22, 1530).
9. ". . . crassitudo . . . gentis Judaicae, quae in rebus carnalibus ponebat fiduciam et gloriam suam." LB VII, 569 D (Paraphr. in Ioan.).
10. Ibidem, 358 A, 377 E (Paraphr. in Luc., 1523); LB V, 513 C, 534 A (Enarr. Psalmi 85, 1528).

11. Ibidem, 102 A (Ratio verae theologiae, 1518). Compare LB VII, 89 D (Paraphr. in Matt.).

12. LB VI, 559 C (Annotationes, 1519).

13. LB V, 86 B (Ratio verae theologiae). Compare: ". . . Ut Judaeorum natio tum omnibus . . . orbis nationibus erat peculiariter invisa, ita vicissim omnes exsecrebantur illi, ceu impuros, prophanos, et impios . . . Tantum erat praecisae pelliculae supercilium." LB VI, 549–550 (In Epist. ad Rom. argumentum, 1518).

14. Ibidem, 85 D (Annotationes, 1516). Compare ibidem, 114 E.

15. For example, in the paraphrases: LB VII, 213 B, 377 A, 377 F, 754 A (1523–1524).

16. For example: LB VI, 60 F (Annotationes, 1527); LB VII, 410 F (Paraphr. in Luc.); ASD V-1, 150 (Modus orandi, 1535).

17. ASD IV-1, 316 (a525). Compare: ". . . Judaeus . . . nihil aliud novit, quam invidere." LB VII, 396 D–E (Paraphr. in Luc., 1523).

18. Ibidem, 502 B (Paraphr. in Ioan., 1523).

19. LB V, 248 E–F (Enarr. Psalmi 4, 1525). Compare LB VII, 108 C–D (Paraphr. in Matt., 1522).

20. Ibidem, 812 D (Paraphr. in Rom., 1517).

21. See Chapter 2, note 17.

22. LB V, 528 F–529 B.

23. LB VI, 926 C (Annotationes, 1519).

24. Ibidem, 549–550 (In Epist. ad Rom. argumentum, 1518).

25. Ibidem, 981–982 (In Epist. ad Hebr. argumentum, 1518).

26. For example, LB V, 87 E (Ratio verae theologiae, 1518); LB VII, 730 C (Paraphr. in Acts, 1524).

27. Credat Iudaeus Apella, Horatius, Sat. I, V, 32.

28. ". . . Difficilis ad credendum natio . . ." LB VII, 3 A (Paraphr. in Matt.).

29. Ibidem, 333 F (Paraphr. in Luc.), 518 E (Paraphr. in Ioan.); LB V, 253 C (Enarr. Psalmi 4, 1525).

30. LB VII, 487 F (Paraphr. in Luc.).

31. Ibidem, 4 A (Paraphr. in Matt.).

32. Ibidem, 600 A (Paraphr. in Ioan.).

33. Ibidem, 384 D–E (Paraphr. in Luc.).

34. Ibidem, 540 C, D–E (Paraphr. in Ioan.).

35. ". . . gens querula et morosa . . ." Ibidem, 718 B (Paraphr. in Acts).

36. Ibidem, 197 E–F (Paraphr. in Marc., 1523).

37. ". . . Nec erat illis religio in crucem agere proximum, a quo tantum acceperant beneficiorum, etiam secundum carnem, ut illis

condonemus, quod mysterium consilii divini nondum intellige-
bant." LB V, 251 B (Enarr. Psalmi 4, 1525).
38. LB VII, 819 C–D, E (Paraphr. in Rom., 1517); ASD V-1, 318
(Symbolum, 1533); LB V, 774 F (Ecclesiastes, 1535).
39. LB VII, 123 E (Paraphr. in Matt., 1522), 460 D (Paraphr. in
Luc., 1523); ASD I-2, 62 (De pueris instituendis, 1529).
40. For example: LB II, 959 E (n. 3001: Dulce bellum inexpertis, 1515); ASD IV-2, 72, 74–75, 78 (Querela pacis, 1517); LB VI,
242 C (Annotationes, 1519).
41. LB II, 963 A–B (n. 3001: Dulce bellum inexpertis).
42. Ibidem; OE III, 282–283 (n. 811), [c. 13 April 1518].
43. LB V, 354 C.
44. LB VII, 1037 C–D, 1073 A–B (1519).
45. LB V, 81 C (Ratio verae theologiae, 1518). This does not
prevent him from condemning the severity of corporal punishments which Proverbs (13:24) and Ecclesiasticus (30:12) demand
for stubborn children. ASD I-2, 62 (De pueris instituendis, 1529).
46. ASD I-1, 406, 408 (De conscrib. epistolis, 1522), 155 (Comment. in Nucem, 1523). Compare though LB VII, 288 D (Paraphr.
in Luc.). There is an interesting exchange of opinions on this
point between Telle, who holds that on this question Erasmus
tends toward Mosaism (Telle, p. 463), and J. C. Margolin (ASD
I-1, 403n), who does not agree.
47. LB VI, 698 B–C (Annotationes, 1519). Comments of the
opposite sort are very numerous; for example: LB VII, 233 E (Paraphr. in Marc., 1523); LB V, 618 D (Christ. matrim. institutio,
1526).
48. LB VI, 702 C (Annotationes, 1519).
49. LB V, 799 D–E (Ecclesiastes, 1535).
50. LB VII, 200 B–C (Paraphr. in Marc., 1523), 324 D (Paraphr. in Luc., 1523). It is interesting to juxtapose these passages
with the description of Christian holiday gaiety in the "Colloquia": ASD I-3, 525-526 (Ichthyophagia, 1526).
51. LB IV, 784 C (Apologia adv. Sutorem, 1525).
52. LB X, 1277 F (Hyperaspistes I, 1526).
53. ASD I-3, 503–504 (1526). Compare also LB V, 155 B (Ex-
omologesis, 1525): ". . . hoc confessionis onus [the subject is
deathbed confession], quod solum plus habet sarcinae, quam uni-
versa lex Mosaica . . ."; ibidem, 646 F (Christ. matrim. institutio,
1526): on vows among the Jews and Christians; LB IX, 1146 D–C
(Apologia adv. rhapsodias Alb. Pii, 1531).

Notes to Pages 53–56

54. LB VII, 806 C–D (1517).
55. See, for example, LB V, 575 D (De misericordia Dom., 1524: God's mercy for the Jews); LB X, 1462 C (Hyperaspistes II, 1527: the holiness of many Jews); LB V, 864 B–C (Ecclesiastes, 1535: the Jews as the best nation of antiquity). For the chosen nature of the Jews see also LB VI, 562 D (Annotationes, 1516).
56. For example: LB VII, 526 E, 529 B, 529 E (Paraphr. in Ioan., 1523).
57. For example: "Iudaei omnes suae gentis fratres appellabant, sed peculiarius cognatos. Dominos autem Iudaeus erat, natus ex Iudaeis . . ." ASD V-1, 242 (Symbolum, 1533). See also OE II, 104 (n. 337, 503–504), [May] 1515; LB V, 473 E (Enarr. Psalmi 83, 1533).
58. LB VII, passim.
59. Ibidem, 131 C–D (1522). Compare ibidem, 228 D–E, 257 F, 265 B (Paraphr. in Marc.).
60. Ibidem, 267 C–D.
61. Ibidem, 266 E.
62. Ibidem, 720 E–F (Paraphr. in Acts, 1524).
63. Ibidem, 637 D.
64. *Kirche und Synagoge*, 1:37–39.
65. Blumenkranz, *Judenpredigt* . . . , pp. 191–192; *Kirche und Synagoge*, 1:98.
66. LB VII, 461 A (Paraphr. in Luc., 1523).
67. Ibidem, 634 E, 636 B–C (Paraphr. in Ioan., 1523).
68. Ibidem, 458 B (Paraphr. in Luc.).
69. Ibidem, 267 E (Paraphr. in Marc., 1523).
70. Ibidem, 141 A, 141 E, 142 C (Paraphr. in Matt., 1522).
71. Ibidem, 267 C (Paraphr. in Marc.).
72. Ibidem, 636 A (Paraphr. in Ioan.).
73. Ibidem, 634 B–C.
74. Ibidem, 140 F–141 A (Paraphr. in Matt.).
75. Blumenkranz, *Juifs et Chrétiens* . . . , p. 270–271.
76. LB VII, 697 D–E (Paraphr. in Acts).
77. Ibidem, 461 F (Paraphr. in Luc.).
78. Ibidem, 261 B–C (Paraphr. in Marc.).
79. Ibidem, 449 A (Paraphr. in Luc.).
80. Ibidem, 323 B (Paraphr. in Luc.). Compare: "Multum debemus Pharisaeorum malitiae, quae subinde Dominum provocat ad explicandam Euangelicam doctrinam." Ibidem, 176 D (Paraphr. in Marc.).

81. LB V, 1266 F (De taedio et pavore Christi, 1504).
82. Ibidem, 1267 A, 1285 A.
83. OE I, 259 (n. 111, 205–210), ⟨October 1499⟩.
84. LB V, 1267 E.
85. ". . . procurata sunt a Judaeis quasi [NB!] sollicitis, ne qua pars vaticiniorum . . . videretur praetermissa . . ." Ibidem, 215 E.
86. Ibidem, 215 C.
87. LB VI, 444 D–E.
88. LB V, 249 C.
89. LB X, 1490 A.
90. ". . . Accessit . . . etiam concordia. Quidquid potuerunt Scribae versutia, Pharisaei peritia, Seniores auctoritate, Anna et Caiphas muneris dignitate, populus clamoribus ac tumultu, id omne expeditum est in Christum . . ." LB V, 543 C–D.
91. Ibidem, 543 B–C. Compare LB IX, 670 A–B (Supput, errorum Beddae, 1527).
92. LB V, 543 F–544 A.
93. Ibidem, 383 A (Enarr. Psalmi 33, 1530).
94. Markish, *Znakomstvo s Erazmom,* pp. 158–159.
95. Blumenkranz, *Les auteurs chrétiens . . .* , p. 86. *Kirche und Synagoge,* 1:108–109.
96. It is apropos to recall the classic formula of orthodoxy; when asked the question "Do you believe?" the orthodox man answers, "I believe, Lord help my unbelief."
97. ". . . ruinae fuit occasio . . ." LB VII, 863 A (Paraphr. in Cor., 1519).
98. Ibidem, 115 C–D (Paraphr. in Matt., 1522). Compare ibidem, I E–2 A.
99. Ibidem, 59 C.
100. Ibidem, 124 B. Compare: "Qui nec tot tantisque . . . testimoniis commoverentur, nec benefactis ac benignis verbis allicerentur, nec minis terrerentur, nec aeternae vitae desiderio provocarentur ad fidem, nec gehennae metu resipiscentur ab incredulitate, certe palam esset omnibus eos suo merito perire . . ." Ibidem, 451 B–C (Paraphr. in Ioan., 1523).
101. LB X, 1412 A–1413 B, 1429 D–1430 A, 1437 F. sq.
102. Ibidem, 1412 C.
103. This follows Augustine precisely. See Blumenkranz, *Judenpredigt . . .* , p. 190.
104. LB X, 1412 E–F.
105. Ibidem, 1413 B.

106. Compare with John Chrysostum, probably the most pronounced enemy of the Jews among the Church Fathers, who even today has a powerful effect on anti-Semitic propaganda and practice; his main argument against the Jews and against dealing with them was deicide. *Kirche und Synagoge*, 1:163.

107. *Kirche und Synagoge*, 1:36.

108. Blumenkranz, *Judenpredigt* . . . , pp. 181–183.

109. Blumenkranz, *Les auteurs chrétiens* . . . , pp. 38, 59, 85.

110. For example, LB VII, 166 D (Paraphr. in Marc., 1523), 469 D Paraphr. in Luc., 1523).

111. Ibidem, 283 D (Paraphr. in Luc.).

112. LB V, 244 B.

113. ". . . quibus apud Judaeos vetitum erat jejunare." LB V, 739 E.

114. LB VII, 672 F.

115. LB V, 8 A–B.

116. Ibidem, 206 A–B (Enarr. Psalmi I, 1515).

117. Blumenkranz, *Judenpredigt* . . . , p. 185. The Augustinian tradition survived until the sixteenth century; Erasmus' contemporaries in various countries termed "Hebraei" also those Christians who taught the Hebrew language. Use of the word in this sense also occurs with Erasmus: OE III, 307 (n. 836, 7–8), 26 April 1518; OE VII, 246 (n. 1806, 41), 30 March 1527. A less clear example occurs in LB VI, 438 F (1519), where the subject could be either a Christian or a convert.

118. LB V 118 D (Ratio verae theologiae, 1518).

119. LB VI, 838 E.

120. ASD IV-1, 287, 297, 305, 310, 325.

121. OE VIII, 117 (n. 2136, 24), 30 March 1529; OE IX, 259 (n. 2486, 14), 16 April 1531.

122. LB VII, 702 B (1524).

123. Ibidem, 704 D.

124. For example, ibidem, 708 B, 712 B, 728 B–C.

125. For example, Acts 6:1. See LB VII, 689 E: in this case the paraphrase does not remove the ambiguity.

126. Ibidem, 829 A (1517).

127. Ibidem, 890 A (1519).

128. Ibidem, 752 C (1524).

129. Simon, passim.

130. It was only in the Middle Ages that the Church finally and decisively announced its claim to the called "the true (or new)

Jews," not just "the true Israel." Blumenkranz, *Juifs et Chré-tiens* . . . , p. 239.

131. This fantastic etymology springs from the time of the Church Fathers and becomes a common point in the Middle Ages, Blumenkranz, *Les auteurs chrétiens* . . . , p. 202.

132. For example, LB VI, 11 F (Annotationes, 1516).

133. LB V, 249 C (Enarr. Psalmi 4, 1525).

134. Ibidem, 261 F. Compare also LB VII, 311 B (Paraphr. in Luc., 1523), 639 D (Paraphr. in Ioan., 1523), 665 A, 734 D (Paraphr. in Acts, 1524); ". . . Judaei sunt, quicumque profitentur nomen Jesu, et mentem habent a terrenis cupiditatibus circumcisam . . ." LB V 1352 A (in hymnum De Epiphania Jesu commentariolus, 1524); ". . . Unde nobis exorietur Esdras aliquis, qui hanc linguarum confusionem redigat ad linguam Iudaicam, hoc est linguam profitentem veritatem Euangelicam?" ASD IV-1, 366 (Lingua, 1525); ASD V-1, 240 (Symbolum, 1533), LB IV, 940 C–D (Ecclesiastes, 1535).

135. "Populus Judaeorum—spiritualis Israel." LB VII, 303 A–B (Paraphr. in Luc., 1523).

136. LB V, 609 E (Epistola consolatoria, 1527).

137. "Filii Sion." Ibidem, 509 A (Enarr. Psalmi 85, 1528).

138. "Habet Israel, hoc est Ecclesia . . ." ASD IV-1, 302 (Lingua 1525).

139. ASD V-1, 272 (Symbolum, 1533). See also LB V, .315 C (Enarr. Psalmi 22, 1530): the church as successor to the synagogue, the concept of succession.

140. Ibidem, 703 A (Christ. matrim. institutio, 1526); 548 C–D, 549 A (Enarr. Psalmi 85, 1528).

141. LB VI, 693 D (Annotationes, 1516); LB V, 621 D (Christ. matrim. institutio); ASD V-1, 106 (Virginis Lauretanae liturgia, 1525).

142. Ibidem, 272–273 (Symbolum, 1533).

143. Ibidem, 273.

144. LB V, 1230 A (Paean Virgini Matri dicendus, c. 1500); LB VII, 516 D (Paraphr. in Ioan., 1523).

145. Ibidem, 242 F–243 A (Paraphr. in Marc., 1523).

146. Ibidem, 252 D–F.

147. Ibidem, 450 C (Paraphr. in Luc., 1523).

148. Ibidem, 397 E (Paraphr. in Luc.).

149. For example, LB VI, 727 C (Annotationes, 1535); LB V, 320 D (Enarr. Psalmi 22, 1523), 477 A (Enarr. Psalmi 83, 1533).

150. ASD V-1, 106 (Virginis Lauretanae liturgia, 1525).

151. LB VII, 166 B (Paraphr. in Marc., 1523).

152. LB V, 1333 B, 332 F, 478 B, 98 C. Here and further on are just *examples* to show the use of the various epithets.

153. LB VII, 356 E.

154. Ibidem, 387 A.

155. ASD I-1, 638; LB V, 1190 C.

156. Ibidem, 530 F; LB VII, 527 B, 535 E, 739 B; LB V, 548 F.

157. Ibidem, 374 A.

158. LB VI, 818 F, 547–548; LB IX, 1199 A.

159. LB V, 375 C.

160. Ibidem, 547 B; LB VI, 133 D; LB VII, 89 C.

161. Ibidem, 6 F.

162. Ibidem, 535 B–D, 536 B.

163. LB IX, 1130 C; LB V, 1079 C, 1192 D.

164. LB VII, 7 B.

165. Ibidem, 740 A.

166. Ibidem, 723 A.

167. LB IX, 830 C, 892 A. The review of the French edition of my book mentioned above (Chapter 2, note 90) accuses me of faulty interpretation of this passage, since the subject is not "Jews in general, but Judeo-Christians," who had demanded that Apostle Peter permit them to observe as they had before the commandments concerning the cleanliness of food (kashrut). In the following chapter I demonstrate that when he speaks of Jews, Erasmus means a people, a national group, national psychology, a national affiliation, and not a religion. This is true in regard to the Jews contemporary to Erasmus, and it is a hundred times even more true in regard to the Jews of Gospel times, when Christianity had not yet separated from Judaism, of which the Judeo-Christians are an example. Their "invincibilis importunitas" (which might also be translated in another way, such as "indomitable impertinence") comes from their Jewish nature; this is a trait inherent in every member of their tribe. This is precisely Erasmus' idea of which the array of epithets I offer can leave no doubt.

168. LB VII, 76 A.

169. Ibidem, 246 C.

170. Blumenkranz, *Judenpredigt* . . . , pp. 187–189.

171. Blumenkranz, *Les auteurs chrétiens* . . . , passim.

CHAPTER V

1. LB II, 968 A (Adagia, n. 3001).
2. LB V, 142 F.
3. LB VI, 9 B.
4. OE II, 491 (n. 541, 133–152), 26 February 1516 (7). [CWE, 4:266–268—A.O.]
5. Kisch, *Erasmus' Stellung* . . . , pp. 6–7.
6. OE II, 501 (n. 549, 11–13), 10 March 1516/7?/[CWE, 4:279—A.O.]
7. ASD IV-2, 80.
8. LB VII, 808 F–809 A.
9. Blumenkranz, *Judenpredigt* . . . , p. 177.
10. OE II, 501–502 (n. 549, 36–44), 10 March 1516/7?/[CWE, 4:281—A.O.].
11. OE III, 108–109 (n. 686, 5–13). For complimentary or positive remarks on Adrian see also: ibidem, 114 (n. 691, 20–22), 30 October 1517; 134 (n. 707, 10–11), ⟨November⟩ 1517; 150 (n. 721, 9), ⟨November 1517⟩; 151 (n. 722), 30 November ⟨1517⟩. [CWE, 4:279–281—A.O.].
12. This is a persistent Spanish tradition, dating right back to the first forced conversions of 612–620. *Kirche und Synagoge*, 1:105. There seems to be no discussion of a direct influence by this tradition on Erasmus, in spite of the hostility to the Marranos which may be heard in the two passages cited above; to these might be added another, contemptuous mention in a letter of 2 November 1517 (OE III, 116, n. 694, 5–6). Even so there is ample justification to juxtapose his position with the views of the jurist Ulrich Zasius, Erasmus' contemporary and acquaintance. Zasius held openly that baptism did not turn a Jew into a non-Jew, that "the acceptance of faith does not destroy the native elements." *Questiones de parvulis Iudaeorum baptisandis*, 1508, p. 29b, as cited in Kisch, *Zasius* . . . , p. 69.
13. For example, "Ego nec Reuchlinista sum nec ullius humanae factionis. Ista dissidii nomina detestor. Christianus sum et Christianos agnosco; Erasmistas non feram, Reuchlinistas non novi Cum Reuchlino praeter civilem amicitiam nihil intercedit . . ." OE IV, 121 (n. 1041, 13–16), ⟨c. November 1519⟩.
14. OE II, 78–79 (n. 334, 185–198).
15. OE III, 589 (n. 967, 69–70), 18 May ⟨1519⟩ [CWE, 6:368—A.O.]

Notes to Pages 70–73

16. Compare Ferguson, W. K., *Europe in Transition, 1300–1520* (London, 1962), p. 544.

17. OE III, 117–118 (n. 694, 37–95) [CWE, 5:167–170—A.O.].

18. Ibidem, 122 (n. 697, 13–15) [CWE, 5:175–176—A.O.].

19. During Darius' seige of Babylon the Persian Zopyrus cut off his own ears and nose, pretending that he had been mutilated by King Darius, and so gained the trust of the besieged Babylonians, to whom he feigned he had run away. Herodotus, III, 154–158.

20. OE III, 125 (n. 700, 18–25) [CWE, 5:179—A.O.].

21. Ibidem, 127 (n. 701, 20–38). This is the same letter to Johann Cesarius from which a phrase was quoted in Chapter 3 (n. 39) [CWE, 5:181].

22. Ibidem, 128–129 (n. 703, 8–21) [CWE, 5:183–184—A.O.].

23. Ibidem, 143 (n. 713, 7–10) [CWE, 5:204—A.O.].

24. This appears in the literature of western Christianity in the eleventh century: *Kirche und Synagoge,* 1:110–111.

25. Poliakov, 1:80.

26. Sorting out the doubtful qualities of this "judeophilia" is not part of my present task. In addition to what I said in Chapter 1, I might add the opinion of a present-day scholar: "Even Reuchlin, who had had Jewish teachers, disavowed any sympathies with Jews and distinguished them from their ancient teachers and sages." W. L. Gundersheimer, *"Erasmus,* Humanism and the Christian Cabala," *Journal of the Warburg and Courtauld Institutes* 26 (1963), p. 41.

27. Geiger, *Reuchlin,* pp. 263–264.

28. OE IV, 45–46 (n. 1006, 114–143).

29. Ibidem, 45, lines 99–100.

30. This phrase is also seen as ironic by S. Dubnow (*Weltgeschichte des judischen Volkes* [Berlin, 1927], 6:196), and by our contemporary G. Faludy (*Erasmus of Rotterdam* [London, 1970], p. 146). It is seen as seriously meant by Kisch (*Erasmus' Stellung . . . ,* p. 9) and Poliakov 1:245–246.

31. Erasmus complained in one of his letters: "Quorundam odia non queo satis admirari, cum hactenus meis scriptis nemo factus sit uno pilo nigrior." OE III, 551–552 (n. 950, 10–12), 23 April 1519. Allen remarks, "Though very sensitive himself, Erasmus was throughout his life curiously unconscious of the effect that his own biting words could produce on others." Ibidem, 522 n.

32. OE IV, 44, lines 39–48.

33. OE III, 253 (n. 798, 19–28) [CWE, 5:347–348—A.O.].
34. OE II, 599 (n. 593, 15–20), [July 1517] [CWE, 4:398—A.O.].
35. See P. Mestwerdt, *Die Anfänge des Erasmus* (Leipzig, 1917);
A. Hyma *The Youth of Erasmus* (Ann Arbor: 1930).
36. LB V, 132 B. This passage was cited at greater length in
Chapter 3.
37. LB VI, 120 E–F.
38. See *Kirche und Synagoge*, 1:108–109, 121–122, 126–127, 218–
219; Blumenkranz, *Les auteurs chrétiens* . . . , p. 134.
39. The small number of missionary passages (directed against
the Jews) in Erasmus' various works are distinguished by their
abstractness, "academic quality," their calmness of tone and total
absence of fervor and hot-headedness, without which the missionary calling is not possible. See LB VII, 3 A (Paraphr. in
Matt., 1523), 469 B–C (Paraphr. in Luc., 1523); LB V, 248 F–249
C (Enarr. Psalmi 4, 1525); ASD V-1, 230, 232 (Symbolum, 1533);
LB V, 934 D, 989 E–F, 1001 E (Ecclesiastes, 1535).
40. OE IV, 102 (n. 1033, 109–111). Compare LB V, 906 B–C
(Ecclesiastes): theologians of the old school, inveterate Scotists
and Thomists are totally ill-suited for battles of words with Jews
or heretics.
41. OE IV, 81 (n. 1021, 95–99), 10 October 1519. Compare
ibidem, 439–440 (n. 1183), 28 Jaunary 1521.
42. Ibidem, 114, (n. 1039, 41–46).
43. LB VII, 892 C (Paraphr. in 1 Cor.).
44. LB V, 216 B–C.
45. Ibidem, 217 D. Compare also 204 D (the Jews clutch their
empty rituals and detest the Gospel).
46. "In alma urbe foenerant Judaei, saltant Mimi, divinant
Arioli, concionantur Theriacopolae et quid non sit in alma urbe?"
LB IX, 385 B (Apologia ad conclus. Stunicae).
47. Ibidem, 424 E (Apologia ad Caranzam).
48. Poliakov, 1:230–232.
49. LB VII, 76 B–D (Paraphr. in Matt.).
50. Ibidem, 240 C (Paraphr. in Marc.).
51. Ibidem, 246 C–D.
52. Ibidem, 224 E.
53. Ibidem, 401 E (Paraphr. in Luc.).
54. Ibidem, 416 F–417 A.
55. Ibidem, 426 F.
56. Ibidem, 427 E.
57. Ibidem, 432 D.

58. Ibidem, 516 C (Paraphr. in Ioann.).
59. *Kirche und Synagoge*, 1:210.
60. Kisch, *Zasius* . . . , pp. 8–11.
61. LB VII, 638 C–D.
62. LB V, 1220 D–1221 A.
63. Ibidem, 1223 B.
64. Allen, OE II, 416 n.
65. As I have noted, Erasmus also at times called experts in Hebrew "Jews" (Hebraei).
66. OE V, 409 (n. 1425, 3–14), 23(?) February 1524.
67. LB V, 236 B, 240 B (Enarr. Psalmi 3).
68. Ibidem, 247 A–B.
69. Ibidem, 247 C.
70. Ibidem, 271 A.
71. Ibidem, 276 D.
72. Ibidem, 287 E–F.
73. Ibidem, 700 B–C.
74. LB IX, 459 D–E (Divinat. ad not. per Beddam).
75. Ibidem, 463 C.
76. Ibidem, 493 E.
77. LB V, 640 F–641 A.
78. OE VI, 402 (n. 1744, 90–91), [c. 2 September] 1526.
79. LB IX, 563 B (Supput. errorum Beddae).
80. LB VII, 80 E–F (Paraphr. in Matth., 1522).
81. LB IX, 582 D (Supput. errorum Beddae).
82. LB X, 1412 F (Hyperaspistes II, 1527).
83. ASD I-1, 694 (Ciceronianus, 1528).
84. LB V, 474 C–D.
85. Ibidem, 474 A. This idea is repeated in other of Erasmus' works not connected to the Marranoes. See Markish, *Znakomstvo s Erazmom*, pp. 176–177.
86. Kisch, *Zasius* . . . , pp. 38–39, 89–90.
87. LB V, 546 A–C.
88. Ibidem, 551 D–E.
89. Ibidem, 551 A–B.
90. Ibidem, 553 E.
91. Ibidem, 752 C–D.
92. A good deal has been written about Erasmus' monarchism and his aversion to democracy. See, for example, Markish, *Znakomstvo s Erazmom*, pp. 204–207.
93. OE VIII, 113 (n. 2134, 208–220).
94. Ibidem, 194 (n. 2178, 59–63).

95. There were rumors of bands of brigands, partly or wholly made up of Jews, from the sixteenth century on. See Poliakov, 1:253.

96. ASD IX-1, 286 (Contra pseudeuangelicos).

97. LB V, 329 F–330 A.

98. Ibidem, 355 E–F.

99. It is apropos to cite here some of Erasmus' judgments on the Turks, since they serve as an interesting and convincing parallel to the "Jewish pronouncements." "We threaten the Turks with war, as though the sword could and will create Christians, while we also carry a Turk within our own breast" (*Hieronymi lucubrationes I*, 59: in Epist. ad Laetam, 1516). "In my opinion, one ought not make war in the heat of temper even with the Turks. First of all, I maintain that the kingdom of Christ was born, spread, and grew strong in an entirely different manner, and perhaps the kingdom ought not to be defended save in the manner by which it arose and spread . . . If we are to speak of faith, then it multiplied and gained renown through the patient suffering of martyrs, not the spears of soldiers; if there is to be a battle for power, for riches, and property, it is necessary to ponder again and again whether the matter is a Christian one. In the current circumstances of affairs . . . it is possible that we would sooner degenerate into Turks than that they would turn into Christians through our efforts" (ASD IV-1, 218, Institutio principis Christiani, 1516). "It must be wondered whether they reason rightly, those who strive to convert the Turks to Christianity solely with the aid of machines of war. No, rather let resound among them the voice of the theologians, resembling the apostolic [voice], let the purity of [our] life shine forth—then they will become truly Christians" (LB V, 114 B, Ratio verae theologiae, 1518). "Those who are now attacking the Turks, to destroy and plunder them, prefer to take the enemy dead rather than alive. Further, we sooner are chasing Turkish money than the Turks themselves" (LB VI, 250 F, Annotationes, 1519–1522). "We must wish the Turks and all other enemies of Christ's name rather the Lord's mercy than destruction" (ASD V-1, 168, Modus orandi, 1535).

100. LB V, 356 A–C.

101. Ibidem, 364 B.

102. Ibidem, 372 E.

103. Ibidem, 380 A–B.

104. Ibidem, 390 A–B.

105. Ibidem, 401 A.

106. OE IX, 181 (n. 2448, 81–82).
107. Ibidem, 243 (n. 2472, 25–30).
108. Ibidem, 251 (n. 2479, 16–25).
109. LB V, 427 B.
110. Ibidem, 458 B.
111. OE IX, 455 (n. 2615, 406–411).
112. LB V, 1216 E (Precatio pro pace Ecclesiae).
113. LB IX, 821 C–822 B (Declar, ad cens. Lutetiae).
114. Ibidem, 907 A–B.
115. ASD V-1, 212.
116. Ibidem, 240.
117. Ibidem, 273.
118. Ibidem, 305.
119. Ibidem, 302.
120. ASD IX-1, 456.
121. "Et hodie profecto non leve damnum est, Christiana Religione in tantas redacta angustias, quum Turcae et Mahumedani, Judaei, aliaeque nationes, quae Christum vel ignorant prorsus, vel ex parte sunt amplexae, nostris moribus redduntur alieniores ab Ecclesiae Catholicae consortio." LB V, 779 B–C.
122. Ibidem, 813 D.
123. Ibidem, 835 F.
124. Ibidem, 1048 F–1049 A.
125. Ibidem, 813 E–814 D.
126. Ibidem, 813 F–814 A.
127. Ibidem, 950 A–B.
128. Ibidem, 954 F.
129. Ibidem, 1009 A.
130. LB VI, 442 C.
131. See, for example, the article on Erasmus in Isaac Landau, ed., *The Universal Jewish Encyclopedia in Ten Volumes* (New York, 1969), 4:156, where Erasmus has attributed to him a nearly burning love for the Jewish people.
132. Kisch, *Erasmus' Stellung* . . . , pp. 28 ff.
133. OE I, 17, lines 34–39.
134. See about him in L. Feilhenfeld, *Rabbi Josel von Rosheim* (Strassburg, 1898).
135. LB VI, 623 C–D, 626 E–F (Annotationes, 1527–1535, 1535); LB VII, 124 B (Paraphr. in Matt.), 410 A (Paraphr. in Luc.).
136. ASD V-1, 294 (Symbolum, 1533).
137. LB VII, 447 B–C (Paraphr. in Luc.), 95 E–F (Paraphr. in Matt.).

138. LB VII, 813 A–817 A.
139. LB X, 1380 C (Hyperaspistes II, 1527).
140. OE VI, 489 (n. 180, 236–247).
141. Lines 248–252.
142. Lines 270–280 (pp. 489–490).
143. Ibidem, 390 (n. 1379, 244–245), 27 August 1526.
144. It is also possible to interpret this as an attack on "Judaism," the direct heir of the Judaism of Gospel times. However, in the given context such an interpretation does not seem convincing.
145. LB V, 105 C–D.
146. Markish, *Znakomstvo s Erazmom,* pp. 164–168.
147. LB V, 100 D–E.
148. LB VII, 72 A–B.
149. Ibidem, 443 E–F.
150. OE IX, 165 (n. 2443, 310–317), 7 March 1531. The same thing occurs but without the "Jewish parallel." Ibidem, 170–171 (n. 2445, 45–64), 11 March 1531.
151. See, for example, LB X, 1504 E–F (Hyperaspistes II, 1527); LB V, 1060 A–B (Ecclesiastes, 1535).
152. LB X, 1437 A (Hyperaspistes II).
153. LB V, 44 F–45 A.
154. Ibidem, 1068 E–F.
155. *Hieronymi lucubrationes I,* 155 (In Epist. ad Eustochium).
156. LB VI, 343 C (Annotationes); LB VII, 448 B (Paraphr. in Luc.).
157. Ibidem, 681 B (Paraphr. in Acts).
158. OE V, 499 (n. 1469, 34), 26 July 1524.
159. LB V, 260 B–C (Enarr. Psalmi 4).
160. LB X, 1505 F (Hyperaspistes II).
161. OE VIII, 29 (n. 2091, 148), January 1529.
162. LB VI, 180 F (Annotationes).
163. Ibidem, 458 F.
164. Ibidem, 458 E.
165. LB IX, 838 F (Declar. ad cens. Lutetiae).
166. LB VII, 718 B.
167. LB VI, 442 D–E (Annotationes).
168. LB V, 204 C (Enarr. Psalmi 2).
169. OE III, 110 (n. 687, 20), ⟨c. October 1517⟩; 112 (n. 689, 16), 26 October ⟨1517⟩; 113 (n. 690, 11–12), 26 October ⟨1517⟩; 120 (n. 695, 6–7), 2 November 1517; 260 (n. 805, 22, 25), 26 March 1518; 400 (n. 867, 207), ⟨15 October 1518⟩; 416 (n. 877, 33), 19 October ⟨1518⟩.

170. OE X, 314 (n. 2876, 10), 7 November 1533.
171. This is a general point of view, almost a "commonplace." See J. Huizinga, "Erasmus über Vaterland und Nationen," *Gedenkschrift zum 400. Todesjahre des Erasmus von Rotterdam* (Basel, 1936), pp. 34–49.
172. For example, LB V, 15 B–C (Enchiridion, 1504); LB IV, 87–88 (Apophthegmata, 1531); LB V, 844 F–845 A, 907 A (Ecclesiastes, 1535).
173. ". . . Christianum orbem unam esse patriam, Christianam Ecclesiam unam esse familiam eandem gentem, eandem civitatem . . ." (ASD IV-1, 75 Ad Philippum panegyricus, 1514). "Hic [Luc. 4, 25–26] nimirum erat animus Israeliticus in muliere non Israelitica. Adeo apud Deum plus habet momenti animus quam genus" (LB VII, 328 B, Paraphr. in Luc., 1523). "Quod ad Nationes attinet, non est in Christo neque Graecus, neque Barbarus . . . Omnes, si volumus, sumus ejusdem nationis, de qua scriptum est in Deuteronomia [4:7]" (LB V, 908 B, Ecclesiastes, 1535). "Proinde quisquis per baptismum insitus est Christo, ponat veteres affectus, non cogitet, hic Judaeus est, ille Graecus, hic servus, ille liber . . . Absint igitur illae voces hominum, hic Graecus est, hic Barbarus, hic Judaeus . . ." (LB VII, 925 A–B, Paraphr. in 2 Cor., 1519).
174. LB VI, 633 B (Annotationes, 1516).
175. ASD IX-2, 68 (Apol. ad annotationes Stunicae, 1521).
176. LB IX 539 B–C (Supput. errorum Beddae, 1527).
177. LB VI, 121 F (Annotationes, 1519).
178. Blumenkranz, *Les auteurs chrétiens* . . . , p. 149.
179. See the text at note 175, above.
180. ASD IX-2, 94 (Nescio quid suspicionis mihi parit, quod Stunica tam impense favet Hebraeis, ut his omnia velit deberi, quum res nihil tale postulet), 124–125 (Ceterum quod argutatur, quibus elementis Hebraice scribatur nomen Iesu, quando ad me non pertinet . . . aliis Iudaeorum amicis excutiendum relinquo) (Apologia ad annotationes Stunicae, 1521); LB IX 413 E (Apologia ad Caranzam, 1522); 363 D, 372 D (Sic solet Rhetoribus increscere per gradus oratio, nisi forte Stunica servat ordinem Hebraeorum, qui scribunt praepostere) (Apologia ad Blasphemias Stunicae, 1522); 380 B (Alioqui posset in litteris Hebraicis, quas a teneris unguiculis imbibit, non poenitendam operam locare juvandis studiis) (Apologia ad Prodromon Stunicae, 1522); 397 A (. . . Stunica . . . maluit hoc laudis asserere suae linguae) (Epist. apologetica adv. Stunicam, 1529). The re-

viewer of my book already mentioned (see Chapter 2, note 90) writes that "Erasmus' text [which? I cite seven passages here— S.M.] clearly shows that in Erasmus' eyes his critic, who had begun to read Hebrew from early youth, had also 'Judaized' his soul" (Chomarat, p. 199). I am not persuaded from my opinion though; it seems to me that even the last of the passages I cite, where Erasmus calls the Hebrew language (ivrit) "His [that is, Zuñiga's] language," is evidence enough for my position. As for the reviewer's objection that "nothing permits a suspicion that Zuñiga was of Jewish origin" (ibidem), I don't suspect him of such a sin. Further, I don't think that Erasmus himself seriously entertained suspicions along those lines, for otherwise he would not have let pass a chance to accuse his enemy of it directly, instead of limiting himself to venomous hints. The foul and troublesome character of the great humanist is no secret to anyone who has studied Erasmus; I do not think that my reviewer was an exception.

181. Bludau, p. 132.

182. W. K. Ferguson, *Erasmi Opuscula* (The Hague, 1933), pp. 316–317n.

183. Ibidem, 316–317 (lines 2–20).

184. Ibidem, 323–324 (lines 67–73).

185. ASD IX-1, 150 (Spongia, 1523).

186. OE VI, 351 (n. 1717, 33–36), 6 June 1526; 354 (n. 1719, 38–48), ⟨c. 6 June⟩ 1526. ASD I-3, 680 (Colloquia: Opulentia sordida, 1531). OE IX, 395 (n. 2578, 31), ⟨fin. November 1531⟩.

187. Allen, OE VIII, 363 (n. 2275, Introduction).

188. LB X, 1679 E, 1684 B–C (Ad febricitantem responsio, 1529); OE VIII, 364 (n. 2275, 6–10), ⟨February 1530⟩.

189. OE IX, 456–457 (n. 2615, 477–484).

190. See, for example, the polemic with Noël Bédier: LB IX, 507 A (In Beddae censuras elenchus, 1526), 601 F–602 A (Supput. errorum Beddae, 1527).

191. *Hieronymi lucubrationes I*, 199 (In Epitaph. Lic. Betici).

192. LB V, 126 A–B.

193. OE III, 589 (n. 967, 69–74). [CWE, 6:368—A.O.].

194. OE IV, 47 (n. 1006, 161–163).

195. Ibidem, 100 (n. 1033, 35–36); the context is almost exactly the same as in the letter of 18 May.

196. LB VI, 761 F.

197. ASD I-2, 336–337.

198. LB V, 798 D.

199. OE IV, 379 (n. 1160, 1–6).

200. The same is supposed in Gundersheimer, p. 50.

201. See the beginning of this chapter, in the material for 1516–1517. On Ricius as cabalist, see J. L. Blau, The *Christian Interpretation of the Cabala in the Renaissance* (New York: 1944; reprinted 1965), Chapters 5, 9.

202. For example: LB IX, 843 A; LB V, 1142 B, 1136 E, 982 A, 537 A, 754 F; OE VII, 182 (n. 1879, 39–41). Blumenkranz (*Les auteurs chrétiens* . . . , p. 216) notes that the series "heretics-pagans-Jews" comes from antiquity, while "heretics-philosophers-Jews" comes from the pre-Renaissance of the ninth century.

203. Blumenkranz, *Judenpredigt* . . . , p. 195.

204. For example: LB V, 240 B, 1148 D–E, 1171 A, 836 C.

205. LB VII, 501 A.

206. LB V, 548 F.

207. Ibidem, 530 F–531 A.

208. Ibidem, 580 D–E.

209. OE V, 319–320 (n. 1381, 304–312).

210. LB VI, 573 D–E.

211. LB IX, 516 A–B.

212. LB V, 554 E.

213. Ibidem, 1216 E.

214. Ibidem, 399 D–E.

215. Ibidem, 364 (Enarr. Psalmi 28, 1530).

216. Ibidem, 358 A.

217. LB VII, 383 B–C, 393 D–E (Paraphr. in Luc., 1523).

218. Ibidem, 464 C–D.

219. LB V, 245 F–246 A (Enarr. Psalmi 4, 1525), 488 D–E (Enarr. Psalmi 83, 1533).

220. LB IX, 689 B (Supput. errorum Beddae, 1527).

221. LB VII, 571 C (Paraphr. in Rom., 1519).

222. ASD II-5, 136 (n. 2153, 1515).

223. LB V, 1081 B.

224. This tradition begins with Augustine. Blumenkranz, *Judenpredigt* . . . , pp. 195–196.

225. LB V, 476 E (Enarr. Psalmi 83, 1533).

226. Ibidem, 904 B; LB I, 732 D.

227. OE V, 221 (n. 1342, 740–745), 1 February 1523.

228. For example, LB VI, 194 E (Annotationes, 1516): "Quemadmodum et hodie Judaei Rabeni Magistrum vocant, sed insignem et eminentem."

229. ASD I-4, 26 (De pronunciatione, 1528). "Magistri Nostri"

was the title of doctors of theology who did not consider the name "doctores" ("ones who instruct") compatible with the modesty of a theologian.

230. LB V, 138 C (Ratio verae theologiae, 1518).
231. LB IX, 928 C (Declar. ad cens. Lutetiae, 1532).
232. *Erasmi Opuscula,* 319, line 8.
233. LB IX, 522 C.
234. LB VI, 743 E–F (Annotationes, 1522).
235. LB VII, 401 A–B (Paraphr. in Luc., 1523).
236. LB IX, 521 E, 928 A.

CHAPTER VI

1. OE I, 353 (n. 149, 43–47), ⟨16 March⟩ 1501 [CWE, 2:26—A.O.]. The closest mention of that same decision of the Council of Vienne is in OE I, 411 (n. 182, 180–183), ⟨March⟩ 1505. In that letter (lines 168–169) this is emphasized particularly: "Veterum librorum fides de Hebraeis voluminibus examinanda est."
2. Lines 21–26.
3. ASD I-2, 114.
4. See, for example, Markish, *Znakomstvo s Erazmom,* pp. 157–158.
5. LB II, 355 A–B (n. 855: *Illotis manibus,* 1515).
6. OE II, 106 (n. 337, 603–608), ⟨May⟩ 1515.
7. LB VI, **2.
8. Ibidem, 325 F (1516). The year before he put Chaldean in the same rank as Latin, Greek, and Hebrew (LB II, 402 E, n. 1001: *Festina lente*).
9. OE III, 336 (n. 844, 215–216), 15 May 1518.
10. LB VI, 107 F–108 A (Annotationes, 1516).
11. Ibidem, 107 E.
12. *Hieronymi lucubrationes* IV, 55 C.
13. Ibidem; LB VI, 107 D–E (1516). Erasmus repeats the same story (taken from Jerome) a third time, in the dedicatory foreword to his edition of Saint Hilary: OE V, 188 (n. 1334), 5 January 1522 [3].
14. LB VI, 107 E.
15. OE II, 213 (n. 396, 71–76), 1 April 1516; LB VI, 7 B (Annotationes, 1516).
16. OE II, 99 (n. 337, 320–323), ⟨May⟩ 1515.
17. Ibidem, 108 (n. 337, 672–676).

18. Ibidem, 170 (n. 373, 170–175), In annot. Novi Test. prefatio, [December] 1515.

19. Ibidem, 154 (n. 364, 8–15). Later, in 1522, in his main "utopian" work, the dialogue *Convivium religiosum*, Erasmus makes this constituent element even more noticeable; the garden of Eusebius (Erasmus' Christian-humanist variant of the garden of Epicurus) is decorated with instructive maxims in Latin, Greek, and Hebrew (ASD I-3, 234).

20. LB V, 77 E–F.

21. Ibidem, 78 A–B.

22. Ibidem, 78 C.

23. Ibidem, 78 C–79 A. Praise for Agricola's diligence is also in Adagia (LB II, 166 D, n. 339: *Quid cani et balneo?*).

24. Ibidem, 79 B–C.

25. Ch. Béné, *Érasme et Saint Augustin* (Genève, 1969), p. 372. Béné also notes that this view of the three holy languages and their role in the *Ratio* is taken directly from Augustine (see pp. 230–233).

26. LB V, 855 A–C.

27. Ibidem, 1051 F–1055 A.

28. Ibidem, 1052 A.

29. LB IX, 95 C–D (Apologia ad Latomum).

30. OE VIII, 433 (n. 2315, 171–177). For a translation see Chapter 3, the passage marked by note 74.

31. LB IX, 82 C.

32. ASD I-3, 270–271 (Colloquia: De . . . Reuchlino . . . , 1522); LB IX, 769 E–773 B, 782 A (Apologia adv. Sutorem, 1525); OE VI, 115 (n. 1526, 5–8), 2 July 1525; OE VII, 335 (n. 1955, 3–4), 20 February 1528. I would quote particularly the letter to Lazare Baïf, a French humanist and courtier of François I (from 13 March 1531): "Gaudeo quod meditaris esse trilinguis," Erasmus wrote, then immediately following this phrase he lists Baïf's proposed teachers, putting Hebrew first, then Greek, and Latin third. OE IX, 178–179 (n. 2447, 26–29).

33. ASD I-1, 46–47.

34. ASD I-4, 32 (De pronuntiatione, 1528). Béné (p. 367) distorts the sense of the entire text, only giving the doubts of one partner in conversation and omitting the answer of the other.

35. LB II, 1053 A–C.

36. LB IX, 104 F–105 A (Apologia and Latomum, 1519). In the same, purely neutral sense—*Erasmi Opuscula*, p. 152 (Hieronymi vita, 1516).

37. LB IX, 25 B (Apologia ad Fabrum, 1517).
38. LB VI, 142 E (Annotationes, 1519).
39. See, for example, Huizinga, *Erasmus,* pp. 122, 124.
40. LB V, 230 C–D (Enarr. Psalmi 2, 1522).
41. Geiger, *Das Studium der hebräische Sprache . . . ,* p. 4.
42. LB VI, 113 F (Annotationes, 1522).
43. LB V, 267 D (Enarr. Psalmi 4, 1525).
44. Ibidem, 1054 F–1055 A (Ecclesiastes, 1535).
45. OE III, 151 (n. 722, 16–18) [CWE, 5:214—A.O.].
46. OE V, 597–598 (n. 1523, 152–154), 10 December 1524. Compare ASD IX-1, 392 (Epistola ad fratres Germaniae, 1530).
47. LB X, 1268 F–1269 A.
48. LB X, 1487 E–1488 A; 1506 B. In the first of these passages we read: "Vide vero unde petat suppetias, ad idiomate Hebraeorum!" I think it is in this context that words from a letter to the Hellenist Jacques Toussain (13 March 1531) must be evaluated, about the introduction of Hebrew and Greek as subjects in the College Royal, in Paris (Erasmus mistakenly supposed that the king had founded a Collegium Bilingue, on the model of the Louvain Collegium Trilingue): "Quin et illud cordatioris consilii videtur, quod isthic duarum modo linguarum professoribus destinatum sit stipendium, Graecae et Hebraicae, quandoquidem Latina iampridem sic effloruit, ut peculiari professore non egeat" (OE IX, 183, n. 2449, 31–34). In addition to the flattery due a royal Maecenas, this passage also has sarcasm, which becomes wholly obvious and unambiguous in the concluding part of the phrase, where he speaks of the unprecedented flourishing of Latin.
49. LB VI, 478 C (Annotationes, 1516). See also LB IX, 400 A (Epist. apologetica adv. Stunicam, 1529): ". . . Christus ipse Syris Syriace loquens apud Hebraeos exacte loquentes soloecissabat"; LB VI, 171 D–E (Annotationes, 1519): "Neque vero mihi dissimile veri est, Christum populari sermone usum, quae tum promiscue multitudini erat in usu: praesertim, quum apud populum verba faceret."
50. Even though the assertion that the Gospel According to Matthew had been translated from Hebrew originated with Jerome, Erasmus thought it unfounded: *Hieronymi lucubrationes* I, 301; IV, 55 D–56 A, 69 C; LB VI, 47 C–D, 99 F (Annotationes, 1519, 1527); LB IX, 746 E–750 D (Apologia adv. Sutorem, 1525). Erasmus rejects the hypothesis that there was a Hebrew original of the Epistle to the Hebrews even more decisively (LB VI, 47 D).

51. LB VI, 476 D–E (Annotationes, 1516). See also ibidem, 477 F; LB V, 120 D–E (Ratio verae theologiae, 1518).

52. LB VI, 551–552 (In epist. ad Rom. argumentum, 1518). See also ibidem, 1024 D (1516); OE III, 137 (n. 710, 10–11), 13 November 1517; LB X, 329 D–E (Apologia ad Stunicam, 1525).

53. LB VI, 1038 C (1516).

54. Ibidem, 476 E (1516).

55. OE VIII, 259 (n. 2206, 36–54), 19 August 1529.

56. ASD I-1, 643.

57. Ibidem, 644.

58. ASD II-5, 234 (n. 2288: *Extrema extremorum mala*).

59. LB VI, 907 E (1516).

60. Ibidem, 404 F (1522).

61. See also ASD V-1, 226–227 (Symbolum, 1533).

62. LB VI, **2 (back).

63. LB IX, 394 A (Epist. apologetica adv. Stunicam, 1529).

64. Ibidem, 393 D.

65. Ibidem, 659 E (Supputationes errorum Beddae, 1527). See also OE VIII, 260 (n. 2206, 101–103), 19 August 1529: ". . . Hieronymus, qui in Veteri Testamento tropos Hebraicos fere omnes audacter sustulit frustra reclamante Augustino."

66. LB VII, 663 E (Paraphr. in Acts, 1524).

67. LB VI, 815 E (Annotationes, 1516).

68. Ibidem, 244 F (1516).

69. Ibidem, 206 E (1519).

70. Ibidem, 41 F–42 D (1516).

71. Ibidem, 1079 B (1519).

72. LB V, 1089 B (Ecclesiastes, 1535).

73. LB VI, 407 C–E (1519–1522).

74. Ibidem, 234 C (1516).

75. See, for example, Markish, *Znakomstvo s Erazmom*, p. 160, 166.

76. LB V, 1030 B–F (Ecclesiastes, 1535).

77. Ibidem, 401 A–B (Enarr. Psalmi 33, 1531).

78. LB VII, 480 E; ASD IV-1, 310–311.

79. OE IX, 204 (n. 2465, Introduction).

80. Ibidem, 217 (n. 2465, 430–432), 27 March 1531.

81. Ibidem, 302 (n. 2513, 571–575), 25 July 1531.

82. Ibidem, 221 (n. 2465, 603–605).

83. Ibidem, 223 (lines 678–680).

84. *Hieronymi lucubrationes* I, 163 (In Epitaph. Blessilae).

85. LB VI, 144 E–F, 414 F, 467 F–468 E; compare also 622 D–E.
86. For example, ibidem, 259 D–E.
87. LB IX, 25 D, 27 A–B (Apologia ad Fabrum).
88. Ibidem, 196 C (Apologia ad notat. Lei).
89. Erasmus also attests his faithfulness to Jerome later: LB IX, 555 F (Supput. errorum Beddae, 1527).
90. LB IX, 774 B–C (Apologia adv. Sutorem). Compare LB V, 258 F (Enarr. Psalmi 4, 1525).
91. OE VI, 466–467 (n. 1789, 12–17), ⟨March 1527⟩, 490 (n. 1800, 300–309), 24 March 1527; OE VII, 132 (n. 1858, 157–163), 23 August 1527.
92. LB V, 468 D (Enarr. Psalmi 38).
93. Ibidem, 1054 D. Béné (p. 405) notes that Erasmus is repeating Augustine here: De Doctr. Christ. III, II (2). It is striking how closely Erasmus approaches his fated opponent Luther on the paths of antiphilology: "Das Erklärungspringzip, das . . . er beobachtet, ist hicht die Grammatik, sondern die Kenntnis der heiligen Dinge . . . Ohne das Neue Testament würde man sich nicht der hebräischen Sprache zu bedienen wissen; denn ihre Punktation, von der die Bedeutung abhängt, entbehrt der Festigkeit und Bestimmtheit, sie hat zur Zeit des Hieronymus noch nicht existiert, und ein Protest ist gegen sie statthaft, solange sie nicht mit dem Evangelium übereinstimmt." Lewin, pp. 55–56.
94. LB V, 497 B. In the Septuagint translation: ὅτι ἔλεον καὶ ἀλήθειαν ἀγαπᾷ κύριος ὁ θεός, χάριν καὶ δόξαν δώσει.
95. LB VI **4 (back).
96. Ibidem, ***2.
97. The following skeptical evaluation of Augustine as a scholar in general and as a Hellenist in particular is not without interest: ". . . vir ille quidem, quod negari non potest, sanctus, integer, acuto praeditus ingenio, verum pro ingenii simplicitate impense credulus, neque perinde munitus praesidio linguarum, etiamsi non omnino rudis fuit Graecanicae litteraturae, at non eousque doctus, ut Graecos Interpretes expedite posset evolvere." LB VI, 419 D (Annotationes, 1516).
98. Ibidem, 119 D (1527).
99. LB IX, 87 E (Apologia ad Latomum, 1519). Compare also OE III, 321 (n. 843, 355–359), 7 May 1518; LB VI f° ***2 (De duabus postremis editionibus . . .).
100. LB IX, 767 C–D, 791 F–793 E (Apologia adv. Sutorem).

Notes to Pages 133–137

101. Ibidem, 744 B. See also LB VI, 814 C–D (Annotationes, 1519).

102. OE I, 410 (n. 182, 116–119), ⟨March⟩ 1505; *Hieronymi lucubrationes* II, 10 (Erasmus Roterodamus divinarum literarum studiosis omnibus); LB VI, 56 D–57 E (Annotationes, 1527); LB V, 1054 B (Ecclesiastes, 1535).

103. LB IX, 160 E–161 A (Apologia ad notat. Lei, 1520).

104. Ibidem, 156 C–D.

105. See, for example, LB VI, 107 C–D (Annotationes, 1516), 1015 F (1527); LB V, 1096 D (Ecclesiastes, 1535).

106. LB V, 202 C (Enarr. Psalmi 2, 1522).

107. See also LB IX, 25 E (Apologia ad Fabrum, 1517); LB V, 375 E–376 A (Enarr. Psalmi 33, 1531); ibidem, 429 D (Enarr. Psalmi 38, 1532).

108. Lewin; Chapter 5, "Luthers Verhältnis zu jüdischen Schriftauslegung" (pp. 51–61).

109. LB V, 511 A–B. Almost the same appears in LB V, 428 F–429 D (Enarr. Psalmi 33, 1531).

110. For example, LB X, 1307 C sq.

111. Ibidem, 1308 C.

112. LB IX, 517 B–C (Supput. errorum Beddae, 1527).

113. OE IX, 150 (n. 2439, Introduction).

114. "... vir Hebraice longe doctior Reuchlino ..." OE II, 244 (n. 413, 13), 5 June ⟨1516⟩.

115. Ibidem, 333n.

116. LB VI, 438 F, 989 D–E: "Audivi quemdam Hebraeum ... Quidam Hebraeus Hispanus, homo mea sententia, non vulgariter exercitatus in suis litteris, ait ..."

117. The monograph by A. Bludau (*Die beiden erste Erasmus-Ausgaben des Neuen Testaments und ihre Gegner* [Freiburg, 1902]) pays no special attention to Hebrew material.

118. OE II, 167–168 (n. 373, 66–75), In annotationes Novi Testamenti praefatio, ⟨December⟩ 1515.

119. Ibidem, 176 (n. 377, 7).

120. Ibidem, 253 (n. 421, 53–58).

121. *Briefe und Akten zum Leben Oekolampads* ... Bearbeitet von Ernst Staehelin, 2 vols. (Leipzig 1927–1934), 1:27 (n. 21).

122. OE III, 252 (n. 797, 4).

123. LB IX, 131 B–C (Responsio ad annotationes Lei).

124. Ibidem, 249 E (Responsio ad annotationes Lei novas).

125. *Erasmi Opuscula*, 278.

126. ASD IX-2, 66 (Apologia ad annotationes Stunica, 1521).
127. Ibidem, 112.
128. Ibidem, 122.
129. To complete what has been cited above: ibidem, 82, 140, 150, 172.
130. Staehelin, 1:66 (n. 38, Anm. 4).
131. Compare in the letters: ". . . lapsus etiam alienos mihi odiosissime impingens [sc. Stunica], puta typographorum et Oecolampadii . . ." OE IV, 535 (n. 1216, 41–42), 26 April 1521.
132. To judge by the texts of the Leyden collection. Naturally, to draw final conclusions, this must be checked with the first editions and other editions done in Erasmus' lifetime.
133. LB IX, 770 F (Apologia adv. Sutorem).
134. OE I, 405 (n. 181, 36–38), [December] 1504.
135. OE II, 50–51 (n. 324, 31–32), 1 March ⟨1515⟩ [CWE, 3:63—A.O.]. The same words occur in ASD II-5, 40, 485 (n. 2001: *Herculei labores*, 1515); OE II, 77 (n. 334, 122–130), ⟨15 April⟩ 1515; ibidem, 87 (n. 335, 271–275), 21 May 1515. The same idea is in ibidem, 218 (n. 396, 280), 1 April 1516: ". . . Hebraicas litteras degustassem verius quam didicissem." All of these confessions are connected to publication of the works of Jerome, which Erasmus could not have undertaken without the assistance of Hebraicists; in this instance too the assistants are termed "Theseuses."
136. Ibidem, 168 (n. 373, 75–76), In annotationes Novi Testamenti praefatio [CWE, 3:200—A.O.].
137. Ibidem, 259 (n. 423, 61–63).
138. Staehelin, 1:33 (n. 27).
139. LB IX, 47 A (Apologia ad Fabrum, 1517).
140. LB VI, 613 B–C.
141. Ibidem, 684 C.
142. LB IX, 47 A–C.
143. LB V, 217 A (Enarr. Psalmi 2, 1522).
144. Ibidem, 255 C–D (Enarr. Psalmi 4, 1525).
145. Ibidem, 279 A.
146. Ibidem, 400 F (Enarr, Psalmi 33, 1531).
147. LB IX, 417 F (Apologia ad Caranzam 1522).
148. LB X, 1278 F–1279 A (Hyperaspistes I, 1526).
149. LB IX, 245 A.
150. Ibidem, 244 F–245 B (Responsio ad annotationes Lei, 1520). Compare also ibidem, 222 A–B.
151. For example, ibidem, 235 A.

152. ASD IX-2, 79–80 (Apologia ad annotationes Stunicae, 1521).

CONCLUSION

1. Vl. Zhabotinskii, *Fel'etony* (St. Petersburg, 1913), p. 81.

AN AFTERWORD, BY ARTHUR COHEN

1. Friedrich Heer, *God's First Love: Christians and Jews over Two Thousand Years,* trans. from the German by Geoffrey Skelton (New York: Weybright & Talley, 1970), p. 110.
2. Myron P. Gilmore, *The World of Humanism: 1453–1517* (New York: Harper & Row, 1952), pp. 199–201.
3. Richard Marius, *Thomas More: A Biography* (New York: Alfred A. Knopf, 1984), p. 8.
4. Shimon Markish, *Erasmus and the Jews* (Chicago: University of Chicago Press, 1985), p. vii.
5. Ibid.
6. Shimon Markish, *Znakomstvo s Erazmom iz Rotterdama* (Moscow, 1971).
7. Guido Kisch, *Erasmus' Stellung zu Juden and Judentum* (Tübingen, 1969). See Markish's discussion of the Kisch throughout his work, passim.
8. Markish, *Erasmus and the Jews,* p. vii.
9. Jacob R. Marcus, *The Jew in the Medieval World: A Source Book, 315–1791* (Cincinnati: Union of American Hebrew Congregations, 1938). Luther's essay of 1543, "Concerning the Jews and Their Lies," is sufficiently excerpted by Marcus, pp. 167–69.
10. Arthur A. Cohen, *The Natural and the Supernatural Jew: An Historical and Theological Introduction,* 2d rev. ed. (New York: Behrman House, 1979), pp. 6–9.
11. Arthur A. Cohen, *The Myth of the Judeo-Christian Tradition and Other Dissenting Essays* (New York: Harper & Row, 1970), passim.
12. Jules Isaac, *Jesus and Israel,* trans. from the French by Sally Gran (New York: Holt, Rinehart, & Winston, 1971); *The Teaching of Contempt: Christian Roots of Anti-Semitism,* trans. from the

French by Helen Weaver (New York: Holt, Rinehart, & Winston, 1964); *Génèse de l'anti-sémitisme* (Paris: Calmann-Levy, 1956).

13. Cohen, *The Myth of the Judeo-Christian Tradition and Other Dissenting Essays*, pp. 74–75; cf. particularly 75n.

14. The interpretation of the classical epical literature in terms of its formulaic character is convincingly set forth in Albert B. Lord, *The Singer of Tales* (Cambridge: Harvard University Press, 1960). See also Erich Auerbach, *Mimesis* (Princeton: Princeton University Press, 1953), pp. 3–23.

15. Marius, p. 268.

16. Cecil Roth, *The Jews in the Renaissance* (Philadelphia: Jewish Publication Society of America, 1959), pp. 137–64 on the Christian Hebraists.

17. Markish, *Erasmus and the Jews*; cf. Erasmus, *Enchiridion*, LB V 32F.

Index

Index

Index